SUPERHEROES IN THE STREETS

**RACE**
**RHETORIC**
**& MEDIA**

Davis W. Houck, Series Editor

# SUPERHEROES IN THE STREETS

Muslim Women Activists and
Protest in the Digital Age

## Kimberly Wedeven Segall

University Press of Mississippi / Jackson

The University Press of Mississippi is the scholarly publishing agency of the Mississippi Institutions of Higher Learning: Alcorn State University, Delta State University, Jackson State University, Mississippi State University, Mississippi University for Women, Mississippi Valley State University, University of Mississippi, and University of Southern Mississippi.

www.upress.state.ms.us

The University Press of Mississippi is a member of the Association of University Presses.

Selections from chapters 3 and 5 were originally published in a slightly different form in Segall, Kimberly Wedeven. "Media Sites: Political Revivals of American Muslim Women." *The Oxford Handbook of Politics and Performance*. Ed. Shirin Rai, Milija Gluhovic, Sivija Jestrovic, Michael Saward. New York: Oxford University Press, 2021. 235–50.

∞

Library of Congress Cataloging-in-Publication Data

Names: Segall, Kimberly Wedeven, author.
Title: Superheroes in the streets : Muslim women activists and protest in the digital age / Kimberly Wedeven Segall.
Other titles: Race, rhetoric, and media series.
Description: Jackson : University Press of Mississippi, 2024. |
Series: Race, rhetoric, and media series |
Includes bibliographical references and index.
Identifiers: LCCN 2023050765 (print) | LCCN 2023050766 (ebook) |
ISBN 9781496850379 (hardback) | ISBN 9781496850386 (trade paperback) |
ISBN 9781496850393 (epub) | ISBN 9781496850409 (epub) |
ISBN 9781496850416 (pdf) | ISBN 9781496850423 (pdf)
Subjects: LCSH: Muslim women—Political activity—United States. |
Women in Islam—United States. | Feminism—Religious aspects—Islam. |
Muslim women superheroes.
Classification: LCC HQ1170 .S355 2024 (print) | LCC HQ1170 (ebook) |
DDC 305.48/6970973—dc23/eng/20231106
LC record available at https://lccn.loc.gov/2023050765
LC ebook record available at https://lccn.loc.gov/2023050766

British Library Cataloging-in-Publication Data available

There is nothing more American than forgetting the past. It is through the obliteration of memory, an obliteration perpetrated with great deliberation by the state upon the citizenry, that American identity is fashioned. But conditional citizens will insist upon remembering.

—LAILA LALAMI, *CONDITIONAL CITIZENS*

# CONTENTS

# PREFACE

Because the journey of a scholar is never a straight path, any analysis of digital protest is also and inevitably a map of one's life and political activism. Writing here about online icons of superheroes and their foundations in protest and radical feminism—what I shall call *radical superheroism*—reflects my own experiences in South Africa, Syria, Iraq, and elsewhere, as well as my work with grassroots organizations, demonstrating for their rights, especially in the wake of the murder of George Floyd and ongoing police violence against minorities. In response, an estimated fifteen to twenty-six million protesters have flooded the streets with rallies in support of Black Lives Matter, protesting systemic inequities ingrained in our history and misbegotten governmental policies. Though hundreds of thousands marched in the civil rights movement, the Black Lives Matter protests may be the "largest movement in US history," according to the *New York Times*.[1] Yet even these numbers fail to take into account still further marches for immigrant rights and women's movements. And that's not counting the millions more who watched these proceedings. Or those who streamed live on Twitter/X, YouTube, and Facebook.[2] Or the *Black Lives Matter* signs that have sprung up on almost every block and lawn, painted on rocks, crafted out of cardboard, scrawled or spray-painted in bright letters, purchased off the internet, picked up at rallies, placed in dorms, or sold at community centers. But what is often overlooked within these protests is the range of people on the march—Black, Arab American, Southwest Asian American, white, and mixed-race Muslims in solidarity with their brothers and sisters. In fact, over 70 percent of US Muslim women have supported Black Lives Matter.[3] In this study, which starts with famous celebrities and concludes with interracial solidarities of Muslims, often stereotyped by the media and US propaganda alike, these activists have raised their banners and protest signs aloft not only on our highways but also in digital networks—in the selfies of their marches, in political posters and Instagram videos and virtual webinars, in images of red-white-and-blue superstars, transfiguring the superhero icon.

In following their activism, what is needed is more understanding of how their online icons have denounced international wars, protested racism, condemned government policies on immigration, and also draw attention to their own public protests and their online trail—all in ongoing efforts to lay claim to their rights.

As shown in my work on digital/public protest—in my first book, *Performing Democracy in Iraq and South Africa: Gender, Media, and Resistance* (Syracuse University Press, 2013), and in my publications on de-imperializing gender for the *Journal of Middle East Women's Studies* and *The Oxford Handbook of Politics and Performance*—even as mass media has singled out women who identify as Muslim, these protests are not new.[4] What is distinct, however, are the pace and capacity of these digital forums, as these activists, posting and positioning icons, have taken to tweets in this digital age, uncovering a kind of cultural amnesia in the West that has buried the atrocities of wars, which have left as many as fifty-nine million people displaced.[5] In the meanwhile, this so-called war on terror has shifted into a mission to save Muslim women, morphing into a "liberal orientalism" or even an "imperialist feminism."[6]

And, alarmingly, the failure of mass media has created intense pressure on US Muslims, demanding that they explain themselves against the backdrop of terrorism, requiring, in effect, constant evidence of "good Muslim citizenship."[7] Recognizing this crisis, this work sees the importance of prior Arab American studies by Nadine Naber and others on racial formation and responds by culturally and historically and individually locating each activist, positioned carefully and clearly, and refers *only* to these multiracial digital activists.[8] At the same time, this work extends these studies with its unique focus on digital activists and online icons. In this way this work also fills a critical gap, for, as Sunaina Marr Maira argues, while an entire 9/11 generation has been profiled, their individual stories are "missing," and their online strategies are unaccounted for within public discussion and academic research.[9]

Several scholars have read drafts, offering advice, giving support, setting up workshops, including Sherine Hafez, Carol Fadda, Shirin Rai, Nadine Naber, Stanley Thangaraj, Danielle Haque, Waleed Mahdi, Lisa Majaj, Nouri Ghana, and Sara Shaban. Many others have walked beside me, especially Aneelah Afzali, Theresa Crecelius, Shama Farag, Nashwa Zafar, Dina Al-Bassyiouni, Miyase Katirciouglu, Uma Achour, Rokaih Vansot, and many others who welcomed me into the American Muslim Empowerment Network. And I dedicate this book to my extended family of Hispanic, Native American, South Asian, Jewish, Dutch American, Japanese American origins and all that they have taught me. My gratitude as well to Anika, Will, Mary,

Erik Segall, always beside me on this path, and also to Luke Reinsma and Lisa Williams, my writer's conscience. And to two more scholars, whose work has accompanied me as well, even though we have met only once, for as early as 2009, Nadje Al-Ali and Nicola Pratt analyzed how US war propaganda targeted Muslim women, ignoring their long-standing activism and the rights of Iraqi women. They pushed back, asking "What kind of liberation?"[10]

Expanding this question, what's missing, according to Sylvia Chan-Malik, unlike media stories of only Arab/Black Muslim Americans, are more studies of historical frames of resistance—current experiences of the solidarities of US Muslims.[11] And what studies have been done have been sequestered in academic "silos," as Linda Tuhiwai Smith writes, colonizing expectations of racialized identities in the US, or research that fails to engage with community empowerment projects.[12] Furthermore, there is a gap in digital studies when they spotlight the numbers of hits, but not the strategies of activists in the streets. Addressing these crucial gaps in research and public understanding, this work takes up this call to attend to the experiences of this emergent generation of women who have become activists, their interracial solidarities, their grassroots resistance, their celebrity positioning, and their use of online icons as innovative political claims in public *and* digital networks.

SUPERHEROES IN THE STREETS

# INTRODUCTION

The adoption of new methods and strategies to affect power relations
has added fresh urgency to our need to understand how societies are
responding to the more permeable forms of information flows.
—MAHMOOD MONSHIPOURI, *INFORMATION POLITICS, PROTESTS,
AND HUMAN RIGHTS IN THE DIGITAL AGE*

Images catch my eye. Superheroes. Wearing red gloves spangled with white
stars, Ilhan Omar, one of two US Muslim women in Congress, circulates her
digital image on Instagram not as a superwoman with an invisible jet, but
rather as another kind of Wonder Woman, landing on 1.3 million sites, gar-
nering fifteen thousand likes—and a barrage of racist attacks. Dreaming up
yet another protest, Sana Amanat, an editor at Marvel, cocreates her own red-
white-and-blue superhero—Kamala Khan, leaping into popular print and
digital comics, hitting the streets, entering video games and miniseries and
movies, battling the assaults of online trolls on Instagram and Twitter/X. In
the meanwhile, posing with a flag for a headscarf in a protest against attacks
on US Muslims, Munira Ahmed appears in posts in hundreds of digital communities. But when Shepard Fairey recreated her flag-draped photo in "We
the People"—along with those of her Black and Latinx sisters—the poster is
carried by thousands upon thousands in mass protests, only to be revived as
a contested site in virtual communities. Recognizing the importance of such
activists—their fight for immigration rights and Black Lives Matter, their
online images reinventing creative signs of superheroes—this work calls
for more attention to their public and digital activism, especially their use
of online icons as protest strategies—which I am defining as superheroism.

As in the study of Ms. Marvel as a superhero icon, this work's focus on
resistant images as icons offers a way to trace these activists and their protests
and contestations—both on the streets and in online images. But before we
learn more of these star icons—like the rap star Mona Haydar, like the sport

3

protest by US Olympic fencer Ibtihaj Muhammad—let's start at the site of the superhero as a protester, after which we'll consider its digitalization. The first chapter, then, follows Sana Amanat's dream of creating a unique super-hero—Ms. Marvel, Kamala Khan. What is less known, however, is that this online icon was designed as a form of resistance, in response to Amanat's own past. In her online talk on TEDx Teen, she remembers the media assaults and bullying of her post-9/11 childhood. What Amanat recalls, especially, was a boy's tap on her shoulder when she was in middle school. "Tell your people to stop attacking us!" he called out. Feeling wounded by his words, she felt stunned.[1] For, although she had been born in the United States, she was attacked by a racist script: *her* identity seen as a threat. To survive, Amanat retreated into a world of misfits—like Storm, a powerful Black woman sport-ing a mohawk, born in Harlem, raised in Egypt—who use their differences as sources of power. These early superheroes helped Amanat to cope, she says in a YouTube video watched by over 74,000 viewers; more importantly, they helped her to challenge the systemic racism that had shattered her own identity. Which is, perhaps, why her strategies of superheroism are based not in the beautiful but in the grotesque—an enormous fist, for example, rising in protest, pounding the pavement. Unfortunately, although Amanat contin-ues to battle online attacks, when Marvel slotted her new superhero into a video game of Avengers, Kamala Khan entered a digital world mysteriously bereft of racial conflict. More than sites of individual activism and historical resistance, then, their icons have also become sites of a larger contestation.

So, what is an icon? And why are these online icons important? Often associated with large-scale concepts, emotional symbols, even collective sites of meaning, an icon is an image that speaks to more than an individual, for it has gained significance as a symbol, write Marita Sturken and Lisa Cartwright.[2] Like the Statue of Liberty, a national icon becomes associated with historical events, influencing how we view histories, and often follows standardized codes associated with the views of the nation.[3] Furthermore, Nicole Fleetwood, in her important work on Black icons, details how racial icons have a heavy load, because these images have been resisting oppressive stereotypes.[4] At the same time, the press and the commercial, she continues, turn these icons of the superstar into a fetish.[5]

And these icons have become part of the news. Press photos—for instance, of these protesters—construct a scene, Robert Hariman and John Lucaites write, and these images are a way for a nation to think of themselves, to show how they view situations.[6] These press photos suggest a need to res-cue Muslim women, and, at times, sexualize their bodies, as scholars have argued—the results of a continuous "colonial feminism," as Leila Ahmed writes.[7] Or of a Muslim woman in need of saving, as Lila Abu-Lughod states.[8] Pressing against such narratives, the racial icon, the newest Ms. Marvel, Kamala Khan, as a famous image, demonstrates the importance of reinventing national investments in digital comics, digital film, video games, YouTube clips, Instagram posts, and other digital forms. And other famous celebrities, like rap star Mona Haydar, and even extremely popular digital activists, like Blair Imani, self-declared as "Black. Bisexual. Muslim," have been using icons of racial superstars and interracial coalitions to revision feminist structures—not images of suffragettes or world war superheroes, but a sisterhood of riveters and coalition icons, celebrating their solidarity and reposting in Facebook, in Instagram, in YouTube clips.

Even as these online icons resist the trope of rescue—which is itself a kind of political activism—the pressures faced by celebrities, highlighted as famous individuals in this book's first chapters, and by grassroots activists, highlighted as coalitions and group images in the final chapters, are significantly and clearly distinct. The focus on famous activists as well as the political attacks that they experience could discourage other activists.[9] And there's the problem, as Jessica Taft argues, that star icons make the gap between doing activism versus being a famous activist seem impossibly wide.[10] Testing these theories, this book leans into activism, by comparing and contrasting these star icons and these solidarity icons. True, posting their images and photographs online, star icons often use their sites of social media and influence to encourage their fans toward specific causes.[11] But the problem here is that the iconic image of the individual superstar, an image moving in the millions in the digital world, cannot possibly represent the complex array of identities of US Muslims. Equally problematic, given the dearth of representations of US Muslims, celebrities like Sana Amanat, and her unique experiences reflected in her superhero icon, or Ibtihaj Muhammad, a US Black Muslim Olympic fencer, with her glamorous Nike commercials and her new Barbie doll, can be coded as unique, outside the norm, or exceptional because they are American. In response, this work has been invested in tracing how these celebrities use radical superheroism as a strategy to fight against the corporate platforms—for instance, of videogames, of commercials—refusing to be used by corporations and their press.

Superstar icons that spotlight a famous individual need attention, given their vast reach in audiences as well as corporate pressures, however, what is also needed, as attended to in the final chapters of this work, are comparative studies on online icons that mirror much-needed solidarities. Like the group photo and film images as an online solidarity icon, as well as the superhero icons and protest products of Aneelah Afzali, a Pacific Northwest

US Congresswoman Ilhan Omar, "The American Superhero Project." Photograph by Nate Gowdy for The American Superhero Project. Reproduced with permission.

activist with whom I've worked as a scholar-activist during the past several years, the digital activism of these individuals has taken ahold of their own virtual networks in the digital world. Just as importantly, these US Muslim activists have been reinventing the news about their protests and refusing the media's scripts about racial identities,[12] in effect using radical super-heroism as resistance aesthetics. Adding to the larger debate on the tension between these famous images who are adored by the masses and the largely overlooked solidarity movements that seek to rescue those very masses, this work analyzes the digital activism and the public strategies of these women and their use of famous images, or icons.

And why are these national icons important? Even as Wonder Woman, Captain America, and other white superheroes memorialized world wars; even as white superstars enacted certain codes of power; even as Rosie the Riveter and her crew glamorized certain kinds of labor—even then, they invited an erasure of ongoing violence, racism, and war. Feeding false narratives of women in need of rescue, false heroisms in ongoing wars, their stories continue to ignore systemic racism and militarization.[13] Of course, this spectacle of white superheroes—this desire for a "good war"—is a form of forgetting, but this longing for a heroic world war is as simplified a projection as a nostalgic film, as Elizabeth Samet writes.[14] It is precisely because the sentimentalities of these white superheroes and superstars continue to wreak havoc that changes in public perceptions, that new icons, new structures of power are required. In response, in each of these chapters, in Amanat's superhero, in Muhammad's star athlete, in Haydar's rap star, in Afzali's group icons, these women activists create protest productions (and digital products) in order to reimagine who is in the streets; in order to question who receives citizenship and benefits and jobs and who does not; in order to ask where our money is going; and in order to ask as well what the twenty-year war in Iraq and in Afghanistan—two of the eight major wars since 9/11—has wrought.[15] As we trace these online images, as part of this journey together, these national icons offer us a way of re-envisioning history—who we were in this decade of warfare and protests; of restructuring politics, who we are in the midst of social injustice and systemic racism; and, just as critically, of reforming our trans/national imagination—who we the people might become.

## MAPPING SUPERHEROISM

In order to map superheroism, beginning with Ms. Marvel, *Superheroes in the Streets* follows women activists using icons of superheroes and superstars and other national icons. Starting with celebrities like Olympic fencer Ibtihaj Muhammad in chapter 2, like rap star Mona Haydar in chapter 3, locating protest icons and their narratives in public and digital forms, this work turns to the streets to join grassroots activists like Aneelah Afzali in chapter 4, finally suggesting how, in chapter 5, group images envision racial solidarities in this era of historic protests. But how are these sites networking with politics? Analyzing how individuals position their own heteroglossic identities and histories, *Superheroes in the Streets* attends to individual identities, as seen in chapter 5, in the case study of Afzali's collaborative workshop, navigating various locations and territorializations of self-images and purposing of websites and Instagram platforms, all the while tracing these protest icons, these red-white-and-blue images as well as Afzali's hopes of multiracial solidarity for an American Muslim.

Since activists with millions of hits have a pervasive impact on our society, as in the superhero and star icons of the first two chapters, the second chapter explores problems when sport stars are advertised as commercialized wonder women alongside the "Fashionable 50" of *Sports Illustrated*. Ibtihaj Muhammad, for example, the Black Muslim fencer for the 2016 Olympic team, has been captured in a video that travels in online commercials— a Nike Muslim Wonder Woman. But even though such images of sport stars participate in trans/national markets, Aihwa Ong writes, their images are more than an online form of global belonging.[16] These Nike commercials tend to idealize athletes in terms of hyperphysicality, coded within gendered, racialized, and even religious scripts. And when these Nike Muslim athletes circulate in commercials with millions of hits on YouTube, they become, in a sense, living icons. In turn, digital activists have been pushing back against these commercials, posting on Instagram and for #BLM, complicating how the virtual movement of these superstar images, like an activist's raised sabre, points to strategies, to a radical superheroism, foiling cyberspace.

Given that superheroes like Wonder Woman often began their careers as sex objects, and that racial icons are just as often exoticized, it is critical to consider the ways that celebrities have used their icons in the digital world and how their own self-images reposition sexualities, in this case a rap star and a digital activist. Chapter 3, then, begins with Syrian American rap star Mona Haydar's resistance to exotic stereotypes in her wildly popular YouTube videos, her strategy rooted in icons of political figures like Malcolm X. After this we turn to the equally popular videos of the digital educator and self-described "Black. Bisexual. Muslim. Activist" Blair Imani and her feminist icon Blairsie the Riveter. Tracing their reinvention of icons—in political figures and in racial riveters—in their videos on Instagram and YouTube, this chapter explores their resistance to hyper/invisible sexual images. And it describes these sites of political contestation, especially as their digital activism and their ideas of racial solidarities and postcolonial sexualities enter into social media.

While digital activists like Haydar and Imani use these sites to signal bonds between racial groups, as well as each individual's own heteroglossic identities, we can sense the kinds of pressures that weigh upon them. Their resistance in online icons grounds itself in their own histories and in Black protest traditions—a radical base for these icons. In similar terms, it is essential to understand how grassroots activists like Aneelah Afzali, director of a solidarity network, also make use of superheroes in their own digital activism. Chapter 4, then, shows how individuals like Afzali navigate and negotiate their protest identities—their strategies online, their tactics on the streets, and their workshops as well. Which brings us, in chapter 5, to the promising activists who attend these workshops, where they learn to use their own protest images as part of solidarity icons—in group photos, in films of workshops, and in multiracial panels—all of which will provide us with a greater understanding of what I am calling *radical superheroism*.

## WHAT IS RADICAL SUPERHEROISM?

Designing an online series of protest photos on a red-white-and-blue placard, Afzali posts her own superhero images on Facebook—her own photos in a shirt with Lady Liberty, her own images of her nieces in shirts that read, "I am SUUUUUPER GIRL." She even used the idea of the superhero in an editorial on immigrant rights in the *Seattle Times*. Still, although her online forms make the news, this is about much more than citizen journalism.[17] Challenging who produces and who consumes the news, digital activists like Afzali use a personalized approach—to put together, take apart, and reconstruct a view of protest, as the media critic Mark Deuze puts it.[18] For in reconceiving and even adding pieces to the news, Afzali's layering of images and news—an image-woven bricolage—she builds her oppositional media. In her digital activism, for example, she calls on her followers to defend her when confronted with racist attacks at her mosque and in her online comment section, thus inviting her own team to take on public roles—all of which is part of virtual and public solidarities.

Leaning into solidarities like this requires a corrective vision, for the battle is in large part against visually oppressive images—this Islam-*media*-phobia. So much more than empty gestures, this resistance must reduce harm, Moya Bailey writes, and these healing practices need to be projected digitally.[19] Such digital activism—as evident in the use of the superhero—positions political stances and draws together alliances. Take the collaborative work of Afzali and myself in an activist-training workshop. Dean Spade has praised the productive relationships that such workshops provide, encouraging in this case connection within a multiracial group of US Muslim women—Arab American and South Asian and Black and white and mixed race alike.[20] At our training workshop, Afzali calls for these women to represent their perspectives in public. "We need more representation out there!" Afzali urges. So much more than the painting of posters, the hoisting of placards, the postings of events on social media, these strategies of resistance, these super-hero images that she posts, these iconic protesters she invokes encourage these women to turn their backs to insults and to lean in with their allies, breaking down the walls of immigration laws—in short, to take to the streets.

Marching together, these women are part of a solidarity, reimagining themselves not only as protesters on the streets but also as an empowerment network, posting their digital images, attending protests as a collective body. And in their group photos, and in their film clips of panels and of protests, their images are of a multiracial solidarity, as shown in chapter 5. As digital activists, their own images, their T-shirts emblazoned with superheroes and national icons, their posters of US Muslim women wrapped in the US flag, their banners swathed in red-white-and-blue—these images are posted as digital media, reinventing the way Muslim women recapture the inter/national news.

In all these ways, these digital activists are defining national identities as well. Whether in workshops or online, Afzali tells her followers that one of the most important goals of activist training centers on renaming—on identifying themselves as American Muslims. But even as this forms a powerful bond, it presents difficulties as well, for it's challenging to claim nationalism in a nation filled with injustices. Nevertheless, at our activist-training workshop on Saturday, March 2, 2019, Afzali exhorted the women to adopt the term *American Muslim* when speaking before others. One of the reasons we identify ourselves as "American Muslims," she said, pausing, is that "we're otherized, seen as un-American. . . . We're seen as outsiders." Looking around the room at her thirty participants, all part of this US Muslim solidarity, she continued. "I don't care if you came here this year, or a century ago with your family. The reality is that if you are here now, then you're an American. And we need to reclaim that," she said, inviting them to join a public protest against the immigration ban. These public claims were also part of her digital activism, posting her video project, ending with each of these women claiming, "I am an American Muslim." Like the use of online superheroes, this protest production, the video on her website, is a signature of political power in her digital activism.

In this era of ours with its Islamophobia, research indicates, Afzali said, that people respond better to an *American Muslim* than to the ethnicity that *Muslim American* emphasizes. Asking them to consider this identity as a preface to the stories they would tell of their own experiences, she went on to talk about the spike of hate crimes, in response to the Muslim ban. She had been working with the attorney general's office, she said, but wanted a second forum of public action. So she was seeking women to tell their stories in film archives, in panels as part of a university forum, in a mosque visit, and in digital activism—in all these ways, taking back the streets and pushing back against images in mass media.[21] The practice of restricting immigrants from Muslim countries and the misinformation about Islam will remain in high gear, she said, until "more of us are equipped" to fight against these misconceptions. And, even as these bans were lifted, this misinformation continues, as stereotypes of women in Iran, in Iraq, continue to enforce icons of women in need of rescue, as propaganda of the US.

These protests against propaganda, racist legislation, and hate speech demand a reorientation toward history as well—a new set of heroes. US Muslims have long been part of this country, Afzali explained, even before it was a nation. Early travelers included Muslims, like Mustafa al-Zamor, an enslaved African, the first Black and Muslim explorer, part of the expedition to Florida in 1527.[22] Estimates vary, but at least 400,000 out of the 12.5 million Africans taken to the Americas were Muslims.[23] Their influence continued in protest, Sylvia Chan-Malik writes.[24] And, as James Baldwin has pointed out, even the story that riveted us in our living rooms in the 1970s, Alex Haley's *Roots*, begins with Kunta Kinte, who came from a devout Muslim family in West Africa.[25] So "American Muslims have been here for hundreds of years," Afzali said. There are also historical records of Muslims fighting in our wars, she added, emphasizing the collective pronoun—"in *our* Civil War, in *our* First and Second World Wars." So unlike the use of white superheroes to valorize these wars as part of a whitewashed citizenship. Nevertheless, the very issue of citizenship has been an ongoing struggle, she went on to say. In the late 1880s, although many US Muslims were naturalized, they continued to be disenfranchised because they were not white. Which left them not only ineligible for benefits but also racialized and marginalized in ways that have excluded them from bonds with other people of color.[26] So, it's not only the term *American Muslim* and its trail of icons that are at stake. It's a retelling of histories, a reimagining of the very history of the United States.

More than an internet strategy, these radical histories encouraged Afzali to reevaluate her own ideals as well. It took her a while to call herself an American Muslim, to feel comfortable with that term, especially since she is also proud of her own cultural identity and heritage: "You don't want to give that up." But when you tell your own story to a predominantly white American audience, you need to choose how to tell it and what portion to tell. Since audiences put them at a distance—as the other, she explained—activists need to create a circle of inclusion. So "when you say *American* Muslim"—emphasizing the first of the two words—"you're already changing their perception of you." That said, Afzali admitted, such patriotic claims are hard, especially since US foreign policy has a history of continuing violence—whether in Iraq, in Vietnam, in Guantanamo's black holes, or, most recently, in Afghanistan. "It's a challenge," she declared. But to claim an American identity is to lay claim, as well, to the democratic values to which Afzali aspires: one person, one vote; civil liberties; and freedom of religion. "So that's the way that I do it," she concluded. Reclaiming radical roots in democratic worlding, racialized citizenry, and interracial bonds, in online media and on the streets, she is, in effect, naming political desire, framing identity. And when she posts superheroes on her Facebook page as part of her digital activism, she is also a political tactician.

What also needs critical attention are the ways that the recent Black Lives Matter protests have crossed paths with Islam—as seen in the diversity of the crowds and the double hashtags of Afzali's banners and posters of #BlackLivesMatter, #IslamicTeachings. Not only in line with Malcolm X and with the Black consciousness movement, her empowerment network is rooted in synchronicities of faith and politics—a protest against racism. "All mankind is from Adam and Eve," a banner reads. "'White has no superiority over a Black, nor Black has any superiority over a white, except by piety and good action.'—Prophet Muhammad." Afzali and her members protest juvenile jails and immigration bans. In alliance with the Poor People's Campaign, her American Muslim Empowerment network's annual march against racism and police violence also celebrates the emancipation of the slaves. Not on Juneteenth, however, when the Union finally brought the news to Texas, but much earlier, when, quite clearly ahead of his times, long before 632 CE, the Prophet Muhammad freed slaves.

In these online icons, including these photos of multiracial groups, we are following these public pathways and Afzali's Facebook trail into traces of radical superheroism. What has continued especially to impress me is Afzali's breathtaking vision as she networks and coordinates antiracism in women's movements. This is what radical feminism looks like. Not a white rescue mission, it is, rather, a US Muslim multiracial group of women joined in public and digital protest and rooted,[27] as I have argued elsewhere, in long-standing practices of protests as well as innovative strategies of digitalization.[28] For even as she marches in support of Black Lives Matter, her radical claims motivate her work.

Presented in online icons, this trail of digitalization is grounded in strategies—what this work calls a radical superheroism—in alliance with the Black Lives Matter protests. Speaking on the ways that racist hierarchies have widened the gulf between Arab Americans and their sisters and brothers, calling, along with Su'ad Khabeer and others for more antiracist

Miyase Katircioglu, Yasmin Aden, "#BlackLives Matter, #IslamicTeachings." Photograph by Theresa Crecelius. Reproduced with permission.

work,[29] Afzali showed the film *13th* on February 11, 2017. In response to this documentary about the ways that the Thirteenth Amendment continues to create virtual slaves of the newly incarcerated, Afzali evoked Islamic traditions of hospitality, in an online lecture that "we must clean our own house before inviting in others." But this film documents her own history as well. Raised in the US, she has no memory of her infancy when her family waited in Germany for visas. In short, as an activist, her strong sense of justice has been born out of issues with race in one country alone: not in Afghanistan, not in Germany, but in the United States. Addressing antiracism in her digital activism, she calls her US Muslim sisters and brothers to "Action in Solidarity with Black Communities." Invoking the murder of George Floyd, she also quotes the Qur'an, wherein "killing even one person unjustly is like killing all of humanity" (5:32).

At the bottom of one of her posts, Afzali stands proudly, megaphone in hand, a white scarf accenting her protest T-shirt, "All Lives Can't Matter Until Black Lives Matter." Her online message tallies only twenty-seven days this year in which police did not kill someone in our country. And in 99 percent of the killings by police from 2013 to 2019, the officers involved were never charged with a crime. As a digital activist, posting images of herself as a protester, posting images of superheroes and other national figures, she is not just creating a posture, a performative gesture. Afzali has supported celebrations of Juneteenth programs at the mosque, and, in collaboration with women of color and transwomen, another of her online virtual protests in 2020 was for The Womxn's March: The Next Revolutionaries. Even during the pandemic, her COVID-19 mask in place, her placard aloft, four months later she helped organize #Say Her Name: Protect Black Women. In short, there is no disconnect here between Afzali's ethical roots in Islam, her feminism, and an online activism that spurs on her protests in behalf of social justice. It is a political synchronicity founded in her innovative digitalizations, in her fusion of protest traditions in politics, and in healing—grounded, that is, in her radical feminism.

As in this detailed example, then, throughout this work these icons are used as part of digital strategies; and these forms of radical superheroism, in leaning into protest traditions of anticolonialism in Islam, into liberation strategies of Black consciousness, into interracial coalitions, challenge the current structures of the nation-state. In conclusion, the final chapter reflects on the historical importance of this digitalization of complex identities of these superstars and superheroes and solidarities—what I theorize as digital heteroglossia. As shown in chapter 1, these superheroes have long been situated in terms of racism and sexuality. But, as Ramzi Fawaz argues in *The New Mutants*, their sites can begin to challenge the national imagination as well. Instead of the iconic figure of heterosexuality, for instance, the mutant bodies of superheroes—with their ever-changing gendered forms and transformations—offer a "queer figure."[30] Still, while recognizing these interventions, this work takes issue with any hint that these superheroes have ushered in a "radical imagination" as part of sixties neoliberalism. On the contrary, I would argue that until recently US Muslim women have been relatively excluded from this postwar superheroism, and their protests have been further swallowed by the propaganda justifying recent wars. And these mutated superheroes have yet to imagine structures of economics, politics, and immigration laws, which in many ways remain mired in the Second World War and its (white) heroes.

Responding further, continuing to focus on icons of radical superheroism and their pathways in the internet, the conclusion situates the dynamics of online icons of political figures, like US representative Ilhan Omar, a well-known figure of public protest and an online presence, and Amani Al-Khatahtbeh, founder of MuslimGirl.com, who ran for office for the US House to represent New Jersey in 2020, following her postings on a new generation of super-riveters. For instance, Al-Khatahtbeh's digital activism and extraordinarily popular Muslim women's blog has spread onto Facebook, Instagram, and Twitter/X, enlisting a racially proud riveter in her fight against hate crimes. As these activists have faced increased digital surveillance, even death threats, these political icons have been part of a critical resistance and demand for reform. Tracing the creative resistance of these online icons—wonder women and riveters and coalition icons alike—this final chapter describes the many ways that these digital activists fight back.

## THE *POLITICS OF SUPERHEROISM* AND ITS DIGITALIZATION

Even though these superheroes and superstars are in some ways new racial icons, they are critical to our histories and legacies. As a critical lens, the idea of superheroism allows us to consider how these iconic figures are very much artifacts of power. As Stuart Hall and others have written, digital activists are one spoke in a wheel of how power operates in our society, as part of a circuit, in production as well as in consumption.[31] This is no small change, the pace and numbers of people that can access these online superstars and other national figures. And these kinds of super-figures and the accompanying marketplace have brought to the stage several US Muslims as national icons—nothing short of a historic shift. Locating these ideas, digital icons and radical superheroism as a paradigm invites a series of key questions, addressed in each chapter, all as part of what I see as the *politics of superheroism.*

1. **Digital Production:** How do these online icons travel from public protest modes, such as printed posters and texts and banners, into digital activism? Following their digital sites and online interviews, how can we further chart these productions as part of their political motivations and visions for change? And how do these digital superheroes press against mainstream narratives, especially in terms of race and gender?

2. **Digital Reception:** How are these digital stars and digital icons received, and how are they attacked by online trolls and cyber-assaults? How many followers are part of their organizations or online sites, and how do they participate?

3. **Digital Consumption**: How are celebrities faced with pressures from corporations, and how do they respond to these economic pressures? And how do media sources consume these online icons?

4. **Digital Representation**: How do algorithms influence which representations, which icons, are most commonly seen? And as part of online sites, how are these resistance icons being influenced by social media platforms?

5. **Digital Identities:** How do these superheroes and their websites suggest these activists' heteroglossic identities? How do these dynamic and variegated icons challenge the mass media's myopic insistence on a single, uniform identity, and other stereotypes of Muslim women?

6. **Digital Regulation:** How do these protest icons showcase unjust regulations? How do these online icons and their sites resist immigration bans and policing of US Muslim communities? And are these digital sites being regulated or deregulated?

## SUPERHEROISM: A UNIQUE LENS ON DIGITAL ACTIVISM

This mode of analysis, mapping and describing online icons as part of political strategies, offers an important way to connect public protest and digital activism—a gap in most research between the street and its many tweets. True, all of this online activism has long been criticized as a waste of time, pointless clicks. But in this era of historic protests, it is ludicrous to argue for "anti-clicktivism," argues Sasha Constanza-Chock in *Out of the Shadows, into the Streets*, since it is both "tweets and the streets"—kinds of visibilities, bodies as an occupation—that bring attention to publics and their networks.[32] Similarly refusing the dismissive criticism of digital activism, Sarah Jackson and others speak of how online awareness encourages understanding of structures of power and of interracial alliances.[33]

But this study of superheroism participates in an even larger debate in the field of digital studies. For while there are those who view digital activism as a utopic space—giving voice to voices as yet unheard,[34] still others view the internet as a dystopic space—where the cyber-assaults, the corporations, and the algorithms of racism have created only damage.[35] Traversing these two models, this book's approach to superheroism as a mapping device traces these pathways of digitalization for both its potential and its pitfalls. Thus, this work uncovers these radical superheroes—in these online icons and their reception in the digital world—charting the potential of the internet as well as its problems, such as online attacks.

But the real problem with many studies of digital activism is that the research only situates the digital movement in social media without attending to the stories of these activists, including their motivations, their creative forms of protests, and their critical visions for structural and social change. True, in *Networks of Outrage and Hope*, Manuel Castells theorizes digital activism as a resistance power and an attempt to shift power relationships.[36] But even while identifying the public square as a multispace between digital networks and occupied sites, there is no clear conception of how digitalization and public protest interact. In short, tracking digitalization, the trail of the tweets, without regard to the motivations and politics of the activists becomes part of an apolitical mode—a technological fetishization.

The approach of superheroism, then, offers a unique lens in digital studies, answering the challenge by Natalie Fenton, a scholar of digital activism, to study the political.[37] Because these kinds of in-depth research are rare, she contends, there is not much understanding of how the internet works and how it influences others, especially the links of politics and networks. Which is why *Superheroes in the Streets* starts with experiences of celebrity activists, who are most entangled in power politics, before considering grassroots activists, their strategies, their protest identities, their political productions, their specific pressures. On the one hand, the celebrities face more cyber-assaults, and, as shown in the subsequent case studies of Muhammad's sport icon, Haydar's rap icon, and Imani's LGBTQ+ icon, more corporate pressure. On the other hand, as shown in Afzali's case, for grassroots activists, the challenge for groups—Black, Arab/Afghan/Pakistani/Iranian American, white, and mixed race—is in claiming collective identities, for instance, claims of national identifications as American Muslims, or even of interracial solidarities in their digital activism.

This study allows for more careful analysis of commercialization. Many scholars of digital activism have, in fact, warned of the ways that Instagram and other online sites are being used to sell products, link to commercials, as in Muhammad's commercials for Nike, and have become more economically than politically motivated. In *Pain Generation*, for instance, L. Ayu Saraswati warns that social media is in danger of "self-branding" as part of a corporate product, which, then, can lose sight of resistance movements.[38] In several studies, however, Jackson and others have argued that forms of protest that are part of creative and digital work should not be free.[39] This conflict within the field of digital activism is addressed in this book with a careful study of celebrities, such as sport activists or rap activists, negotiating the pressures of corporations; and of grassroots activists, navigating strategies for inter-racial alliances.

*Superheroes in the Streets: Muslim Women Activists and Protest in the Digital Age*, an interdisciplinary intervention in American studies, analyzes these tensions between celebrity and grassroots icons, and between claims of national identities in solidarity movements. Responding, then, this work considers these famous activists and their digital icons. As Erica Austen and others find, these celebrities can urge large numbers to engage in specific actions.[40] But famous icons of sport stars as well as rap stars cannot possibly represent the multiplicities of US Muslims. This work addresses this problem. This book suggests a subtle tension between the icon of the famous individual in contrast to the online activism based in the grassroots with their group photos, their filmed panels, their identities in multiracial coalitions, whose important work in public and digital media needs more attention. At the same time, clearly, all of these star icons that are circulating and reproducing in a fast pace in a digital age, contrast the rescue images of the press, doing important political work; however, this work further asks, what distinct kinds of work are celebrity versus grassroots icons doing? To answer these questions, this work begins with case studies of US Muslim celebrity women, like sport star Ibtihaj Muhammad, rap star Mona Haydar, and digital activist Blair Imani, and their millions of hits. It then tracks grassroots leaders like Afzali, taking to the streets with her thousands of followers, as in her activist group. In this case study of activism, in their trail of group photos and filming in front of the police station, the public hall, the capitol, these images are national icons, because they are icons of civic authority.

There has been a great deal of research on how digital activism has been used in North Africa and the Middle East.[41] But in addition to a prolific number of global studies, the field should investigate how media depicts US Muslim women activists. Even when mass media does turn its attention to these protests, as in these next few examples, its lens often remains singularly out of focus. At a Black Lives Matter rally, for instance, NBC documented how one activist was forced to remove her headscarf during her booking photo at the police station.[42] Of course this rights violation needs to be corrected—in fact, a change.org petition garnered forty-five thousand signatures on this issue. What is even more notable, however, is the complete invisibility of her actions in and ideas about the protest. Not until the second paragraph do we learn her name: Alaa Masri. And it is never clear what happened. Was it she who sprayed red paint on the hands of the statue of Christopher Columbus? Or daubed "BLM" at its feet in the park in Miami? Although charged, along with six others, with suspicion of battery against a police officer and disorderly conduct, Masri's role at the protest is never clear. There are no interviews. Focusing only on her religion, the online article further erases diversified communities such as Black American, Arab American, and South Asian US Muslims alike. Obviously, removing her headscarf is a critical civil rights issue. But by focusing only on her clothing, this news item not only overdetermines her religion but also erases her racial identity and further dismisses her political views—her reasons for attending the march, her ethical framework, her experiences of racism, and her possible role in the anticolonial graffiti. In this instance the press homed in on only one aspect of Masri's identity, so that the dominant lens of racism, targeting her religious affinity, reproduces oppression against its citizens. Too often mass media leaves no room for US Muslim women and their communities.

These online images code race and religion and politics in a web of sexualities as well. Let's consider an article in London's right-wing *Daily Mail*. The frozen image accompanying the tabloid's online video highlights but one woman, her face covered except for her eyes, shouting during the Gay Pride March in 2019. Although the accompanying article acknowledges that many religions, including Islam, were represented in the pride march, the headline, "Muslim Woman Wearing a Niqab Shouts 'Shame on All of You Despicable People' in Shocking Homophobic Rant at Pride March in London"[43]—the headline focuses our attention on THE Muslim protester, her *blurred image* juxtaposed to that of a woman draped in a pride flag. In its online video on Twitter/X, she repeatedly "screeches . . . 'shame on you,'" endlessly chasing the woman wearing the rainbow flag in a frenzied rerun. In highlighting this SOLE protester, what we are missing, Jasbir Puar argues, is the larger discussion that to label Muslims as homophobic, or as sexually repressed, or as silent and oppressed—all of these sexual stereotypes contribute to Western arrogance and actions, fueling modern wars.[44] Mass media has weaponized these images. Shared and reproduced on Twitter/X, this Muslim female protester is yet another object of the internet's gaze, feeding its algorithms and lies.

Even using the keywords *Muslim* or *Muslim protest* to find images on the internet invites racial profiling—what Safiya Umoja Noble calls the oppression of algorithms[45]—in this case, gendered images of Muslimness, typecast in protests, as objects, as extremists. Some view the internet, in particular, as inclined to treat all users as unwitting victims—mere data banks to be mined by algorithms—unable to find their communities or to navigate their own digital archives. But while these activists have been finding connections, digitalization still spreads and commodifies racial images and racism. These racist kinds of media, treating these Muslim women as if they were helpless, unable to use computers or to leave the house, ignore historical representations[46] of these women as cunning negotiators of political power.

Long after the tear gas has cleared and the signs for immigration rights and Black Lives Matter now occupy living room windows, the resistance of US Muslim women persists as they continue sculpting national icons and innovative modes of inclusion. Recognizing the recent flood of images in mass media that highlight the burning of the hijab in Iran, as if these women needed saving, since there is no historical context of these women's ongoing resistance, then, this work on public protest in a digital age traces how these US Muslim women activists have reinvented the streets, rewriting racialized codifications, refusing fetishized objectification and dehumanized stereotypes alike. By naming and posting superheroes and superstars alongside personal intimacies and structural intricacies, these women have further staked out their social and political claims, even as these remain contested digital sites. In iconographies not seen since the Second World War, the latest wonder women are marching not on the battlefields but in virtual worlds and on the streets, their posters and banners held aloft, a critique of the political, racial, and sexual alike. These superheroes stride not only across screens—as in Ms. Marvel's commercialized universe—but more importantly in the hearts of radical feminists and their online icons and digital strategies, driven by celebrity power, upheld by grassroots foundations—a racially inclusive digital revolution.

# Chapter 1

# MS. MARVEL'S RESISTANCE ICON

Within this "new generation of activists and bloggers," there is
a "radical transformation affecting the way stories are told, dissent
is expressed, and canons are produced in the new millennium."
—TAREK EL-ARISS, *LEAKS, HACKS, SCANDALS: ARAB CULTURE IN THE DIGITAL AGE*

Highlighting the importance of the superhero in her TEDx talk, Sana Amanat, as one of the creators of the new icon of Ms. Marvel, says her safe place as a child was in the virtual world of the Mutants: they too were "different."[1] She loved how they owned it and defended it. No matter what. And she saw how the absurdly strong man with shaded skin and hair of blue was treated as a beast, just as she had been dehumanized as a Muslim, despite her own citizenship in the US. When she was a teen, she saw how the news media about terrorists led toward more social targeting. Muslims are accused of hating Americans, so it was as if her face were suddenly present in a barrage of images across the television screen that had a "big red X painted over it." Her sense of self began to "blur." In response, she insists, "I'm an American," but, of course, "I don't hate myself." Given the challenges in a society that has either criminalized or ignored people of color, it is not enough to shift from neglect toward presentations of Black and Brown bodies in the digital world.[2] Even as this superhero icon leaps into the big screen of *The Marvels*, Kamala Khan takes flight in the miniseries, in video games, in commentary on YouTube, in millions of posted images on Facebook, on Twitter/X, on Instagram. But it is important to trace the origin of these comics and the context, since this series began the same year the police shot Michael Brown.[3] Based on experiences of the editor Sana Amanat, cocreating with a fellow US Muslim, the writer G. Willow Wilson, her superhero Kamala Khan engages in this historic era of protests, her superpowers rooted in her raised fist and hands-up sign, as well as her own heritage, a radical superheroism.

The origin story portrays the superhero as a *protester*. Kamala learns to accept her powerful, massive fist and its gigantic, swinging arm of justice as an extension of herself. She owns her identity. But her massive fist is used only when others in her community are threatened. When her brother, Aamir, is arrested with charges that he doesn't have the right papers, she joins a public gathering in her neighborhood, her multiracial community, demanding her family member's release.[4] At this point she throws down her fist against the newly authorized immigration agents. Unlike with many superhero protagonists, however, who tie up criminals and hand them to the police, there is clarity here about the abuse by the police and about unjust laws and their enforcement, especially against those who are deemed as different. As this superhero takes to the streets, her journey shows us the structural violence of her society. This strategy recognizes powerful villains as well—the dissemblers and the inventors and the corrupt politicians who deceive the populace. But when this superhero takes to the street, as part of her rite of passage, using her mighty fist, her power of resistance, she also learns to rely on her community in times of need. And she stands up for them. In fact, her writer designed her as a young activist, for "that is exactly what her real-life counterparts are doing in Black Lives Matter, Immigrant Rights, and other social justice movements."[5]

Thus, this growing fist of power symbolizes collective resistance against racist structures. In the panel that depicts the interrogation of her brother, Aamir, for instance, he lists all the ways that the police have targeted him only because he looks Muslim. It is against this kind of racism that this superhero strikes back. And in a subsequent panel, her fist takes up an enormous space, a sign of the power of activism. It is, of course, a referential sign as well, for these panels reflect the recent massive protests in the United States. In a sense, then, in this superhero milieu, there is a remembering of these protests. The significance of her powerful gesture, although clearly a symbol of liberation, is also a means of retelling history. All the more affecting with a teenage heroine, these comics remind us of this epic movement when vast numbers of multiracial youth have taken to the streets. Just as in the story of Ms. Marvel, her supportive community, these citizens, come from numerous backgrounds. Therefore, this new Ms. Marvel, the key representative of this collective—with her central gesture of the sign of solidarity and of power— is equally at home on the streets and in the mosque, a force of justice that saves her brother as well as other targeted individuals. As Ms. Marvel hits the streets of New Jersey, she rescues many in her society, and these actions are a claim on race, place, and space—a reterritorialization. What we see here is neither the usual super-icon of whiteness nor the conditions that deny citizenship as a kind of erasure[6] nor an object of rescue; we see instead, much more inclusively, a racial rescripting of belonging. As a kind of radical feminism, rooted in the streets and grown in her community at the mosque, her actions highlight the role of US Muslim women activists. No mere protest icon, her figure symbolizes a history of resistance, one that is rarely recorded.

## BEYOND ICONS OF IMPERIALISM: REDESIGNING FEMINIST SUPERHEROES

Before analyzing the origin story of Ms. Marvel, it is critical to understand how a superpower of a raised fist has long departed from the world war superheroes. In the Marvel comics of the forties and fifties, the "superhero-as-American-Dreamer was essentially white, suggesting that the aspirations of heroism as well as of power and success were beyond the grasp of minorities," writes Mauricio Espinoza.[7] But in the sixties and seventies, largely white male superheroes became more unstable, according to Ramzi Fawaz, shifting shapes in ways that obscured gendered codes—a "queer" embodiment.[8] Nevertheless, while shifting sexualities may be reimagined, what the superhero genre has ignored are the many complexities of racism and its empire. For there is no memory in these comics—almost no visual record of the racism against US Muslims, no memory of the violence of the US government in Iraq or in Afghanistan.[9] Given the ways comics sideline those who have been assaulted by US imperialism, only such an "act of remembering," to quote Melinda De Jesus, refuses the erasure of peoples, who have been marginalized in comics, in classes, in most histories.[10] Any revolution in comics must contest the relative absence of figures of color in generations of Marvel comics. In response, these poses on the pages and panels of Amanat and Wilson's comics situate Kamala and her community amongst racism on the streets. Restaging these memories, then, these moments of being targeted, for instance, is Amanat's response to injustice.

This superheroism is different from sexualized superheroes. Given that mass media and the cultural media of superheroes have interlaced legacies of gendered and racialized discrimination, Amanat and Wilson had their work cut out for them. The role of media and its mediation of history was also very much on the author's mind. With a major in history from Boston University, Wilson also studied religions, first converting to Judaism, later to Islam. When she went to teach US history at an American school in Egypt, she met a young physics teacher, Omar Haggag. At the school she was interested in teaching the histories of North Africa and of the Middle East but was required to stick to the United States. Complaining over this, she found agreement from Omar Haggag, who saw this history curriculum as being highly regulated.[11] Given their mutual interests in history and in politics, they started dating and later married. After they moved to the US, where her husband became an advocate for immigrants, and G. Willow Wilson started writing scripts for Wonder Woman and Ms. Marvel, they also agreed about an international qualm. Superheroes were an "attempt by the world's only superpower to normalize its violence," he said.[12] A historian, familiar with the ways that the Western world had controlled the Suez Canal and colonized Egypt, Wilson agrees that most superheroes reflect the ethos of the US as a *superpower*. Resisting this expansion of imperialism, she has been creating, instead, a consciousness in her new protagonist, including her most common gesture as a symbol of protest against the powers that be: a symbolically large fist. This power matters as well to Amanat, who sees her superhero as critical for young dreamers, fighting their way through mass media, finding their forms of activism on the streets.

Reinventing wonder women, however, is challenging, since this genre dates back to the world wars with gendered caricatures and colonized groups, depicted as savages forced to fight for the Nazis.[13] And in this war against the Nazis, these hypersexualized white women in bondage as well as women tying up men in bondage were often situated in a jungle, sexualized even as they were eradicating Brown folk who were fighting for the Third Reich.[14] In this period superheroes and prisoners of war alike step into the mire of sexual fetishization. In fact, early women superheroes, like Wonder Woman, who began her career as a nurse in WWII—not only a feminist icon but also a femme fatale and a woman in bondage—fit within this propaganda.[15] Second World War damsels of destruction were also in distress, these origin figures were often incapacitated with headaches and fainting and memory loss, like some stereotype of war-shocked southern belles. After the war thousands of cheap, tawdry crime comics further stereotyped sultry, lascivious, duplicitous femme fatales. But these visual patterns of the past also align with present trends in mass media, which, true to form, now claim that we must save the women of Afghanistan from the Taliban—or even worse, from their own systems of belief—while turning a blind eye to our own role in this era of atrocities.

Similar patterns in comics emerged even as recently as 2002, with Sooraya Qadir, an Afghan Muslim, a super-mutant called Dust. Although she tells her mother that she has *chosen* to wear the veil—unlike the forced veiling under the Taliban—her veiling is seen as oppressive by those around her. She is depicted as the girl who cannot integrate, will not tolerate rock music, and is called a religious freak—a mutant who is not accepted.[16] But like a stereotype of a terrorist, she becomes psychotic and tries to kill the other mutants, a loss of control that further demonizes her, writes Martin Lund.[17] Even as she wears the niqab, she is, at times, displayed without her face veil or clad only in her undergarments—a sexually charged unveiling.[18] When the comics move into a future state, she belongs in the West only in a sexualized form with a scanty outfit—an object of orientalist imperialism.

With their sexualized women and their ultramasculinities of violence, these are the gritty adult comics with their white supremacist images and settings, which Wilson wanted to subvert. She sees her superhero icon as a fight over "who gets to be American and who gets to represent America." "Superheroes have always been a big part of that conversation," she adds, "kind of our collective iconography." But unlike the lasers and the explosive powers of other superheroes, Kamala's powers are always negotiable. Sometimes this superhero becomes small and runs away. But it is she who gets to decide when to engage, what to do, what part of her small body to shift, when to raise up her gargantuan, almost grotesque, fist. Gesturing toward years of collective resistance, her fist is prominently upheld in the civil rights movement and many other protests—its primary goal not mass destruction but justice on the streets. As an icon of superheroism, her extended body with its upraised fist as well as her hand reaching out to save others is a symbol of a resistance movement.


## SUPERHERO ICONS:
## THE REINVENTION OF FEMINIST SCRIPTS

Since superheroes are a national image, then superheroes who attend mosque and know their hadiths promote new ways to belong—new modes of citizenship via popular culture. For over nine months Sana Amanat and G. Willow Wilson worked side by side envisioning the setting of Jersey City in this newest version of Ms. Marvel. Many of their panels contain specific details of Amanat's youth—sniffing food, for instance. But even these small gestures show how assaults of identity and ensuing anxieties and her transformations all catalyzed her activism. In her TEDx Teen talk, facing her childhood fears, taking an activist's stance, Amanat boldly begins, inviting the audience to judge her, introducing the idea of labels, such as Muslim. As the only South Asian female comic editor, she wanted to create a character that she could identify with. When introducing Kamala Khan, she places her own yearbook photo on the screen. Asking us to imagine, she uses the third person to describe her character and herself. "She never felt like she could fit in. She didn't look like the other girls, couldn't fit in with her class." The initial scene shows Kamala sniffing pork sandwiches at the convenience store, even though she never eats pork. In this scene, significantly, a white bully enters the outlet. Insecure about her identity, Amanat recalls constant stereotype threat, obliging her to mask her identity in a futile attempt to fit in. But while other superheroes mask to protect their status at work and in street politics, this masking was in response to microaggressions. As a result, Amanat imagines this series as an attempt to unmask—as an attempt to "embrace what is beneath your mask," a reclaiming of one's complex feminism embedded in sites that are political, social, religious, gendered—a much-needed revisioning of white wonder women, a form of inclusion, a racialized citizenship.

Superheroism reinvents icons of feminism—the original sex symbols of the world wars—but even more intimately, radically rooted superheroism is a record of trauma as well as a kind of healing. Remembering her childhood, Amanat recalls the trauma of mass media and daily encounters. Given mass media's view of her people as a threat, she started feeling like "a splintered version" of the person that she wanted to be. So her superhero is equally besieged—as in assaults in the streets. Not surprisingly, superpowers do not emerge until we see how Kamala is equally splintered by racial aggressions. When Zoe Zimmer, a white student at her school, makes insulting compliments, Kamala's best friend, Nakia Bahadir, understands the barbs, but Kamala feels torn with ambivalence. Zoe's assault takes several angles. Telling Nakia that her headscarf is "so pretty"—she likes the color—she quickly follows up with a discourse on orientalism. Was she pressured to wear the scarf? she asks. She's even concerned that Nakia could be targeted for an honor killing. But, in fact, Nakia responds, her father, who refers to it as a phase, is pressuring her to take it *off*. Zoe, however, manages to turn Nakia's moment of empowerment into an insult. "Cultures are so interesting," she responds, patronizingly. Superheroism is a march into the politics of the streets. With her feigned concern, Zoe, the "concern troll," for instance, functions as a symbol of racial assaults.

But in the next scene, there is an initiation, a strategic entrance into superpowers. A teen on a new quest, Kamala transitions from a sense of alienation within her own nation, in an initiation that brings her greater vision, anticipating her awakening into power. Critics have variously interpreted this scene as a religious experience, an intergenerational bond, or even a hallucination in dual languages.[19] What is not noted, however, is that this is, much more poignantly, a moment of initiation not just into the limited rites of white superheroes but into a new type of uber-citizenship. Nor is it an erasure of her cultural inheritance. Nor is it in English. It is, rather, a ceremony, ritually grounded in a song with lyrics in Hindavi—a song about a maiden arising. The singers are icons—her heroine, recently known as Captain Marvel, Carol Danvers, singing the opening verses, Iron Man and Captain America translating. The song is by Amir Khusrau, a Sufi who grew up in India. Often considered the father of poetry in Hindavi, he wrote about a young woman who gathers bouquets as she waits year after year on her dreams, for her beloved. Unlike the "hypermasculine" rituals of kingship in Black Panther,[20] this ceremony blesses her status as superhero—grounded in pop icons and in cultural complexities—in a heteroglossic virtuality. Providing Kamala with national recognition, these icons of her desire for belonging set the stage for a powerful initiation. Around her the superheroes speak all languages, embodying nationalities and religious identities as well. "We are faith," they say. Reminiscent of the white icons of Norman Rockwell's *The Four Freedoms*, the panel embraces the freedom of multiple religions—the red-white-and-blue of the full-page panel in an antiracist rendition—celebrating the new heroine's status as all-American hero. At the same time, it places her in Marvel's iconography, as part of a rite of passage, in its heteroglossic nationalism, an embrace of a superhero who symbolizes a *multiracial* nation.

An erasure of neither culture nor religion, this initiation into super-citizenship, in a ceremony to swear in the youngest member of the superheroes in Hindavi and in English, reinvents ideas of racialized citizenships. What it is not is a scene of assimilation—*pace* the critics—which would erase her ideas of cultural affiliations.[21] Instead, this ceremony brings with it its own set of questions. Leaning forward, Captain America, the ultimate symbol of nationalism during the Second World War, asks, "You thought that if you disobeyed your parents—your culture, your religion—your classmates would accept you." But "what happened instead?" They "laughed at me," answers Kamala. Beginning to see the light, Kamala realizes that in seeking invisibility, in breaking her parents' curfew, it was as if she had "kicked the dumb inferior Brown people and their rules to the curb." She doesn't even know who she is supposed to be, she further reflects. Her first stage of activism, then, in an antiracist posture, embraces her heritage, even though she has yet to accept her own complicated self. In this Socratic process, Danvers, her virtual heroine, asks her who she wants to be. "Beautiful and awesome and butt-kicking and less complicated," she answers. Confronting her, Danvers leans forward. Warning her that her desire for beauty is coded in whitewashed views, she still offers her a pharmaceutical reboot. But like any drug, she cautions, it will not come without its side effects. And at that, rising into the clouds like so many Elijahs, these new prophets of the digital age wish her luck and whoosh away. Kamala's metamorphosis is incomplete.

But this ritual passage is not yet superheroism. Even after her initiation into super-citizenship, her longing to be someone else creates instability. When she turns into the double of her media idol, Captain Marvel, Kamala takes one look at her bikini and push-up bra, her bare thighs, white skin, and blond hair, and has an identity crisis. Having turned into the spitting image of her idol, she wonders if she can change her mind. The tension and anxiety of the moment, in fact, cause her to vomit. Nauseated, her body convulses and splits: one eye blue, the other brown; half blond, half brunette. Having exchanged her own skin for another's, she doesn't feel confident and beautiful; instead, she's "freaked out and underdressed." Leaning over the sidewalk, losing all the contents of her stomach, it is a purging, an abnegation, an internal violation. At this early stage, her struggle is with her vision of a national identity, which does not include herself. It is here, in the midst of this struggle, ethics are recoded. As it turns out, being an activist means fighting not only for others but especially for yourself, which includes embracing ethical stances and political activism not coded in whiteness.

Superheroism, here, embraces oneself and one's connection to others: a radical superheroism interlaced within her heritage and her action in the streets. Kamala manages to recover her former self, only to discover that when she tries to restore her super status, nothing happens. As she discovers, she can transform herself only when there is a need to rescue others—a principle based on her faith, on her rendering of the Qur'an. So, when she comes across her tormentor, Zoe, drunk and drowning in a river, Kamala has to return to her ethical tenets before she can change. Reciting from the Qur'an, "Whoever saves one person, it is as if he has saved all of mankind," she recalls her father's words as well, that people who help others are also blessed. So Kamala finally finds her direction. It is only from this radically relocated superheroism—this ethical stance, rooted in faith and family, and in her action, this commitment to help others—it is only then that she begins to awaken into her power.

Nevertheless, this superpower resists these stereotypes. Even though she reaches out to rescue Zoe from the river, it costs her, since her arm, having grown more powerful, is grotesquely distended. Worse yet, she has yet to come to terms with her identity, since she still looks like a blond, white superhero, like her virtual female heroine, Captain Marvel. Afterward, she recognizes what makes her happy isn't her white skin, but seeing others survive—even if it's others, like Zoe, who have targeted her. But now there's a news media report that someone else is mimicking Danvers, Ms. Marvel's mundane counterpart. A new superhero? "Being someone else isn't liberating," she later recognizes, mulling over her affiliations. "It's exhausting." Symbolized by a set of panels, the oppression of the mass media, resembling televisions, calls this new superhero a copycat, for in Kamala's rescue mission, she wore the face of a white superhero and a mask of another. Drenched after rescuing Zoe, she puts on a dry sweater and pants from the cart of a homeless man, and then she faces her parents, who are justifiably concerned, given that it is the middle of the night. In her refusal of empty mediations, her self-recognition grows. For this superhero icon, protest is part of her resistance aesthetic.

But this icon requires reimagining feminism. Finding her own racial script as a superhero and her own vision of citizenship—set into four key panels—requires reinventing several resistance movements. Starting with world war white feminisms, this icon mimics the flexed muscle of Rosie the Riveter. In the first panel, trying to come to grips with her newly found powers and potential to help others, she stares at a poster of the original Ms. Marvel, her arm flexed in the classic Rosie the Riveter pose, still trying to find herself in the face of Danvers. It is as if she were looking in a mirror. Reflecting on her powers, the slouched teen stands in front of this image of the wartime poster, which carries a nationalizing aura. Superheroism as a reinvention of icons links experiences and historical events,[22] and we decide how much time has passed between Kamala's staring at her poster and panel two, where she holds her enlarged hand up to the poster.[23] Not only drawing us into ordinary objects, even more critically, the muscled arm is a specific cultural context.[24] As we connect this gesture with its story in the US, this national simultaneity locates the young teen in histories: in the world war context and its white icons.

But this series dares to imagine a new icon of protest. Its strategy reconceives the postwar feminist image. Kamala's critical gesture of stretching her hand toward this prototype of feminism alters the poster's dynamic. In the third panel, it is she who becomes the new source of backlit patriotism. Glowing with yellow light, Kamala looks upward. Preceded by a white pilot and a Black lieutenant, she is the newest icon of women's protest: the latest Ms. Marvel. Indeed, this pattern of glowing light is the trait of her predecessors, like the fire-bombing fists of the first Ms. Marvel, Carol Danvers, a white pilot who loses her memory; or the Black lieutenant, the photon-powered second Ms. Marvel, Monica Rambeau, fluent in three languages. In fact, even as the third panel illuminates Kamala, her hand glowing with power, the light begins to block out the image of Danvers, her predecessor. In this

G. Willow Wilson and Adrian Alphona, *Ms. Marvel No Normal*.

iconography, then, a radical feminism of US Muslim women's activism offers an alternative light on history, which will glow as well, one that relies on neither hypersexuality nor amnesia, neither bondage, mass destruction, nor military leadership, but on the space of inclusion of the newest superpower: US Muslim women and their innovative strategies and their heroic agencies.

For this superheroism, their strategy shapes icons in a journey through symbols of protest. In fact, awakening into her superpower is incomplete until she manifests her iconic sign of the collective resistance movement, in the gesture of the upheld (and gigantically symbolic) fist. In the fourth panel, the largest on this page, her fist rises in protest, a symbol of power. Not limited to the white icon of the women's movement with the flexed muscle of Rosie the Riveter, this portrait powerfully gestures toward greater inter-racial collectivity. Not just a panel, it is a protest sign, as significant as those in movements such as BLM, captioned, "Maybe I'm finally part of some-thing. . . ." As we pause between captions, the ellipsis invites us to imagine something "Bigger." Her raised fist is enormous, no longer a sign of a young teen, or of trying to break the glass ceiling, but of the power of helping others, of racial citizenry, of a political collectivity, a radical superheroism.

As a kind of finale, this largest panel shows the ultimate gesture: the sign of racial solidarity, the power sign of the raised fist, the symbol of street protest. But what we see in this poster of feminism is also a larger vision of the self, a newly found self no longer encased in the straitjacket of a super-hero costume. Instead, Kamala finds her sense of a heroic self when wearing the sweater that she got on the street—hardly the classic accoutrement of a superhero. Far from the sexy images, far from the Danvers's leather, this is the street wear of a homeless man pushing a cart on the street. What's more, her new sweater sports a brown-skinned face, symbolizing what Richard Rodriguez has famously called the *Browning of America*.[25] No longer are we following white superheroes and their Anglo-codes of normativity. In awakening after helping others, she is not costumed in Wonder Woman's bikini or in her future lightning-bolt burkini, but in the recycled wear of the homeless—a measure of care and concern with the presence of the streets.

This superheroism is a process, and a critical turning point, not only in holding out her white-skinned and distended hand to rescue Zoe (which, as critics have noted, reverses the stereotype of white men rescuing Muslim women, for it is she who rescues her white tormentor)[26] but also, in this final moment, in holding up her own hand in a fisted symbol of power. Thus it is that in stepping from one pose to another, these panels build toward protest signs, adding new awareness of what we expect from a feminist icon. And as we follow our young superhero, we are forming new attachments.[27] Not

unlike bridging the gaps between social media platforms, political prefer-
ences, and selfies on digital platforms, we fill in the gaps between images
of Kamala eating her breakfast, leaping off buildings, helping others, and
growing into herself. Thus, this strategy simultaneously creates shared attachments and political intimacies. But as part of these attachments, there is a
question of this incomplete icon, who at this stage is heroic only in this
white embodiment.

These changing embodiments of her superhero icon and its racialization have been variously analyzed. Coming into her superpower is part of
a critical transition, which scholars have variously interpreted. The critic
Mel Gibson, for instance, argues that the "two worlds of her Pakistani and
Muslim family background and her New Jersey teenage peers, [make] the
narrative, in part, about issues around assimilation and integration."[28] This
talk, however, of two worlds unwittingly replicates mass media's images of
Muslims who cannot integrate into the Western world unless they erase part
of their own identities. Reproduced in kinds of mass media, these binaries
of Islamic versus US culture have been espoused by scholars—what Bernard
Lewis calls a "clash of cultures"[29]—at the expense of Muslims. So too, in
an otherwise brilliant article about Danvers, Richard Stevens suggests that
Kamala struggles against the "strictures imposed by her family's culture"
and the excess of US norms.[30] In this reading, Kamala is assimilated in an
intergenerational bond not with her parents but with Danvers.[31] But Danvers
has lost her identity and her memory. Not only does this white superhero
shift into her powers, in her origin story, during fainting spells, awakening
without memory of her actions, as Stevens's provocative research points out,
in the initial figure, it is even more troubling, for there is a "thinly veiled rape,"
robbing her of memory when an alien is implanted within her.[32] In her origin
story (and big screen debut), Carol Danvers has forgotten her identity and
her history. So interpretations that focus *only* on Kamala's adoration as a fan
of this white superhero create a lens of assimilation. What's missing here is
Wilson's insistence that this is an "anti-assimilation story." In the origin story,
her power emerges in a scene that weaves in Hindavi script, her support is
from the mosque, and her miniseries highlights her grandmother's bracelet.
In short, Kamala's superpowers have been rooted in her cultural inheritance.

The story of Kamala Khan is more than just being a fangirl, because her
own identity, her personal voice, her cultural complexity is very much a
part of her unique and radical superheroism. When our young superhero
tries on the body of Carol Danvers, she becomes ill. This rite of passage
is part of developing her *political consciousness*. Afterward our superhero
refuses Zoe's taunts and reclaims herself and her family before taking to the

streets. Reclaiming her racial identity, refusing the white body, Kamala claims her identity through caring for others, especially through fighting anti-immigration police, who are rounding up those without the correct papers. Embracing familial and multiracial bonds, she finally becomes healed. In fact, her healing is possible only when she is more herself. And the more she heals, states Wilson, the less she can "take on the shapes of other people." In fact, Wilson is far more concerned with *not* assimilating—with embracing one's complex self and with healing from the damages caused by the dominant culture. In this superhero strategy, Kamala regains her brownness, and, unlike the face-changing of the X-Men's Mystique, only her size varies. Rejecting Zoe's standards—what I view as a refusal of assimilation—this series shows how she uses her powers as a form of coping. Thus, radical superheroism leans into healing, claiming one's complex self, and developing a more powerful political consciousness.

This emphasis on activism returns us, finally, to her creators—in the fullest sense, activists themselves—who have cultivated this emergent Ms. Marvel while reflecting on their own experiences. In fact, this is in many ways Sana's story, acknowledges the writer.[33] Unfolding in solidarity with Wilson's own memories as well, this teenage super-activist is very much based on the author's desire to elicit more powerful images for her own multiracial daughter. When her eldest daughter, "half North African and half European," was born in 2011, her conception was part of a historic shift when more multiracial children than white had been born. But even as our population has become more diversified and more hybridized, these young citizens are still subject to the mainstream media's images of discrimination, of fetishized orientalism, or, just as powerfully, of neglect. So, even as the majority on the streets are no longer white, these new majorities are still sidelined in mass media and rare in digital activism—an experience encapsulated even as the author holds onto the smallest of hands. "My husband is Egyptian," Wilson says. "I'm American."

> We both come from the racial and religious majorities from our respective countries where we grew up. It's been a struggle for both of us to learn how to be a minority and prepare kids who are going to be both/and, neither/nor in the ways that Kamala is. When I had my older daughter, I said, "God, I have to get to work! By the time she's old enough, there has to be a body of books for her."[34]

The newly discovered teen power rises from these hybrid identities—superpowers that *all* emerge within multiracial family and friends and in public protests. In creating Kamala's powers, then, the author's own experiences with her daughter and her desire for her country are part of her tactic—a racially inclusive new feminist icon.

Similarly, superheroism as a process of claiming belonging rises in an intergenerational bond. This strategy—with its many iconic faces—revisions the feminist icon in a mother-daughter relationship. When our superhero opens her hands, she stares down at them, trying out her new powers, longing to be a pop icon—to be Taylor Swift. As the young superhero looks in the mirror, she realizes that she has turned herself instead into an image of her mother. Thus, her uncertainty turns into a movement toward family—not toward the pop singer or Danvers, but toward her Ammi, her own mother. Placing her hands to her head, she repeats, "Fix it, fix it," and then she returns to her own body. But this is not a clash of cultures with her mother that she's trying to bridge, even though at times there is misunderstanding, what Wilson calls a generational gap. In fact, after trying to rescue the brother of her friend Bruno Carrelli, Kamala says, "As great as it feels to be powerful . . . I kind of want my mom."[35] She still needs to be cared for, a reassurance that her Ammi provides.

Intergenerational bonds have become part of the protest iconography. And her father, in one of the most moving panels in the series, not only sits next to her in conversation but also holds her in a warm embrace. Although understandably anxious about his daughter's nocturnal wanderings, he becomes a figure of support. "You don't have to be someone else to impress anybody," he assures her. "You are perfect just the way you are." Her bond with her parents is an embrace across generations, her transformations a dual claiming of public citizenship and of the multiplicities of heritages in the US.

Thus, superheroism is an inscription of masculinities, not just femininities. Amanat remembers how the men in her life—Yusuf, Aamir, Mohammad, and the like—were vilified, viewed as extremists in their religiosity, stripped of their complexities, creating insecurity in an uncertain masculinity. And this series protests these roles. So within the virtual world, Ms. Marvel's father and her brother, Yusuf and Aamir, both practicing Muslims, exhibit very different performances of masculinity and of vocation and of faith. In fact, this resistance is imbricated within complex reading communities. While her father reads his newspaper, for instance, his son, Aamir, steeped in religious texts, dressed in a white shalwar and white skullcap, prays at length at the dinner table. Finally, his irritated Baba, his father, replete in silk tie and dress shirt, confronts him, saying that they'll starve if he doesn't stop praying. Besides, he continues, these lengthy prayers look like evasion—avoiding getting a job. In response, Aamir retorts that his father's job at the bank is an offense to religious-based ethics. To which his father replies that the only reason Aamir can continue meditating on eternity is thanks to *his* work. It is these quotidian intimacies of families—these gestures of reading, of praying, of eating, spiced with their loving banter—that enhance our understanding of everyday practices.[36] Within these practices, reading is a powerful action, and this series represents growing ideas of a gendered national readership. Engendering inclusive national bodies, these men with their diverse reading habits, caring for our young superhero, claim tender masculinities.

Since these reading communities embrace radical femininities, it comes as no surprise that Ms. Marvel's Kamala Khan should appear on the cover of the first issue carrying a US history book alongside *Hadiths to Live By*, a sign of her faith. Clearly all-American, with a thing for Taylor Swift and comic books and a fan-girl site of heroes whom she writes about online, Kamala idolizes Carol Danvers, the mother of all Ms. Marvels. In these gestures of reading, then—both in texts and in technology—we expand the ways that we imagine reading at school, at the mosque, at the dinner table, at the computer. Not limited to white icons, far from flimsy stereotypes, overdetermining her piety, for instance, these images of the superhero icon provide an intimate array of multiplicities. With her family's daily gestures that include newspaper print, online virtual reading, and fan sites of female superheroes, alongside bank records, daily prayers, and refusals of simplified gender roles—in all of these ways, this family of heroes, this tender table, carefully turns the pages of a multitude of texts, a superheroism of heteroglossic virtuality.[37]

This icon creates room for multiplicities of identities and of faith. These depictions are nurtured in the soil of the creators' daily lives. In her memoir, for instance, G. Willow Wilson focuses on the small gestures of life, describing a "strange feeling, praying into your hands, filling the air between them with words. We think of divinity as something infinitely big, but it is also infinitely small . . . the warm space between your shoulder and the shoulder next to you."[38] As a strategy, then, the superhero's power emerges from intimacies that include practices of religion as well, as Kamala takes off her shoes to join her imam, Sheik Abdullah. Sitting in front of her imam at her mosque, she describes her transformation. "I . . . I help people," she stutters. With great humility, she says she's trying to get people out of trouble, but it's not going well. And he encourages her in her journey. So even perching at the feet of her superheroes and her imam is an act of activism, for there is a refusal here of mass media's demonization of vast numbers of people and their diverse forms of faith. Instead, this strategy envisions activism in ways that include not only cultural and religious agencies but such intimacies and solidarities of communities in private and in public spaces as well.

Superheroism thus combines the everyday with civil action. After her lesson at the mosque, Kamala not only raises her enlarged fist but pounds it into the sidewalk, protesting against those who police the undocumented. This iconic sign of civil rights, reminiscent of a Black Power sign, is situated within everyday gestures—slurping a Slurpee, for instance—that fight for inclusion even as they create attachment. More than the nostalgic flights of Wonder Woman, these protest gestures are part of a visual aura of power, which is further contextualized by the hadiths that Kamala clutches alongside her US history book—the record of the actions and sayings of the Prophet Muhammad, her ethical grounding in activism. This superhero as part of a national fantasy revises the national body.[39] More than ordinary gestures, then, these critical constructions of racialization perform radical feminism.

## SUPERHEROES IN THE STREETS:
## MASS PROTEST MOVEMENTS

She's no caped Superman, swooping in; no wealthy, leather-booted Batman, dressed by his butler, driving his weapon-laden, souped-up car. No, this hero relies on her parents and bounces back only with the support of her friends, her brother, her imam. Although Kamala initially tackles immigration police alone, she does not come into full strength until she joins with her family and her friends, who are leading a protest in the streets. The madrasa itself, the school at the heart of the religious institution, becomes a sanctuary when the immigration police round up those with extraordinary powers. Equally supportive, her best friend, Nakia, and her sister-in-law, Tyesha, lead a political protest against the immigration officers who have seized the latter's husband—Kamala's brother—and others. This political revival, never the work of a lone superhero, is a powerful and communal movement of solidarity led by these women activists. Holding the megaphones are her bestie, Nakia, with her tight pants and her scarf, a Turkish American who wears her scarf as a symbol of political defiance; and her pregnant sister-in-law, Tyesha, a Black Muslim, an activist, who loves reading sci-fi and who wields the court order against the thugs that are policing an ICE-like roundup of the undocumented. Sheikh Abdullah greets them with outstretched arms and a warm welcome, declaring the mosque a sanctuary. In this issue, titled *Mecca*, mass media, billboards, the police, and street crowds alike target our masked hero. It is not until her family and friends, all part of a multiracial crowd, have taken to the streets, and her brother has been arrested, that Kamala joins them and raises her hands in the air in an all-too-familiar symbol of protest—"Don't shoot!"—epitomizing their mutual stance of solidarity against police violence and mass incarceration and immigration raids.

Superheroism fights discrimination. The politicians in this comic, published in the midst of the Muslim bans, complacently speak of a return to normalcy, law and order, and economic growth. As big developers and their political cronies begin building large, pricey apartment buildings, confiscating the property of low-income shops, people on the street put up posters falsely attacking Ms. Marvel for supporting gentrification. Given the numerous ways that Muslim women have been used to justify US wars, the use of her image for such a campaign is quite significant. In this situation the damage to Kamala's reputation affects her family as well. Most painfully, it is their neighbors with their false smiles, secretly planning to betray them, who have turned them in, overwhelming our teen heroine. It is they who report to the Keepers of Integration, Normalization, and Deference Agency (K.I.N.D.), which sets societal norms and controls those who are unregistered, that is, the unregistered superheroes who have supposedly thwarted law enforcement.

The story alludes to racist oppression, especially the targeting of Muslims, and thus formulates a collective memory in comics that has long been socially obscured. Her nemesis, Discord, is an outlaw who ironically represents the law. Targeting her family and her neighborhood, Discord uses electricity to defeat her, alluding to Abu Ghraib and to the many times that Muslims have been tortured in prisons. Her dismay is made even greater when Discord tells her that politicians and developers are supported by crowds who actually fear her. The blame is placed squarely on those who are different, like those with superpowers, and the very foundations of democracy are crumbling: the rightful mayor cast out, the bureaucrats losing people's papers, and many others, including her brother, Aamir, arrested. Kamala's fighting figure—her gigantic fists pounding the pavement in front of the police, who are rounding up people into a truck—becomes a gigantic symbol of resistance, part of a larger vow to protect the minority from the collective evil of the system.

This is a protest movement that has emerged in response to racist assaults. After being led away in handcuffs, Aamir, his hand rubbing his forehead in dismay, is arrested. Once under the blinding light of interrogation, he is targeted for his traditional garb and beard—both associated with Islam—as well as for an earlier incident, when he was regarded as having (super)powers while he helped others. "Don't I have rights?" he asks, shielding his eyes, worried that the police are not concerned about the facts, that they are merely looking for a convenient suspect. He calls for a lawyer, but his concern for civil liberties is twisted by the interrogator, who assumes he has something to hide. Inevitably, his choice of dress—his beard, his long, white-robed qamis—becomes a constant site of political engagement, and his gesture of despair indicates his frustration with the targeting of those with brown skin.

But Aamir embodies this protest movement. Finally freed from immigration services, when the targeted group looks for a place to hide, it is Aamir who steps forward, bringing everyone to the mosque. Committed to helping the oppressed, to keeping others safe, he seeks out the madrasa as a refuge. When Aamir and Tyesha are finally reunited, they weep and embrace, opening the door into new visions of masculinities, a sensitive husband engaged in interracial bonds. Finally all return to the site of the exuberant sheikh, who opens yet another door for all to enter, inviting inclusive racialized citizenship.

Even more powerfully than Aamir, his wife, holding her megaphone, brandishing her court order, pressing for his release, epitomizes the protest movement. Obtaining the court order, gesturing toward the paper as she declares that this kidnapping of people is illicit, it is Aamir's wife, Tyesha, a figure of power, who has shut down these oppressive raids and rescued her husband. There has been a long history of Black Muslims resisting codes of political exclusion, argues Sylvia Chan-Malik, and pressing against social and cultural norms in racial and gendered codes of "belonging and citizenship."[40] And it is Tyesha who holds the court papers and stands up for justice as part of her identification as a Black Muslim, since her religious ethics are part of her political perspectives and her refusals of racist codes in her life.[41] Superheroism imagines protest as part of a cross-racial movement, and it is rooted in origins of Black Power, in long-standing histories of US Muslim resistance.

But even in these solidarities, there is room for dissent. The ways in which resistance is imagined by these two women protesters, a Turkish American and a Black American, show distinct ideas of protest symbols. While simultaneously inviting a discussion of their reasons for resistance, this strategy of resistance considers veiling as a protest strategy. Wearing the veil as a symbol that is used only to take back the streets is not the same thing, Tyesha says, criticizing Nakia for her resistance vestments. Flaunting her headscarf as a political statement diminishes its original meaning, Tyesha says, accusing Nakia of using her scarf as part of a larger marketing and commodification of the veil, comparing it to Nike's sports advertisements. Resentful, Nakia responds with her own rendering of the Qur'an—a competing hermeneutics about clothing as part of her idealism, her commitment to activism. What's more, she insists, her veiling is not tied to capitalism but is part of a matrix of justice. And it's not she who is following in Nike's footsteps, she adds; it's the marketing world that's profiting from *her*. What we have here, then, even as both of these women take to the streets with their megaphones to fight against illicit policing, are quite distinct strategies: wielding the court order, positioning one's body as a resistance figure. Despite this division, these remarkable female leaders, these two protesters with megaphones, still band together, symbolically leading an enormous multiracial crowd of urban supporters. Their critical resistance, their diverse approaches, their protest is a *heteroglossic resistance*. Never a single protester, these are *superheroes in the streets*, icons of many racial groups, marching in solidarity with collective sites of memory, rooted in public protest.

Superheroism makes space for many views, allowing its heroes a plethora of beliefs, even as protest provides sites of memory, of resistance as our shared history. Nor is it an accident that this solidarity movement is set during the time of Eid al-Adha. For instance, *Mecca*, volume eight of Ms. Marvel, commemorating Abraham's sacrifice in the Qur'an, not of his son but of a goat, begins with a goat purchased for the Khans' holiday dinner, although, as always, they embrace different views of Islam. When the family selects one of the animals, her brother argues for its importance, her father speaks of practicality, and Tyesha expresses gratitude. And Kamala? Kamala feels bad for the poor goat. Nevertheless, these memories are distinct from those of Sana Amanat, who recalls never opening presents at Christmas, never fitting in—not just during holidays, but throughout the year, because her parents were not invited to join the PTA. In contrast to Amanat's experiences, then, new worlds are imagined, cultural memories of Muslim festivities, her family feasting on goat and rice, her brother spilling the biryani, singing traditional holiday songs with her parents and exchanging greetings of *Eid Mubarak*—happy holidays. In all these strategies, superheroism radically reclaims space for her heritage.

Symbolically, the superhero is situated in a new practice—a reterritorialization of memory at the mosque and in the streets, planted in the fields of the public, in seeds of protest. Holding their megaphones to order the disbanding of the illegal security, referring to ICE-like agents, these marginalized sojourners, led by Nakia and Tyesha, are not circling the Kaaba in Mecca but are nonetheless in a modern pilgrimage together, this time through a gauntlet of police in the streets of New Jersey. This massive group, all walking toward the mosque in this modern journey during the time of Eid al-Adha, in an interracial and interreligious full-page panel, again speaks of a political movement that is taking back the streets. Thus, it is a time of celebrating how all will be saved—not sacrificed, not arrested, not tortured, not targeted—for Kamala's devotion to her community and her Islamic roots empowers her against hostile crowds. Holding both their megaphones and their hands aloft, these activists call to us, "Nobody gets left behind," modeling inclusive citizenry.

## DIGITAL REPRODUCTIONS:
## PROBLEMS OF MS. MARVEL'S VIDEO GAME

But what happens when this figure of the protester, this superhero icon, enters into the digital world? So popular has Kamala Khan become—a video game, a card game, an action figure, a cuddly doll, one of the Marvel Rising on the Disney+ channel cartoon—that she turned into a protagonist in *The Marvels*. Challenging mass mediation in this historic era, this most recent Ms. Marvel has launched from print to video to digital platforms, compelling us to reimagine our world. And alongside her role in the blockbuster film *The Marvels*, her presence on Twitter/X and video games, and her Marvel websites and Instagram stories of fully dressed cosplay, enhance the national aura of the newest Ms. Marvel—a movement of technological sentimentalities. But there are problems with this digitalization in video games. Although these new video games and action figures, like Marvel's Crystal Dynamics Avengers, locate Kamala and her companions on the streets, these icons have been largely stripped of their cultural identities. Why these gaps between the video game and the original story? These changes are intentional, for these games are designed to make money. Although her video game character (for clarity, referred to here by her last name, Khan) has familiar attributes of a teenager, which players relate to, there are very few distinguishing characteristics. This *digital stripping*—my term for the capitalist maneuvers of a "corporate game"—relies on a world where there are no racial problems.[42]

This stripped virtuality has extreme binaries. While you get to shoot at "baddies," just as problematically in this postracial world the "goodies," the Avengers, function like a happy family. It is, in effect, not only colorblind but a utopia laid out on a national platform. Shooting in a cityscape threatened by external force, continues the Avenger's end game, the threat to the US empire. Internal targeting of minority populations, raids by immigration officers, dissembling politicians, and economic problems of gentrification—all of this social trauma is lost in this video's metropolis. Given the vast number of game players in the US, this divide between Amanat and Wilson's protest production, the original story of Kamala's comics, and this Avengers video arena—the corporate game, starring Khan—creates virtual challenges and digitized stripping.

Although some critics consider the digital world, with its economies based on time and algorithms, as destructive,[43] others suggest that these new products invite visions of radical change. For instance, Fawaz sees flexible bodies of superheroes as rejecting heterosexual desire, the super-mutants who resist corporate forms.[44] In contrast, Adrienne Shaw sees video games as filtering the worst parts of our social fantasies into virtual worlds.[45] Similarly, Lisa Nakamura argues that racism and sexism are pervasive in video games, and gamers and the industry can be "brutal to women, people of color, sexual minorities, and anyone who signals difference online."[46] Although there are inclusive icons, inclusion in gaming is often set in a dystopia, argues TreaAndrea Russworm, limiting racial empathy, playing on stereotypes of suffering.[47] But there might be unrealized gender potential, argues Jennifer Malkowski, of having a femme fatale in a video game.[48] And when these virtual worlds destruct, video games suggest that our expectations of this virtual world crumble, a form of resistance.[49] Understanding problems and potential, this work provides an alternative model, a paradigm that offers two layers, a double conscious digitalization. The splintering impact that white codes of national identity have on marginalized communities has long been recognized in the idea of "double consciousness," a description by W. E. B. Du Bois in 1903.[50] Using the tools of superheroism, then, we can trace the ways that these icons of racial identities have splintered between subject and object. As digitalizations video games are an in-between space: neither a utopian space of imagination nor a set code.[51] On one level, these new products, these video games, promise to rescript racialization, confronting mass media's obliterations. But these ideals haven't stopped particular digitalizations, such as this Marvel Avengers video game, from eviscerating Amanat and Wilson's story of racialized trauma and activism.

Part of the complexity is that having a Pakistani American on the Avengers team beats killing her. Avengers has a daily range of under two thousand players per day, even though it launched at over thirty thousand players, and it was one of the top ten best-selling games when released in September of 2020.[52] But at least this Avengers game is less popular than the damaging *Call of Duty: Modern Warfare*, a shooter game that comes with "moral choices"—ascertaining, say, whether a civilian woman is a threat with a gun or just taking her baby from the crib—where you are penalized points for killing civilians.[53] Emulating the Syrian Civil War, the US Iraq War, and terrorist attacks on London, these games kill Muslims. Like the mass media that obscures the violence of US occupations, *all* of this video game warfare, unwilling to contend with the millions of dead and displaced Iraqis and Afghanis and Syrians, as well as thousands of scarred veterans, recreates

Afghanistan, Iraq, Syria, and other regions as visual spectacles of empire—callow, immoral, bloodless. Shooting at anyone with a scarf, not to mention gaming penalties, normalizing their deaths, has become a national pastime.

So, on this most profound level, this new Avengers video game would seem to be a vast improvement. At first glance the video game seems to offer, for once, an option of a Brown icon—not just super-whiteness—with her familiar voice and gesture, her mammoth fist raising and pounding and pounding and pounding again. Once Khan is put into motion, the massive simulation is not just played by one individual: thousands are becoming Khan—a powerful form of simultaneity, a national flexibility. Also most of those who play this action figure will have read the comics or seen the cartoon or miniseries put out by Disney+ Marvel. So in many ways, the icon summons nostalgia—not for Danvers, the white pilot, not for Rambeau, the Black lieutenant, but for the star of this video game, Kamala Khan.

But in terms of superheroism, we must look again: for in this video game, Khan is no longer an antiracist teenager but a weapon. Although there are games based not on hits and kills, with more imaginative options that are based not on deaths but on moving via levels, most video games have been criticized as "a victory of the quantitative over the qualitative."[54] And this is one of them. Problematically, says the animation designer Eli Vanderbilt, Avengers is a numbers-based game with little originality: kill "baddies," bring in the loot—a "boiler plate" game.[55] In contrast to Hulk's supersized ferocity, the diminutive Khan uses her fist as a hammer, but its incessant pounding—so unlike the negotiations of power in her original story, such as becoming more flexible and consulting others, so different than the stop-and-go panels of her comics—transforms her into yet another weapon of mass destruction.

When it comes to comics, it seems that Marvel's Crystal Dynamics was less invested in the story and more in the business aspect of video games. Its strategy is even a bit underhanded. As Vanderbilt puts it, the game play is like a Skinner box. For just as the rat is more likely to keep pressing the bar for a pellet if rewarded only half of the time, so too this video game works via uncertainty. If you hit the target, you may or may not get rewarded with more power or more weapons. What awaits you is a possible bonus, but as you keep playing, bigger upgrades cost money. Because the gameplay is in a loop, players become impatient for their character Khan to get stronger and are more willing to pay for extra resources. In short, it's like a slot machine, designed for addiction, pressing the lever for weapon upgrades. These transactions are the goal of corporate video games. This game's core motivation is business, not art.

Even as Khan's star role is presented—in short videos, intermissions between level 1 and level 2, designed for the game—these videos are a compelling incentive, keeping us invested in the game and attaching us to the teenager. But the opening scene is drastically and significantly revised. Her idea that she might become part of something bigger is no longer her reflection on activism after helping someone on the street. No, this time, Khan, traveling with her father to the Fanfiction contest, values competition. Although her loving father, Yusuf, still counsels her, his counsel is that "competition makes us strong." No longer is activism against immigration policies, or caring for others, rooted in ethics inherited from the Qur'an. Winning, competition, and fandom compose the world of video Khan.

So, while a nostalgic gaze returns to the series, the corporate production diminishes her. In the battle moves, we hear not only the galvanizing roars of the Hulk but the adolescent superhero, awkwardly apologizing for being late. In her very vulnerability and her casual Gen X charm, Khan is an essential part of the team—the warm heart of the Avengers. In one scene, slurping on her Slurpee in the midst of a battle, she even uses her extended arms to make a huge heart in the air. In these intermission clips, then, it is Khan who brings the team together, explaining that they are a superpower because they work together despite their differences.[56] But these differences refer not to ethnicities, but to getting along: the Hulk and Iron Man have been tearing each other apart. This game-world excludes her visits to the mosque and her cultural background.

Not surprisingly, then, Khan's game character has jeans and a backpack, so unlike Kamala's multitiered and shifting dress in her original story. In her origins the homeless sweater signals her activism. And while Kamala sports a scarf at the mosque, she wears her ornate dress—the *shalwar kameez*— at a wedding, congratulating herself for the extra bling. So Kamala's complex identity wears several guises: at the mosque, her long tunic and pants, reminding us of her Pakistani American heritage; her skinny jeans for hanging out; her modest swimwear, a lightning-bolted burkini, for rescue on the streets. In the video game, however, Khan puts on her costume not proudly but with embarrassment. She explains to Iron Man's alter ego, Tony Stark, that she is wearing modest swimwear worn by some Muslim women. It's not about the costume; "It's about the attitude," Stark responds. He replaces her complexity with a feel-good slogan: it's not about culture; it's about confidence. This video icon is stripped—appropriated. True, in her video game, a bare hint of her scarf peeks out. But the bling of the sparkling dress is gone.

Why? Because Marvel Avengers assumes players are not interested in complexity. All players begin with Khan as their role, and what they're interested in is that she's a bubble-popping teen. A big fan of Avengers. There's no sense of her multiracial family and friends. And the audience projects their own sense of self and fanfare onto her. A vapid remark that she's not a true fan of Avengers replaces the comic's racist remarks: the denigration of her parents, the remarks on honor killings, cracks about cultural exoticism. Appealing to the widest demographic, Khan's video player is a two-dimensional figure not meant to have much character at all. In fact, later levels offer the option of the Hulk. But either way, both players are means to an end—no experience on the streets, no racializations. In this format, then, it makes very little difference whether you select the brown- or the green-skinned icon. Like pieces in a Parcheesi set, it is a choice, not a sense of a society besieged with racism. She has been virtually stripped.

The video game erases not only Khan's city streets but her home as well. No banter with her brother, Tyesha is missing, her father is left behind; her game world offers substitute parents. These Avengers, these surrogates, are reading up on parenting and suggesting sit-down dinners.[57] In fact, the advice of her surrogate parent, the alter-ego of the Hulk, Bruce Banner, reminds her of her father. As a result this teen does not grow into her powers but relies on their rescue. In fact, when she gets bigger, Khan passes out, since she can't control her power. And it's no mother, but Black Widow—who claims not to like kids—who rescues her. Although this imaginary super-community is indeed a powerful form of nationalism—in their colorful costumes, the Avengers resemble an ad for Benetton's united colors—it erases signs of Kamala's community. She is a computer geek who has stolen information, in effect orphaned, like a poster child for diversity. Replacing Kamala's trauma and her transformation into activism, hacking codes and finding information Khan will save the world. A model minority. So even as her uncertainty is captured in cries of effort—the game's "arghh's!" and "oh's"—the anxious sounds of a teenager emerge in a postracial world, where she is much beloved. Even her sarcasm is born not of activism but of angst. True, her self-talk— "I'm not afraid of you"—is a form of empowerment, but it is not connected to her racialized identity, and it does not return her, at the end of the day, into the arms of her father.

## SUPERHEROISM: PLAYER DISCRETION ADVISED

Also challenging is Marvel's *Powers of a Girl*, a book that features the newest Ms. Marvel as a rather fair-skinned redhead in Alice Zhang's illustration, who looks like she could walk the beach in California.[58] Despite her full-body clothing, her teen action figure is more curvaceous, a type of sexualization.[59] These consumer products court the idea of *pretty citizens*, their notions of beauty corralling svelte body types. In contrast Wilson explains that they designed the teenager so many people can cosplay Kamala, far from a "size two." Outfitted, in her original story, in recycled wear from the streets, before her handmade costume, Kamala rejects any slick and slim beauty packages.

In fact, the original story gestures not toward the beautiful but to the superhero as grotesque. Although Kamala's superpowers—her upraised fist, enormously sized, or her distorted arm distending itself across the panel, a sight that is awesome and kind of gross, as her friend Bruno puts it—allow her to reshape her body, this is no beauty contest. Even her mascot, a gigantic, slobbering dog, is gross. She's no Wonder Woman never overwhelmed, never less than beautiful, never without her bullet-refracting bracelets, always a show of strength. No, one comic strip after another shows us a heroine seized with dismay, uncertainty, self-doubt. And what she discovers is that in order to fight, her body must extend itself. But while these enlarged figures may not be beautiful, they are essential forms of power during a time that calls for extreme responses. And Kamala is able to use her distorted shape for the good of all. Running into her nemesis, Dissent, she engulfs her with her engorged body, disabling the dissembler. *Gross.* Significantly, it is not only her engorged fist but her enlarged body—symbolic of the collective power and resistance of American Muslim women—that is able, in the end, to stop this assault. Afterward our superhero stands larger than life, while the enemy—well, she is reduced to the size of a Barbie doll. Miniaturized.

If Kamala's body is grotesque, it is a gigantic counterweight to mass media's object of rescue. But in Kamala's case, the grotesque is about the recovery of a body that is overextended in response to bullying as racist assault. Much more than the growth spurt of a teen, these exaggerations show how her body has been assaulted by Zoe's daily microaggressions as well as by political targeting. Refusing racist legislation of citizenship, these grotesqueries, her symbolic engorged fist as part of this thick activism, pulsing with historical remembrance, gives her power in these streets. She has to take a stand, leaving her vulnerable to ridicule as her arm distends itself into a giant fist that at first she can scarcely control. Putting yourself on the streets is not pretty. It's risky business. Her physical gestures, then, are evidence of these painful encounters, her extended features, her public protest.

But these gigantic gestures are also forms of assistance, to help others on the streets. So these distensions that "embiggen" Kamala, in the author's words, are designed not to make her appear more attractive but to show the painful nature of political work. In her original story in the comic series, when Kamala begins to come into her power, she vomits. She discharges her internalized inadequacies and racist exclusions, as she slowly finds her national form in protest, standing in solidarity in multiracial communities. This strategy of superheroism continues as they select a young actress, Iman Vellani, who found out about the show from her aunt on a group chat, and recalls middle school, where her entire world had always been about superheroes. When she dressed up as a superhero in a costume of Captain Marvel, "no one knew who I was," she said.[60] "Everyone thought I was the Flash. So I had to buy a comic book and hold it with me." In this series she is dressed up not as a beauty queen but as a young woman who distends her arm to save her nemesis, the bully Zoe, and stands up for herself in a world that doubts the idea of what the television script calls a Brown superhero. This superhero miniseries, ethically grounded in the radical inheritance of her grandmother's bracelet, and with Nakia running for the mosque board, had 11 million views of the trailer after twenty-four hours.[61] What we have here is no empty battle machine, no green hulk of a hero in a video game, but the anxious face of a young woman, grimacing with the effort of putting herself out there. It may not look pretty, but it is surprisingly visible. Superheroic, even.

But the game world has no room for this resistance figure with her diverse identities and the complex histories of her Muslim community—for Tyesha, her Black Muslim sister-in-law; or her nemesis Zoe, a white "Karen," whom she later befriends, and who later comes out as gay. Unlike with young Spider-Man or other teen Marvels, her advice comes from the center of the mosque, as the imam counsels her. So even as she defends the city, she returns to this religious milieu. When she enters the madrasa, a large banner advertises a community food drive with a call to help the poor, even as Kamala helps others. Unlike these video games, Kamala's original story—stitched into many of the strands of her miniseries—is interwoven with historical complexity.

Products that fail to tell the traumatic context of racism in this country come with a high price. That doesn't mean that there couldn't be some measure of dual awareness for the users. A product that any six-year-old can choose how to animate—the stuffed Kamala doll, for instance—does not necessarily rule out the ways in which this toy might also embrace a youngster's sense of longing. In the same way, those who select the Khan icon, a digital avatar harking back to the original story, might remember the racialization depicted in the original comic series. The avatar is imagined as both being and not being oneself, as Lisa Patty argues, for it is less about identification with the icon and more about the desire of the player to become an image.[62] But the frustrating constraints of this video game, where the tasks must be completed before advancing to the next level, limit any attachment to her. She is just a stage. The game is not a negotiated advancement but a money trap.

Still, player discretion is advised. We need a new set of rules on how to think of this new superhero as within or without history, challenging or glamorizing. The miniseries and Ms. Marvel dolls build inclusion. But in looking at the games and baby cartoons in the Disney world, there is the inevitable danger of glamorizing. Pairing up with Squirrel Girl in the spectacle of Disney+ Marvel Rising, inserting Black and Brown bodies in cartoons and video games without any cultural context is arguably a kind of stripping. Assimilation as a model of citizenry rejects any social and cultural heritage.[63] Superheroism therefore recodes early sex objects into radical feminism, surfacing around solidarities in the mosque community and in activism. Walking the streets—with the potential to purchase and to interact with others—is a relationship of power, writes the sociologist Pierre Mayol.[64] Leaving her home in the morning, chatting with her bestie at the mosque, going to the Circle Q, leaping buildings, negotiating money and space and policing—in all of these everyday enactments, she's navigating relationships in a city that needs her. This is the solidarity movement that is essential when the superhero—disrupting political fake news, dronelike weapons, and anti-immigration arrests—succeeds only when joining her friends and her neighborhood, to take back the streets. These forms of activism become increasingly diverse—Kamala, Nakia, Tyesha, the young women and their allies, including Kamala's friend Bruno, this panoply of political revivals, all pulsing with civic engagement. No longer a lone ranger, she has become part of a community. Holding her hands up and lifting her fist into the air and carrying schoolbooks and walking the streets—these gestures of political intimacy and of collective resistance lead to a rethinking of immigration policies and other patterns of exclusion. Superheroes are no longer white saviors or sex objects in glass planes, but rather these feminist icons, rooted in inheritances and bound in a body of protesters. "Do not be satisfied by stories that have come before," says Sana Amanat, quoting a Sufi poet in her YouTube video. "Unfold your own myth."

# Chapter 2

# ONLINE SPORT PROTEST

## Nike Wonder Women

As we interconnect ourselves, many of the values of a nation-state will
give way to those of both larger and smaller electronic communities.
—NICHOLAS NEGROPONTE, *BEING DIGITAL*

Black celebrity activists reach others online to expand resistance, but what
is needed, Spring-Serenity Duvall and Nicole Heckemeyer argue, is more
research on their *digital activism* in sport.[1] In response this chapter considers how protest is being built not only around fictional superheroes but also
around larger-than-life superstars—and the fans who decode their (digital) protest movements. When, for example, the fencer Ibtihaj Muhammad
learned that she had qualified for the US Olympic Team, she found out online
before she received official notification. At the same time, Google had taken
hold of her story as the first US Muslim woman, who wore her hijab, her
headscarf, on the US Olympic fencing team. From this moment on, she felt
that she was part of something bigger, she says in an online interview with
sport announcer Jemele Hill, even before winning her bronze medal, because
of the many women of color and Muslims who are not always welcome in
sport.[2] As in the raised fist of Kamala Khan as a superhero, sport stars have
also been raising their fists. In fact, ever since 1968, when the Black athletes
Tommie Smith and John Carlos raised their black-gloved fists during the
medal ceremony in Mexico City's Olympic Stadium, international sport has
been a venue for activism. Not in raising a fist or in taking a knee but in lifting her sabre, this Black Muslim celebrity enters into an ongoing tradition
of superstar athletes and their digital protest.

This chapter will track Muhammad's online icons; navigating this high-
way of digitalization, watching for her routes of innovation in Instagram,
her story of resistance; and analyzing the commercial potholes of Nike's

spectacular sport icons with their national frames. Thus, in this chapter, we follow Muhammad's innovative strategies—not just in posting her own self-images but on platforms, as on Instagram and on YouTube. Although the only Muslim on the team and one of the few people of color, she has navigated public and digital media to define where she "belonged."[3] After writing her memoir, with its red-white-and-blue cover, a superheroism image on its marketing sites of her Instagram as well as Amazon, with its patriotic title of *Proud*, she speaks of her story in online interviews, because as a digital activist, her online icon is a role modeling. "Had I had this story as a kid," she said in her YouTube interview in the "Authors Revealed" series, "it would have made a lot of the bullying and moments of sadness and depression easier."[4] She recalls assaults in school. "'Why are you wearing that tablecloth on your head?'" her classmate Jack Bowman kept asking.[5] Never knowing "where or when he'd show up," she remembers his surprising her from behind and punching her. On top of this, "certain girls in the cool club acted like I didn't exist. And the thing was, I never knew if it was because they didn't like me, or they didn't like my hijab."[6] On the fencing court, then, it was gratifying to look like her other teammates while being able to maintain her political and her personal beliefs. But she still encountered racism, including a coach calling her "M1," since she was Muslim, and a team member calling her the "n-word."[7] As a fencer Muhammad wanted to challenge the narrative that Black Muslim women are docile,[8] she says in her YouTube video, showing instead the feminism at the heart of Islam. All of which—the uncertainty of her personal, her racialized, her religious affinities—was part of her motivation to excel and to speak out, her reformulation of public and digital sport activism.

Posted on Instagram, her photograph of herself as a sport icon shows her holding up her sign: "MY HIJAB IS NOT YOUR BUSINESS."[9] The individual celebrity is by herself, her arms lifted as if ready to fly. Her background reflects the bluest of skies. A sport hero. Her caption resists the vote to ban hijabs in sport, calling out "what happens when governments and officials [as in France, as in India, as in Quebec] mask their discrimination with legislation."[10] And she moves from her sport icon into a collective calling: "We must stand together and vehemently denounce discrimination in all of its forms." It receives almost seven hundred comments. She views her online icons as part of a movement, wherein the journey of her sport is made available for the next generation of US Muslims.

And refuting any token position, in a few of her YouTube videos, she showcases other powerful Muslim women. In her captions she uses the trope of superheroes. For instance, her posting zooms in on fellow activist Lina

Khalifeh, who "always wanted to be a superhero."[11] And Khalifeh's antibully-
ing work includes training in self-defense, teaching others to develop "their
inner strength—and inner superhero." Her caption on Instagram further
illuminates the trope of superheroism and the "next generation" of women
fighters: "EMPOWERING THE NEXT GENERATION OF SHEFIGHTERS."
Creating a digital model of her sport icon, Muhammad also selects other
individual activists—part of her digital tactics of Black Muslim feminism,
her strategies of radical superheroism.

This identification of politics and her performed sport—her multiplicity—
is very much a part of rewriting racial scripts as a Black Muslim woman.
Her transformative vision is part of a larger momentum of resistance; she
recalls how this journey felt bigger than her.[12] Refusing the idea of the sole
protester, the *only* Muslim woman, as a token in sport, or an exception, she
has rejected the confusion around Islamic identities, repositioning herself,
not in single images but in an iconicity with multiple performatives, not
only as a woman of color but also as a woman who wore the hijab on the
US Team. Refusing racist assumptions that only Arabs can be Muslims, she
states that she is "American by birth. I'm not Arab." Further marking her
complex identity, she speaks of linguistic markers and racialized positions:
"I only speak English. I'm African American." Reposting and repositioning
clips in videos and snapshots in social media, she claims that she is one of
many activists in sport, even as it is a reclaiming of her multiplicity.

The tension for celebrities is that they need sponsorships even as these
commercials market certain postracial identities. As these forms of activism
open new venues of belonging, Stanley Thangaraj writes, as in the navigation
of and reception by the sporting world, these venues also create opportunities for social mobility, sponsorships, and new possibilities for greater media
visibility.[13] As accessories in Nike's sport arena—and the fashion world of
*Sports Illustrated*, of *Vogue*, and even Covergirl makeup—Muhammad and
her fellow athletes invite us to evaluate how these spectacles are not only
about money, financial leverage, essential sponsors, and marketing but also
about envisioning who belongs in the national spotlight. Although mass
media often shows images of the female Muslim protester as propaganda—in
need of rescue, for instance, as Lila Abu-Lughod has noted[14]—both digital
activism and its commercialization also need to be analyzed for its forms of
protest icons, of sport protest. Pressing back, these activists have been creating and re-creating themselves, in their own YouTube videos, in their own
Instagrams, in digital media, and in response to advertisements—complex
poses of stardom and of online resistance.

As a result, for instance, Muhammad receives emails and online comments on her own digital platform. This celebrity—at once a political star, a commercial figurine, a sport figure, a model for a new Barbie doll, and a Muslim icon—gets a ton of fan mail from Muslim families, not just because she won a medal but for being an inspiration. In her online videos and icons, we see clips of her story of resistance, her choices in digital activism—in her postings, in interviews with Stephen Colbert, and in talking to former President Obama, all asking her about her fencing and her faith. "'I told her to bring home the gold,'" President Obama said.[15] And young girls—usually Muslim or Black—seek her out as a mentor and as a role model as well, which is why she turned her memoir into a Young Readers Edition in 2018. In a stream of online interviews, she stresses that she wants not only to change perceptions outside of the Muslim community but also to inspire those within the Muslim community. And online, we can find her fencing, we can hear her protests, we hear her cry of victory. By following her own self-positioning in such iconographies, we discover her complex strategies of digital superheroism. This chapter shows her sites of digital activism, as we follow her own captions on her Nike commercials, her own videos of many activists, her own international locations.

In commercials, however, these digital athletes are often photographed and reproduced as "tensed in action, super men and super women"[16]—which almost looks like a patriotic frame, resembling the action figures of early wonder women. And Black female athletes, like Muhammad, are often even more scrutinized, for instance, when coded in the press in racist terms as not sufficiently feminine—a "super masculinity."[17] In response, athletes who are women of color have been using digital activism and their own fashion not just as style but as a power move, reclaiming what is sexy.[18] And these fashionable icons enter into their digital media. Despite fetishizations in sport products, their imaginative poses, their powerful outfits, their captions all create online media, reconceiving scripts that are racial and gendered.[19] As her sabre whips toward us, Muhammad has joined this protest movement as an athlete and a digital activist, drawing new attention to US Muslim athletes. Her interruption of mass media's spectacular fetishization, her marking of racialized citizenship in Black pride, her stylized icons are part of her innovative marketing of Black Muslim resistance. In tracing this celebrity and following her digital activism, what we see is a refashioning of sport as protest. As part of her online activism, her digital posts include her prayers, her Olympic uniform with red-white-and-blue, and the cape of the US flag that she wears like a superhero. "You pray" beforehand, she says. You "pray that all the stars align right for that day." In the end she took home the bronze, "very, very thankful" for her team, for her achievements, and for her prayers answered at the Olympics. Thus, her self-positioning as an activist in the digital world includes the complex aura of her faith, her abilities, her team, and her prayers—her prayers also bonding her to other Black Muslim feminists and other international communities. But before analyzing her photos and her captions, her Instagram icons, her red-white-and-blue postings, we need to enter the arena of mass/commercial media. Even as these athletes situate their own protests in icons in social media, their massively replicated icons have been consumed—mediated, commercialized, negotiated—in online media in sport advertisements.

## MASS MEDIA: DIGITALIZING SUPERSTARS

Although little has been written on Muslim women competing at sport in Olympic events, as shown by Sumaya Samie and Kim Toffoletti in *New Sporting Femininities*, there has been some research on how media depicts these sporting embodiments, notably, how the press invariably places these women in a metanarrative of victimization or exoticism, focusing primarily on their scarves—as if these athletes were not modern.[20] Given that there were two US Muslims at the 2016 Olympics, for instance, these critics ask why mass media ignored Dalilah Muhammad's cultural identity but not Ibtihaj's. Why? Because Dalilah didn't wear a headscarf. Thus, media inscribed type-codes of Muslimness. Even when her parents attributed her success to her Muslim faith, the *New York Post* just commented on her hard work.[21] Most problematically, her Muslimness was erased even as this newsflash made her into a token, an exceptional athlete who is from the US and, in contrast to racialized stereotypes of laziness, works hard. But no more attention was paid to how Ibtihaj Muhammad sees her identity. "'My hijab is liberating,'" she said, but her words were drowned in a general discourse on diversity.[22] Extending even further, beyond these critiques, what is also missing is any sense of Ibtihaj Muhammad's refusals of these codes, and of her virtual community, evident in her creative protests as in her own icon and its digital trail. This chapter navigates how her icons have been surfacing in public and digital pathways—not only as part of algorithms of empire that encode typologies of Blackness and Muslimness but in her inscriptions and iconographies of radical superheroism as her very pointed resistance.

## PROBLEMS IN MARKETING PROTEST:
## NIKE'S MUSLIM WONDER WOMEN

When Nike introduced its new sportswear in the spring of 2018, the advertisement began with Ibtihaj Muhammad, her eyes closed, her sabre swooping in ritualistic patterns across her watchful face. She is a celebrity worshipped, inspiring faith—a Rembrandt-lit saint. The piece itself a stunning black-and-white medium shot, as if in a documentary, zooming in on Muhammad and her fencing sword. This Olympic athlete is surrounded by the smoothest of blues, intertwined with the variegation of a near-rap beat, as the fifteen-second film moves between prayerful and absolute feminist power. What if we do, in fact, think of such advertisements as rituals, which, Kathryn Lofton argues, initiate their novitiates into "unconscious politics and overt economics"?[23] Enacting a trancelike awakening of this well-lit superstar, Nike's advertisements not only market those who wear the scarf but also sell ideas of a mystical performance of Islam, thus acting out a type of *religious* production. Even as it celebrates and thus sells female Muslim athletes, commercializing their products, its devotion to female power (and their paychecks) is a marketing of glamorous activism—in some ways fetishizing the veil, but in other ways opening a space that, at the same time, resists mass media's stereotypes of Islam.

At first glance, then, this widespread digitalization that traveled on iPhones and living-room flatscreens is a performance of power and virtue that has begun to circulate a female icon of a US Muslim athlete. Quite far from presenting sport in terms of white masculinities, here lie the virtues of femininities and power in an Islam no longer demonized. And her all-white fencing kit adds a new dimension, an online media of national aura and of Black power, encouraging, in effect, new icons of power. But there are limits to continual flows of angelic white—not an everyday image of racialization, not unlike a caped superhero in a video game, but an incarnation of glamour, a fetishization. While this series of #Believe commercials enhances acceptance of such diverse beauties and their movements, it is not very specific about what it is that we are to believe in.

As in the national branding of world war icons, Nike's wonder women, like Ibtihaj Muhammad or Serena Williams, multiply in cyberspace, shine with mystic power. Our sabre-bearer, an icon, a new superhero in the form of Joan of Arc, her eyes closed, surrounded by soulful rhythms, her fencing sword floating in a Sufi-esque meditative rhythm, seems to be in prayer.[24] This pose is in line with the activism of the civil rights movement, of taking a knee on the sports field, of the prayers of MLK before facing tear gas and racist crowds. But when she shifts into a beat-laden *awakening*, an athletic dream, the images of the slashing fencer in this Nike commercial double, then triple, then quadruple on the screen—a frenzy of fencing parries and thrusts, like a spiritual force, angelically clad in white. This iconization of purity and of power reimagines this striking athlete and activist as the model of the warrior icon. But there is no opponent in sight: at one point, she strikes, then disappears off-screen. In her role in the spotlight, she has become a new lady of liberty, a new belonging of the Black athlete and her faith. In Nike's commercial, she is one of the wonder women. And in this spectacular visual sequence, in one fell swoop, most spectators, while reverencing her as *national idol*, also participate in her marketing as a *religious icon*. This aura of prayer reimagines American Islam and recognizes this Black Muslim athlete as its icon. Blinking in the klieg lights of an icon, an exceptional athlete, our superstar in the States, this spectacle—US exceptionalism—does not neces- sarily defuse stereotypes. Furthermore, given her country's vehement assaults on Black women and on Muslims, what's missing in this marketing is any sign of external aggression—of the unseen opponent.

Not the superhero of the world wars, neither sex object nor woman in need of rescue, then, Muhammad's newly digital performance of Blackness and Muslimness emerges in a more active negotiation, even in a mystical sensationalism, introducing, for instance, the new Nike Pro Hijab, its distinc- tive white swoosh glimmering on her satiny, black head covering in an ad with over 1,100 views. Paradoxically, sport has been idealized as a nonpoliti- cal space, even as attention is given to protesting athletes, and this is not an embrace of all Muslims, focusing, rather, on our exceptional athlete. So vari- ous assumptions seep into these sites of power.[25] But its sites of protest are often viewed as masculine spaces. So, in all of these ways, then, the social construct of the Black athlete has critical importance. Blackness has become a location of political struggle, Ben Carrington suggests, resurfacing in high- powered commercials of Nike, a signature that has remained racialized.[26] Sweeping into Nike commercials, these racially spotlighted celebrities, these spectacular productions of success in sport marketing, following Cole and Andrews, contrast the ways that vulnerable groups have been targeted.[27] In Muhammad's case, her own political agencies and her multiplicities and even her prowess have become reconfigured—her Muslimness, her Black- ness, her feminism—in the spectacular icon of the athletic wonders, one of Nike's wonder women.

In the sport arena, we would hear the quotidian sounds of effort—the clash of foils, the explosive breaths, the thrum of the spectators. But in the

Nike world, musical accompaniment sets the mood for this mystical fencer, this shadow boxer. Producers are paid to reproduce the company's script, as Jonathan Beller argues, a development of the product in order to maintain a certain economic gain.[28] So what we are watching is more than the victory of the popular Olympic fencer, for the filming of the spectacle is a fetishization of her labor—what Beller sees as a *counterrevolution*, no less than the triumph of commodity fetishism.[29] #JustDoIt. When the camera cuts to the next move, in a mystical and nearly magical movement, the athlete herself is transformed into a product, a spectacular fetishization—her supportive fans, her opponent, her experiences of racism, the specificities erased.

What's more, even as the corporation turns toward feminism, branding the swoosh of Nike as a sign of female empowerment, hidden is the exploitation of women workers in Vietnam and Indonesia, paid around two dollars a day to make shoes.[30] There are massive amounts of wealth in racial scripting, setting up sport as a game played for money, the sport production.[31] On Facebook this video is accompanied by a byline, messaging for Nike Muslim women, which promises free Nike Pro Hijabs to those who convincingly tell the editor why sport is important to you.[32] Picking a few of her favorite comments, the Nike editor will reply to her responders, shipping them their new product (limited to US participants only). With over a hundred thousand views linked to Muhammad's Facebook site, not to mention its over one hundred comments, as well as ninety shares, this commercial is part of a greater marketing of celebrities, in a larger reimagination and reproduction of Islam. But it's not about promoting specific political changes. It's about producing a product.

When we heart a product, it is a way to distinguish ourselves, as people participate in or criticize an object as part of an ethics and topic, which is how our contributions toward popular culture build a larger public.[33] When we select products, Lofton continues, we make commitments to certain scenes, responding to the sounds and the scenery of the commercial.[34] Indeed, after giving my own heart to this Nike site, in liking this advertisement, I am not alone. Dina, Suad, and Mennah—my Facebook friends and fellow activists from the American Muslim Women's Empowerment Network—pop up with their own first names, their photos showing up online, all part of a call-and-response, all reaching out. We are in accord. We—and 181,109 others—are one. The movement of the market follows, as well, a political trail—not in action but in virtual communities and solidarity groups and digital bonding.[35] We are all following a protest icon, selecting a celebrity.

Given these extreme politics of these racial icons, how can we consider Nike commercials, with their thousands of hits and likes, a worldwide web of consumers and their communities in the digital world? It's a billion-dollar industry. But first let's start with the commercial marketing of activism. Is this what American success looks like? You know you've "just *do[ne]* it," and just made it when you've been commodified? When you've been turned into a Barbie? Into an online icon? Given that, at $20–$30 a pop, Nike Pro Hijab hoods are more expensive than other sport caps, the market clearly makes money off these activists. Their sleek look, originally marketed in more austere navy and black, has given way to demands for other colors, echoing the multiplicities of women and their various tastes. Emblazoned with the familiar swooshing symbol of Western sport, the very polyrhythmic soul of US capitalism and competition, these sport heroes (and their fellow women on the streets) are active protesters, as they run and foil and box, they are rejecting the stereotype of Muslim women who never leave the house.

But what happens when we explore the history of these icons, the roots of commodification? Although Nike advertised its commitment to these sport products as early as the spring of 2018, detailing its eleven months of work toward their design, they were not the first to offer a line of sport and trendy styles. Tracking various designs, Emma Tarlo writes about two designers in Europe: one in Britain, another in Holland. Despite their common commercial interests, starting in 2005 and 2007 respectively, these designers had distinct objectives. In London, Wahid Rahman focused on Muslims wanting trendy styles, while maintaining a sense of modesty in keeping with their religious ideals.[36] But his shop also purchases Capsters designed by his competitor Cindy Van den Bremen, a social activist from Eindhoven who values accessible forms, such as outdoor, tennis, and skating models, as part of her commitment to multicultural justice. Consulting with Muslim women, Van den Bremen has created simple, practical models that fasten with zippers rather than Velcro, allowing air flow within the fabric and versatility for sundry movements.[37] On the other side of the channel, Rahman's hijabshop .com advertises that 10 percent of his profits go to charity, to helping the poor, a kind of tithe, a corporate *zakat*.[38]

In contrast, a plastic head decked in a Capster sits on the designer's desk in Holland. Lacking any logo or insignia, commercial or religious, the motif is girl power. Van den Bremen's website supports *Women Win*, offering special rates in Africa and the Middle East, indicating the developer's ideals while further promoting its products and branding.[39] In short, the sport cap has been marketed in a variety of ways: not only as a religious/cultural sign or as a practical product, but rather hijab as a form of fashion. Both designers have been called in by institutions, such as governments, prisons, sport groups, Islamic charities, and even by IKEA for its uniforms, all seeking advice on their products. As marketable objects, these sport goods have been thrust into the political and digital limelight.

## NIKE'S MUSLIM WONDER WOMEN:
## GLOBAL PROBLEMS

This section shows how the sport icon—these commercial icons of Nike that contrast national and international hijabi women—simultaneously have been divided. These commercials imagine Ibtihaj Muhammad as a warrior icon, a kind of action figure, like a wartime wonder woman, parrying to jazz music. But this superhero image contrasts its other commercials of Muslim athletes from other countries in an oppressive milieu of Muslimness. This fantasy world allows us to celebrate the Black American Muslim woman and continue these patterns of Islamophobia. Nike's urban billboards and digital commercials only exacerbate mass media's misunderstanding of sport activism in general and US Muslim athletes in particular. Take, for instance, the *New York Times* article "Nike Reveals the *Pro Hijab* for Muslim Athletes," about a commercial that appeared in the Middle East, featuring, among other young women, a horseback rider, a *traceuse* leaping from one building to the next, and then a gang of cool women lounging on their Harleys. We see the figure skater Zahra Lari from the United Arab Emirates, the fencer Ines Boubakri from Tunisia, and Jordan's boxer Arifa Bseiso rising to the surface of a pool in a kind of ecstatic baptism.[40] Writes the journalist Valeriya Safronova, Nike released its commercial featuring female athletes from the Arab region with the tagline, "What will they say about you?" Voiced in Arabic, this campaign introducing the pro-hijab was beamed onto screens in South Asia, the Middle East, and North Africa, and then translated into English. But why, then, did the *Times* account of this commercial include a seemingly requisite photo of Ibtihaj Muhammad winning the bronze in the Rio Olympics in 2016, her cry of victory palpable, raising her sabre aloft, her masked helmet emblazoned with its patriotic colors?

Once again, as in her iconization in the press, there is no context, no story. There is only this image, not of Saudi Arabia, not of Dubai, but of a Black Muslim from Maplewood, New Jersey, even though she is not, in fact, in the commercial itself. In the *New York Times* article, she is but a cipher. A hook. Eye candy. What needs decoding, then, within mass media's celebration of women athletes are the ways that the press encodes Arabness, Muslimness, Blackness. What's missing is the context of Ibtihaj Muhammad's own story, her own tale of political activism and racism. And in these international frames, US Black Muslim sport activists become the sign of having just "made it," as an exception to the general rule of global Muslims.

Let's see these sports icons in the fantasy land that Nike designs overseas. Situated in landscapes that are being associated with the Middle East, these commercials about athletes awakening into their powers offer a particular kind of *political propaganda*. Most troubling, in this staging of #Believeinmore, and in Nike's framing of what "they say," is the question of who are *they*. As it turns out, they are the disapproving elders standing on the sidelines, skeptically eyeing a runner and then a skateboarder zipping past. The jaundiced faces of the Muslim elders that frame the accomplishments of these young, singular brave hearts remain problematic. Staging these boxers, skaters, and horseback riders against the backdrop of a larger culture of Islamic negativity, a mass of conservatives, is once again to (literally) buy into a very Western and, as a result, very skewed take on Islam. For, in the gaze of many Westerners, these wizened elders, the apparent face and framework of belief, once again stereotype Islamic practice as nonadaptive, even archaic. All of which is particularly ironic given that this commercial ends with its focus on belief: "Believe in More." In short, the same commercial that seeks to promote belief in feminism provides us with an implicit indictment of Islamic forms of belief, reinforcing assumptions about static generations and their cultures, indeed, turning the parents into social scolds who do not, in fact, believe—who do not believe, that is, in their own daughters and their own granddaughters. Since this video was translated into English and placed on YouTube (watched by over a million viewers), then spotlighted in the *Times*, Nike has clearly been marketing to a Western audience as well. This is problematic on a couple of levels: in terms of imperialism, in terms of feminism. Muslim women need to be wrapped in Western values and goods to get out of their ghettos. Thus, these massive mediations are part of the national frames that strip Muslim women of their capabilities, replacing their work, as Samie and Toffoletti write, with the rhetoric of the "West is best."[41]

These wonder women of propaganda are controlled productions. Joining thousands in clicking on the resulting YouTube video, we are surprised to find ourselves plunged into translucent waters alongside the liquid beauty of Arifa Bseiso, a young Jordanian fighter.[42] At the same time, in Arabic, an omnipotent voice intones that there will be an emergence of these athletes *who believe*—who believe in themselves. While a playful part of the video, it is also a rite of passage, a rebirth. Her boxer's hands wrapped in linen, her eyes closed, suspended, gathering herself in the watery depths, the fighter in this moment is almost prayerful in her serenity. Hers is an unexpected baptism. And then, her eyes flashing open, there is an awakening. Throughout is an amorphous, male, almost godlike voice-over. It is the voice of empire. Witnessing the awakening into power of these young Arab women—the submersion of a boxer, the runner leaping fearlessly from one building to the next—we become part of their digital transfiguration, baptized in these communal waters. We want to believe. But what we believe in is empire— that the swoosh is sending Muslim girls on their way, an imperialism of rescuing others.

Further missing in this newspaper article and in these commercials are the ways that Arab women have long played sport—a heritage of self-actualization and social progress. Their activities are not necessarily new, nor are Arab women's powers delivered by the Western world, arriving in a box tagged with a swoosh. The caption of Ibtihaj Muhammad's ad is "Be the hero you didn't have," but it's not true that these women haven't had any Muslim feminist heroines. And given many Westerners' misconceptions of the Islamic world, scrolling past this article on an iPhone or watching this commercial on YouTube may reinforce the stereotype that what is holding these young, spirited athletes back is their culture—that the real problem is, in fact, Islam itself. This is not just consumption for the few: Nike isn't just marketing athletic headwear for the Islamic. No, the market is the world at large, and what is being branded is belief itself. "Believe in More," the commercial concludes.

But this is not just about imperialism. There is a problematic coding of feminism as well. At least Muhammad makes a showing in Nike's stirring "*Dream Crazier*" commercial, which celebrates female prowess alongside emotive expressions coded in society as crazy.[43] Many more athletes flash by. And among the panorama of these women—a runner, boxer, weightlifter, snowboarder, and more—there stands Ibtihaj Muhammad, veiled in white, shouting out a cry of victory. There is Megan Rapinoe, star of the US soccer team, said to be "delusional"; an "unhinged" Sue Bird playing basketball for the Seattle Storm. And, finally, Serena Williams, coming back for more after twenty-three grand slams and a baby. Then the Nike slogan that is associated with female power: *It's only crazy until you do it.* But what's "it"? "Do" what?[44] The coding's so vague that consumers are free to rewrite the script. The spectacle of feminism keys into their emotional moments, without showing the ways society punishes them for showing emotion. And here, most troubling, Nike showcases the one Muslim athlete, spotlighted in her patriotic red-white-and-blue uniform, reproducing her victory "war cry" at the end. What is not shown are how emotions of hijabi women are not just labeled. Their emotions have been politicized, sexualized, criminalized, and policed.

And these commercials have been placing icons of resistance that inter-sect Muslimness and Blackness without giving much voice to the kinds of belief of these diverse sport athletes. Female power and racial identities and athletes become part of an array of images promoting individual sport prowess. Narrating, the Black activist Colin Kaepernick walks amid a mon-tage of aspiring athletes—runners, football players, refugees playing soccer, and, in her sport veil, a Muslim boxer. In these spectacular close-ups, lines of gender, race, religion, abilities all flash by.[45] All flow in a mass media currency and spectacular current: not Black pride, not politics, but belief in yourself. Focusing on the individual athlete, what is being redefined is power, not as a political but as a private matter. This is not structural change. This is a *conditional citizenry*, where athletics offers a door to enter, but only for the individual—for Michael Jordan, Serena Williams, Colin Kaepernick, Ibtihaj Muhammad. It is not an antiracism campaign. Not de-imperializing. Rather, what we have here is glamorous belief in glittering accomplishment for the iconic few. That this is a private matter is the propaganda of empire: the survival of the fittest.

These are problematic—postracial icons, voiceless. Again, at the end of this commercial, a female Muslim, completely voiceless in this video, watches us. But this time she is one of many images, and many races, one of many visuals beamed onto the buildings of a city, illuminating diversity in a utopia with no racial challenges. Transformed into luminescent billboards, lighting up a cityscape backlit by those who have faith in themselves, all these young dreamers watch over the small cars below. At the same time, however, these highlighted dreamers obscure the streets, territories policed by immigrant bans and hostile government policies. So even as Nike booms out an essen-tial hope in sport feats, its postracial and postmodern billboards continue to strip everyday lives, eradicating ethical and spiritual values, erasing along the way racist structures—emptied icons.

From swimsuits to sport leggings, tennis shoes, and even fashionable bags, these ads have been reconceiving their markets, buying into *new* ideas of race and place. Still, what is sporty, what is sexy, what is beauti-ful is also political. In recently selecting more sport icons, political icons, supermodel icons who are US Muslims, the mainstream beauty industry has been refashioning its latest look. These are the new fashionastas—*Vogue Arabia*'s fashion shoot of Ibtihaj Muhammad, featured in the "Fashionable 50" of *Sports Illustrated*,[46] which has been updating its swimsuit issue as well. These recent icons are very much in the klieg lights, a spotlight on beau-ties and on swimwear and on goods as part of an economy of Muslimness, accessorizing ethical concerns as well as advertising their claim to being cosmopolitan, because of their iconic fashionistas. Although headlines such as "The Statement Makers," advertised in the *New York Times*, frequently pop up online, seeming to promise racial progress, in the end it's an ad for a handbag. As it turns out, Rothy's "New Kind of Statement Bag"[47] features the supermodel Halima Aden, sporting an enormous (and very expensive) red, politically correct bag, made from recycled marine plastic. Clutching its strap, she stares ahead, not amused but nevertheless rather luminous, almost angelically lit. Her all-black scarf complementing a black Western suit, her sunburnt turtleneck—the only bit of color—accentuating the bag, her cheeks brushed with a glamorous sunny blush, this modern icon, this fashion queen, advertises new beliefs about consumption. "Clothes on my back, clean drinking water . . . those things were luxuries in my childhood," she says, recollecting her days in a Somali refugee camp, in Kenya. "Now, luxury is being able to choose to support brands that are sustainable and ethical." For those concerned with the refugee crisis, climate change, the pandemic and the like, the extravagant amount of money spent on a handbag has turned into an ethical opportunity. No child labor, no minimum wage paid here. As an icon she becomes marketed as part of the solution for our environmental concerns. Her superstar icon functions as a remodeling of places—from Somalia to Kenya—so that her multinational background is not really about refugees. Rather, it is an iconic *new* lens on the cosmopolitan nature of Black Islam in the US—not unlike the branding of the world-class fencer in *Sports Illustrated*—itself, then, converted into a commodity for international consumption.

What is at stake here is no less than a new marketing strategy. These ads combine celebrity icons and ethics, a commercial production of our national values as reflected by women who are Black Muslims. But their experiences of trauma are elided. This same advertisement, for instance, homes in on Halima Aden. "You're a former refugee, an immigrant who some perceived as an outsider when you first entered the fashion industry," says the unnamed interviewer, presenting these stories beyond the runway of swimsuit fashions, for the bag company. "What important things have you learned about yourself since then?" "People will accept you and love you when you're true to yourself," Aden answers. But, as usual, there is neither time nor space made for follow-up on what being true to herself means for this Black Muslim fashionista. What these skimpy lines gloss over are the ways that the flood of refugees is an ongoing, government-sponsored crisis. What is being purchased is a remaking of a place, a refugee camp, into a commodified bag. Circumventing trauma, eliding any sense of ethics, this commercial has long abandoned the trail of political change.

True, breaking barriers in modeling swimwear, Aden talks about how she deals with the bullies. But no stories of racism are written here to build awareness. Instead she is positioned as part of a greater movement. And truly, representing racialized bodies in a world that has scripted power in beauty codes of whiteness is critical.[48] "It's bigger than just you," she says. Traces of her quotes move beyond these lines of fashion. When she feels overwhelmed, she remembers that others are enduring greater trauma, something ten times harder. But the trauma of others remains elusive, undefined. Within these portraits, then, the fashionable and the ethical and sportswear link hands in some troubling postures. In one of her photo shoots, she sits on the floor, among four other models, leaning forward, finally laughing—a rather vulnerable posture, given that she is a former refugee amid four other models, and even more problematically, the only model of the Islamic faith.

As this commercial highlights the challenge of breaking into *Vogue's* runway, into the swimwear sport fashions, the ad relocates her in not only in the context of her childhood at a refugee camp, not only in the international dreamer's success on the runway, but also by turning her luxury item into a solution for an environmentally sustainable future—a monetary lens on Blackness and on Muslimness and on US-based success. Even now Halima Aden, starlit with her luggage, is being carried into digital media of the news and its ads, online formulas of a glowing model of the cosmopolitan, a fashionable remodeling of Black Muslims, reconceiving racial scripts and their online territories. These racialized icons of sport and fashion threaten to break through their prescribed roles even as these icons are carved by media into an American dream, as Fleetwood writes, a sign of overcoming racial inequality—glittering symbols of public perception.[49] But beyond this chimera, the algorithms of empire press on. For what is not accounted for are the ways refugees often move with only what they can carry. Their own bags, their clothing slung over their backs. Not a luxury item. The impact of colonialism with its ensuing wars, as well as the history of turmoil in the near-permanent encampments, as well as their refugee status is a case that is never opened.

Although whiteness is still the primary framework of fashion magazines, these commercials with their racial icons, highlighting iconic athletes, politicians, and supermodels alike, can be recoding, resisting white screenings, appealing to next-gen activists as a form of political repositioning, even as the coding of its production, its interpretive messaging may be undoing that very work. As a form of public discourse, then, landscapes in *Vogue*, in *Sports Illustrated*, in Nike, its new racial scripts, its new politics, its spectacular positioning of an international glamour through US Black Muslim icons—all of this comes at a price, even while bringing attention to these ceiling-breakers, a loss of values, as part of corporate profit.

Nevertheless, it is as individuals that we decode meaning. And these popular icons in countercultural communities have also been at work, refashioning power. For instance, even as a racial icon is seen as a model for a particular group, there can be resistance to the coding of norms. Viewers have choices—kinds of reception, critiques of the branding, decisions about purchasing, argue Brian Wilson and Robert Sparks.[50] And body posture determines perceptions of authority.[51] Like the raised fists and wide stance of a boxer (or sensual glances), these recent power poses can elicit the very presence of Black Muslim feminism.

Further refashioning herself, Ibtihaj Muhammad is one of the key stars in an April 2019 article, "Women Shattering Stereotypes," in *Vogue Arabia* alongside other celebrities, such as fashionista Halima Aden and the politician Ilhan Omar—all stunningly adorned with clothing and cosmetics.[52] These rags-to-riches stories, alongside star-worship of those who have risen to fame, fully accompanied by their merchandising, are, of course, embedded in toxic traditions of the too-slender figure or, as shown, in disjunctive interpretations, as in the marketing of our newly digital hero. Although this mass marketing of Ilhan Omar, Ibtihaj Muhammad, and Halima Aden, as popular icons—these political superstars, burkini beauties, ravishing swordswomen—come with problems in placing the political and the sport and the fashion icon on the same page, it still succeeds in gathering a new form of cultural capital, even as it receives contestation in its responses.

Whether flipping through screen shots or *Vogue* or *Sports Illustrated*, checking out the beach shots of Halima Aden, skimming these issues in the press, buying hijabi Barbies, participating in online chats, surfing across social media, or reposting these images, multiple publics are clearly participating in a greater movement. As suggested in the chapter on virtual revolutions, racial codes of power and beauty are being reimagined. Now you can buy from Amazon an eleven-inch, $29.87 Barbie Ibtihaj Mohammad, with its absurdly small waist, tiny fencing uniform, sabre, and mask. Or buy her cosmetics, while watching her moving interview for Covergirl, spoken in front of the mirror as she applies her foundation, her sparkling eye shadow, her rich, kohl-like, eyeliner.[53] At the same time, these online practices produce value, their posts creating social status and political perspectives, as well as cultural and economic capital for digital activists.[54] These next-gen activists have been recoding values and intimacies in their icons, a powerful digital reconstruction—their own radical superheroism.

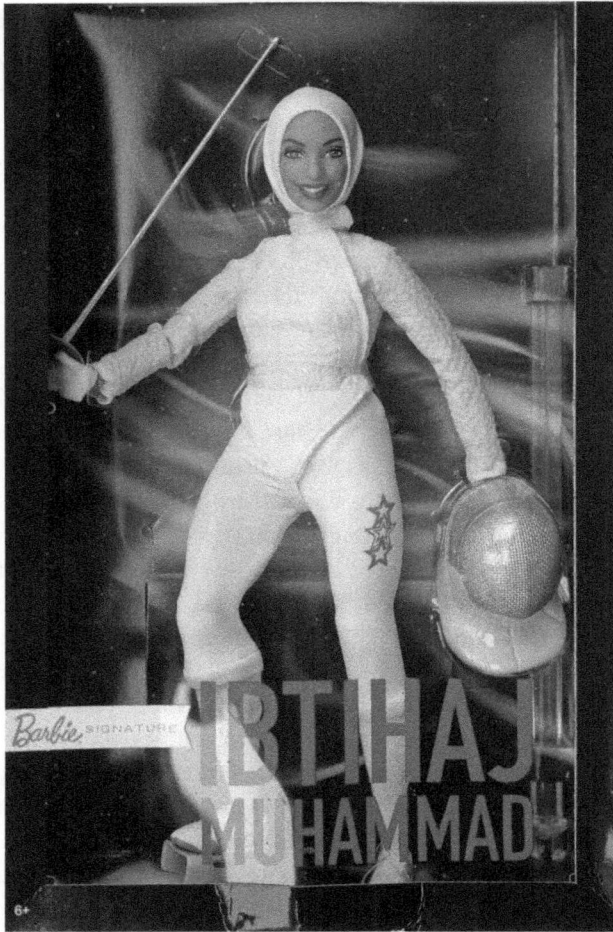

Barbie Ibtihaj Muhammad, Doll with Sabre. Photograph by author.

## RADICAL FEMINISM:
## MUHAMMAD'S DIGITAL ACTIVISM

On one level, then, this branding of the sport icon in commercials rejects overt stereotypes of passive Muslim women: as they are active in sport, they invoke Nike's #JustDoIt. And they #Believe. But believe in what? What is invisible in the celebration of this fencing star is her own naming, her own claiming of racialized citizenship. In her inventive superheroism rooted in her Black Muslim feminist *counter*script to mass media, she's staging her own resistance. As a digital activist, she crafts her own signs and signatures in her promoted activism on YouTube, rejecting stereotypes of sporting femininities, reinventing her star icons. As this chapter demonstrates, in the many photos and captions that reflect the hybridities woven into Muhammad's political postings—her creative speaking into her nuanced affinities, as well as her reinventing of Black trans/nationalism[55]—she demands action and critical thinking on the status and nature of these new superstar icons.

As a political tactic on one of her many sites on the web, in her YouTube videos, she traces her journey from childhood to champion and recalls the many times of her life that could easily have broken her.[56] After repeated bullying she fell into long periods of depression. As the only veiled girl at Columbia High School, she struggled with anxiety, but she records how her family and her faith helped her through—critical steps in her journey as a superstar. When she overcame her paralyzing anxiety on the fencing court, there was a distinctive activism in search of her own sense of Black Muslim feminism.

As an activist Muhammad's selection of self/family images—her own resistance aesthetics—demonstrates her bond to her family and their pride in Black Muslim feminism. In her memoir, *Proud*, she explains her mother's compelling desire to be a Muslim. Her mother, Denise, grew up in relentless racism and police brutality in the city of Newark, New Jersey.[57] When Denise decided to convert, it was her own form of "reinventing her life, rewriting her story."[58] This solidarity turned toward Islam, as Carolyn Rouse demonstrates, because of the potential to refuse racist structures that surrounded them.[59] As her mother states, it was a spiritual sense of compassion with an alternative modelling of social codes, as they were in the streets, offering protection from police brutality—as part of a merciful religion.[60] Black Muslims stood up for their rights and political needs, expressing a solidarity even in their dress, fashionably reclaiming their community, showing their pride in a political identity, sharing their hopes in a way forward amidst the structured racism in the US. By wearing long pants and long skirts, she was in control of how her body would be viewed, Ibtihaj Muhammad recalls. Thus it was that this community of women—resisting toxic white codes—refashioned gendered agencies and street aesthetics in their Black Muslim feminism.

In the YouTube series "The Secret Life of Muslims," Ibithaj Muhammad, wearing a bright red Nike sweatshirt and sleek, black scarf, takes her own political stance. "Being unapologetically Muslim, Black, a woman," she says, "either you like it or you don't." And "I don't really care either way."[61] In an Instagram post, Muhammad noted how so many are pleading for invites to the Metropolitan Museum of Art's fundraiser, celebrating how mostly white supermodels are wearing the *newest* fashion, which has turned toward head

scarves and long-sleeved clothing that is less revealing, more modest. At the
same time, however, when these styles have been worn by women of color
who are Muslim, there is "bashing, banning, dragging" of those who have
long worn these styles.[62] Wearing all black with a wrap on her head and
dark sunglasses, she looks away from the camera. "Your racism, xenophobia,
Islamophobia is showing." Her distant gaze is a refusal. Her caption concludes, "Get it together." Almost seventeen thousand liked her post.

So unlike the feminists of her mother's generation, instead, she developed
her own mode of digital activism. Battling the Scylla of bullying and the
Charybdis of anxiety, the budding fencer rose above it all. "I have to shake it
off," she kept telling herself. "I have to perform." Not too far, actually, from the
Nike commercial, #JustDoIt. But unlike the spectacular ad, in this case, she
was doing her sport in a landscape of post-9/11 oppression. Not only through
dedication but also through continued devotion, succeeding in school and on
her team, while embracing the strength of her mother's practices of Islamic
activism in community, all the while combatting racism in the sport and
academic field—in all these ways, she defines her resistance, as in her digital
aesthetic, in her Black Muslim pride, as part of her celebrity icon. Unlike the
commercialized idea of #Just Do[ing], sport has brought Ibtihaj Muhammad
a sense of personal pride, proud of herself for making it out to the other side.
Her protest icon shows a pride not in the nation with its police brutality and
its endless wars, but rather, a pride in herself in having survived the endless
empire of racialized assaults.

Distinctly *reinvented*, then, Muhammad offers us her own brand of American Islam, her own sense of self and of power, including her own icon of
superpower. On her Instagram posting on the Fourth of July, for instance, she
wears the flaglike cape around her shoulders. She is not facing the camera. It
is a posture of resistance. Her caption details how in 1776 the United States
still held hundreds of thousands of African Americans in captivity.[63] With
9,635 likes, showing appreciation of her digital activism, she is reconstructing her own iconicity, artistically and digitally and historically. Hers is not
the commercial figure of Blackness inscribed in the usual patriotic tints and
hues. Rather in reflecting on her history and her story, as in her first games
at the Olympics, her captions and her iconicity model this online potential
for other Black Muslim women. And in her own way, then, in her public
staging, in her online activism, rewriting her story, her history, her iconicity,
wearing the cape of a superhero, Muhammad expresses her desire to serve
as a model and as a mentor for Black Muslim women. An inscription of her
own resistance aesthetic—her digital icon of sport activism.

Through her online activism, we learn of her roots and resistance—
a much more complex story than mass media's celebration of her place on
the US Team. YouTube's February 2017 episode of "The Secret Life of Muslims" tells the story of her transfiguration into an activist. Having grown up
in Maplewood, New Jersey, not far from New York City, she went to Duke
University, graduating with a double major in international relations and
African American studies, crossing global and national lines, suggesting her
early awareness of colonial legacies and modern racisms. And she minored
in Arabic, further reflecting her own faith and her family's resistance of racist
structures as part of a pride in Black Muslim power. Her posting of trans/
national contexts refuses the divide between the US icon (as exception) in
contrast to global Muslims.

Even as the branding of commercials has sensationalized icons and theo-
rized the individual dreamer, so that, in so many ways, these productions
have lost sight of the origin stories, as in the case of Ibtihaj Muhammad,
digital activists have been fighting back—posting their own radical icons and
networks as part of this era's political consciousness. In this digital world,
Muhammad protests France closing down an athletic company that sold
pro hijab products by Nike. "France has not joined the global conversation
around inclusivity," since they have prohibited the cap at a sport company,
she contests.[64] "Sport is supposed to be inclusive of everyone," she continues,
"no matter where you're from, your sexual orientation, your faith, your skin
color, your gender." This news springs up in our online search, her YouTube
site, linked to the AFP News Agency. Far from the patriotic imagery, she
showcases her own form of Black Muslim feminist trans/nationalism—with
sexual inclusivities in a sisterhood of global Muslims.

In this digital activism, Muhammad includes her friends and her family as well—as part of her heteroglossic virtuality—and what Nike never
adds: her faith practices as a Muslim. Traveling with her family and close
friends, she goes on a pilgrimage to Mecca. During the trip, she posts pictures of herself and her friends in Instagram. Unlike the lone image of the
sport hero, this photo of the group creates their own branding of Black
Muslim trans/nationalism. And two women wear white Nike hats. Almost
forty thousand travel with her, liking her image. And in her series "Travel
Top 5," she features Morocco, educating her virtual community about the
history of French colonization. She turns to the ancient city of Medina
and teaches about the call to prayer. Her heteroglossic virtualities in her
posts on Instagram span from her travels to her politics. Her post receives
18,667 likes, expressing appreciation for the athlete on tour, and self-positioning

in a global community of faith. Beyond the commercial icon of the national superhero who fights for *our* US Olympic team, her online icon is a part of a trans/national community, a prayerful *ummah*, which includes Blackness. Connecting to others, via their digital streams of faith, she lists her hashtag that praises God: #alhamdulillah.

In terms of her online activism, Muhammad's internationalism also claims racialized solidarities. There is, for instance, a political posting, a clip of BLM billboards in Los Angeles, in all caps. It was viewed by 28,062 with eighty-six comments. She captions another video link for her interview with ESPN. "Breonna is all of us. We all see ourselves," she writes. "That could easily have been me." Not in her uniform with a flag, her next photo shows her in a shirt in all caps as well: "ARREST THE COPS WHO KILLED BREONNA TAYLOR." Then she stands in solidarity with Palestinians, another vulnerable group that has faced extreme dispossession, pointing out "colonization, military occupation, ethnic cleansing and apartheid." The post received an avalanche of responses—881 comments—all responding to "we all deserve the right to live life free of violence and free." Locating issues of race in certain places directs her viewers in a specific orientation, making more space, as Sara Ahmed argues, a way of viewing the world.[65] Reframing race and place in her posts, her heteroglossic virtuality is framed by her politics and personality and her own digital activism—a Black Muslim feminist trans/nationalism.

As part of her strategic approach, then, Muhammad's online accounts include other accounts of racism. In many ways the empire of visualities can be contested only with many voices. On her own Instagram, she includes interviews with other Black athletes, such as Ashleigh Johnson, a sport hero of hers, considered the best goalie in the world, a two-time Olympic gold medalist in 2016 and 2020 for water polo. By way of introduction, Muhammad writes that this gold medalist was often the only Black girl in the pool in Florida. How did she find her way to this sport? Muhammad asks. As a kid, "no one looked like me in the sport," Johnson says. She had to fight against the stereotype that "Black kids can't swim." And "people asking about your hair," in ways that make you feel like "you don't belong here," she adds. Her mother fought for her, but she had to believe that she belonged. She narrates problems of access and the "history of exclusion" to people of color in swimming. "You have to represent or show up for your community," she says, a mirror for others—essential sport activism—so they can contact her on Instagram. So even as the mirroring of athletes that look like us is work that Nike does extremely well, what's missing are the intimacies that include explicit structures of racism, heteroglossic voices, identities, and experiences. These interviews as digital activism, are part of this critical mirroring, for

"God has unexpected plans for us!" Muhammad says, her own Black Muslim feminism evoked in this virtual conversation.

What is not seen in this posting and others is the amount of extra labor that is done by those who have been marginalized as US Muslims. Sponsorships are critical to these athletes. But this arena has been largely dominated by white athletes, raking in the money. It is the labor of Black women, during the civil rights movement and Black Lives Matter, as well as on the courts and in Muhammad's public stances, posting in her digital media,[66] that is rarely seen as such and is often minimized or dismissed. Blackness in (sport/political) activism, often understood through the figure of the Black heterosexual male (athlete or politician), excludes women of color and LGBTQ communities. And why should Muhammad, this woman of color, be expected to be above the fray, above the marketplace? Why should this celebrity activist not receive funding as well? But another way to position her activism is through double-conscious digitalization. For not only white-owned corporations are marketed here. Given that sport superstars require sponsorships for funding, she has also started her own company, raising money as a charitable fund. Named after her grandmother, Louella Ballard, born in rural Georgia in 1919, Muhammad's fashionable clothing is a Black-owned business, a way to "give back to our community." Her caption ends with #BuyBlack and #Allahyerhamha, a blessing, may Allah show mercy. It is also a blessing for the dead, in this case, for her grandmother. Recognition, long overdue, of their mutual labor, in a radical Black Muslim feminism.

This protest icon is in her posting of another Nike commercial and her own views of solidarity during the pandemic. Speaking of the cancelled sport events, and then the 2022 Olympics, Nike's "Stronger Together" commercial celebrates the athletes' "competing against the ghosts of ourselves, of history." But as these athletes train in isolation during the pandemic, these video clips reveal a secret—an intimate and tantalizing glimpse. This isn't about breaking records, the campaign says, but about building a place for everyone on the sport field. And again we hear Muhammad's war cry of victory. But in digital resistance, Muhammad's Insta-caption of "#Strongertogether" suggests that "the world moves forward when we move together." This is about more than a place on the playing field. More than a titillating glance into isolated trainings. This is about working together in a pandemic, especially as the wealthier nations have the vaccine (imperialism), and there is less health access for Black communities (racist divisions), even as the drug companies clean up. In her next posting, she's wearing a lavender dress—her power move in fashion—holding flowers on a mountain, as if bringing them to graves. Not the ghosts of history in sport but, more hauntingly, the many dead from the pandemic. "Fully vaxxed," she writes. "Headed back in the house."[67] In a country polarized over quarantines, the glaring health inequities in vaccinations are shown in her next posting, her short video with long lines of Black men and women—all waiting in front of the gym with a close-up of her mask. Her post provides a link for vaccine resources. Lamenting health inequities in this pandemic, devastating and killing generations of communities of color transnationally, her prayers, after fasting, after Ramadan, reflect her political backbone. "We will never forget those who live in the midst of oppression and inequity." In all this—posting her interpretation of "Stronger Together"—she subverts the sport market. And in her feed/back around this sport video, in her many intimate images, her heteroglossic virtuality, this digital activist protests global injustice in her digital activism, creating a radical icon. She actively seeks health justice for her community, an antiracism, and prayerfully posits her own branding of Black Muslim feminism. "The work doesn't end," she concludes, "until there is liberation for all."[68]

Similarly, Nike has created a poster of her—a photo with her sabre and helmet, leaning into her wide stance, the sport icon in her power pose—that reads, "I do it to make history." Enhancing her national aura, the ad walks the line, hinting that it is individuals who make history but not claiming whether this is a general moment in sport or an event in a racialized history. So Muhammad takes on the individualism of this Nike ad, transforming the *I do it* to a collective *us*. "For all of the kids who have been told they don't belong," her subversive caption reads, "this one is for us." There were almost two hundred comments on this post. "For all of my ancestors . . . who were not given the chance to go as far and for my daughters," one woman responded, "so they can see what's possible." Given the massive legacy of slavery and its atrocities as part of colonization, her comment reinvented this commercial as a visible hope for future liberation, to see what's possible." Highlighting comments in her virtual community, reinventing her own iconic status in Instagram in a scripting of a racialized citizenry, Muhammad frames her activism in captions. And she offers her own digital praise to the divine—in an Arabic phrase meaning praise God with its hashtag #lhamdella—a mark of her Islamic feminism as well as her Black Muslim history.

Like the sabre-swinging wonder woman of Nike commercials, this activist has been fashionably produced as an icon and then reproduced as well in mainstream press. As an icon, her images circulate into new spaces of negotiation, online places that are ricocheting into home screens and in platforms and in captions that variously decode and encode. So, Nike's ads—of Blackness, of Muslimness—work only as long as Muhammad is isolated, for she is always depicted (as in her victory cry) as an icon filmed apart from others. In contrast, her digital media in her greater community and her trans/national commitments and her online presence—her heteroglossic virtualities—refuse these exoticized mysticisms. True, in comparison to mass media's slanting, Nike's commercials are performing power, sending its gladiators into the arena of national identity, but its marketing ends in products of beauty, not agency. As a performance of faith, Nike offers a much more creative space of mysticism as a reinvention of Islam. But the faintly exoticized tinge, the angelically robed fencer is still a mythical portrait. And when depicting other international athletes, spotlighting their Muslimness, again, these ads surface within negative stereotypes of Islam. Nike's glamour, reselling her veil, puts her fetishized image on the auction block.

Of course, neither Nike nor the Olympics are concerned, first of all, about inclusivity. Nor do they believe in you. But in her posting on Instagram, it is Muhammad who teaches us the meaning of faith in the States: in an intimate portrait of prayer. "I'll never forget the time I was followed home in grade school by two bullies," she writes on June 8, 2020. "They called me names as they repeatedly shoved me into the snow. I remember being small and having a hard time pulling myself up from the snow because it was deep. They held me by my bookbag, so I couldn't get away. This went on for miles and as the tears fell from my cheeks, I remember praying . . . a passerby would save me." Over one thousand viewers heard her prayers. So when we see the many forms of publicizing this superstar icon, what is needed is her own voice in her digital posts and in her online interviews, tracing her resistance aesthetics. Muhammad's idea of patriotism is not blind. This digital activist fearlessly and adroitly navigates mass media with her own captions, with her own YouTube features, with her own Instagram videos, her own journey across trans/national borders to reorient us into Black Muslim feminism. What is crucial, then, lies not in the hands of the bullies or the hands of the corporations, their directors, and their commercial creators. What truly matter are the critical and creative and digital choices of this sport activist, for it is her hands, in this case, that radically model the resistance ethics and aesthetics of a world-class fencer.

# Chapter 3

# DIGITAL REVOLTS AND RIVETERS

Google influences "our personal information, habits, opinions, and judgments"; as well as the "world through the globalization of a strange kind
of surveillance"—a kind of *infrastructural imperialism*."
—SIVA VAIDHYANATHAN, *THE GOOGLIZATION OF EVERYTHING*

While the last chapter looks at sport icons, this chapter analyzes the online
icons of celebrity activists who use video postings on Facebook, Twitter/X,
and Instagram. But the trouble with posting one's icon—especially these
national icons, these rapping and riveting icons in social media as well as in
YouTube videos—is that these online videos are flying into contested spaces.
Even popular hijabi rap stars and activists, like Mona Haydar and Blair Imani,
have been subjected to questions. "Where are you from?" is still the most
common question people ask of the rap star Mona Haydar. Flint, Michigan,
is unacceptable. When they dig for her heritage, they light up when they
learn that her grandparents are from Syria. "Wow, you are so exotic!"[1] Their
comments, she says, in her interview on YouTube, are a form of racial aggression, because she doesn't fit in their box as an eroticized Muslim woman or,
as others suggest, oppressed.[2] They try to imagine that "under her clothes"
there must be a belly dancer outfit. Not only is there such cyberbullying for
people of color, as the social justice activist Blair Imani points out, but more
pushback, especially for Imani, who identifies as "Black. Bisexual. Muslim."[3]
She navigates with her own icon, not of Rosie the Riveter but of her own
Blairsie the Riveter. Considering how these images, belly dancers and riveters—the latter, an icon of whiteness and prop of war—have been part of
the violence inside and outside the US, this chapter follows video images
of Mona Haydar, an Arab American rapper, refusing these sexualizations,
and the video postings of Blair Imani, a bisexual Black Muslim, reinventing
Black riveters.

"How can you be a Muslim and a rapper"? "How can you be Muslim and bisexual?" they ask. As certain sexualities are set in imaginary locations—a modern empire that stretches endlessly, including even rap stars and digital activists—these sexual objectifications have been used to justify the exceptionalism and militarization of the United States.[4] So these two activists, Haydar and Imani, have a challenge, using videos on YouTube, posts on Instagram, reinventing their rap and riveter icons, refusing suggestions by conservative and liberal politicians alike that these women must be rescued in the name of feminism.[5] Their rapping and riveter icons instead are a means of decolonizing sexualities.[6] Radically re*fashion*-ing these images, reposting, retweeting, trending in thousands, in millions as online icons, with their algorithmic beats, these two digital activists have been creating virtual collectivities. In all these ways, then, in their refusals of sexual empire, their star icons reflect trans/national feminisms.

## MONA HAYDAR'S DIGITAL ICONS: TRANS/NATIONAL FEMINISMS

Exceeding even the branding of a Nike commercial, in a very different way of selling her performance platform, Mona Haydar's rap video *Hijabi (Wrap My Hijab)* has garnered over 7.1 million views on YouTube. Calling out and dancing in a hallway, she and her troupe of rapping activists whirl us into another *branding* of racial solidarities, vocalized together in a refusal of sexual fetishization of women of color, and a powerful anti-imperial feminism, winning an award as one of the top ten protest songs of 2017.[7] She's an iconic digitalization, a celebrity rap star. But she faces online assaults, as they try to turn her into an exoticized object, a sexualized icon. This is not how one responds to an individual or to a feminist rapper or to a social justice activist. "They don't want to see me as American." So she responds online with her own question of their birthplace, retorting, when they say that they are from North Carolina, "Wow, so you are Cherokee!" Detailing this exchange on her interviews on YouTube and in her rap videos, there is a rallying cry of resistance against such racist assumptions and their sexual undertones, since she contends that "Islamophobe Is Just a New Way of Saying White Supremacist."[8]

In her digital activism, this rap star uses radical strategies to call out the ways that her body and her choices are off-limits to prying questions and orientalist imperialism—her protest gesture. It's not about raising a fist or even a sabre. It is, rather, about rubbing her pregnant belly, thereby redefining her body and her sexuality. So, in similar fashion to Nike's activism, the rap video leaves us in its thrall, even as it resists spectacles that turn protest into making money for white corporations. For she clearly states that she needs to be paid for this kind of educational labor. In fact, if you want education, you can use "her PayPal, PayPal, PayPal," she raps. Whether answering questions on the street, filming a rap video, posting digitally, her performance is labor—a refusal to let the Western gaze stare without recognition of the laborer and her work. As a result, her song offers a critique of labor exploitation, especially in her lived experiences:

> Not your exotic vacation
> I'm bored with your fascination
> I need that PayPal, PayPal, PayPal
> If you want education.

The rap singer rings up her daily expenses and their consequences. Tired of providing free entertainment to the masses, she's not an *exotic vacation*. Rather, she details the cost of racisms and their sexualized gaze. Requiring monetary gain for any education that she might have to offer the public about her identity, this rapper, especially given the types of racisms embedded in these questions, claims there is a cost because this information is often used against her—an exotic fantasy land that incarcerates her in sexual fetishization.

What happens when we follow this rap star and her digital trail? Her story crosses borders. When asked about her time staying with relatives in Syria, in her interview with Celine Seman for *Elle* magazine, Haydar articulated her longing to understand her heritage. "I felt disconnected from my roots as a young person," she said. "I wanted to be in the place where my ancestors lived, where they loved, where they resisted their French colonizers."[9] Significantly, reflecting on her childhood visit to Syria, Haydar does not take selfies in the markets, the famous *souks* of Damascus. There are no camel shots in Syria's Badiyat Al-Sham desert, no watching eyes of Hafez Assad's police. Rather, she recalls her heritage within important anticolonial battles against Europeans. It is within this history of resistance that she positions herself, framing the dual claims of her heritage and her activism as a citizen in the United States.

Given her resistance against white domination in both the US and Syria, Haydar's interview with Seman delineates, long before her sense of dual displacement, her initial identity crisis leading to her political awakening.

Staying with relatives in Syria was not as utopian as expected, leaving her at a loss. Having left her home in Flint, Michigan, hoping to find belonging, what Haydar found instead was alienation. She was not a Syrian. Once again she was a foreigner. "Going to Syria when I was a kid, I was always called the American," she recalled. "And then here, I was always considered other, not fully American, and I wanted at least one part of my identity to really crystallize." In response Haydar sought out religious affinities, vowing to root at least a part of her identity in her heritage. In many ways, then, her sites of belonging in the ummah is recoding white nationalism. "I wanted to study Arabic and Islamic studies in a traditional way," she continued. Expressed in high-school poetry and later in rap music, hers has been a *political positioning*, her rap icons—a performance of racialized citizenship, as part of a group, rapping together, deeply rooted in the ethics of belief and Black power—navigating her own trans/national location.

Calling out spectators' views of the exotic sex object, Haydar's video begins with three loosely clothed, European beauties, frozen like statues in a harem. But then the rap video disrupts this image with the song of an expectant mother, Haydar herself, and then with dancing. Disassembling exoticism, these women gather in public spaces—in hallways or living rooms—in a series of poses that resemble a portrait, a claustrophobic harem from out of Manet's odalisque painting *Olympia*, wherein "you only see Oriental," as the rapper croons. All of this protest of these rap singers and rap dancers—simultaneously replicating and rejecting this exotic framework—in stark contrast to the three white women. By interrupting this pantomime of the frozen harem with a protest message, and, as powerfully, staging an emotive affect and resistance aesthetic, moving to the beat, these dancing activists produce a new site of iconographies. These rap singers and dancers, often imagined existing outside the realms of desire and pleasure, are asserting their claims on these spheres with how they wrap and how they rap. These video rappers, not in the streets but in the hallways, in the digital world, follow their lead singer in a multiracial band.

Disrupting the harem fetish shows how this idea of women trapped in a space for men's pleasure is a concept as Western and distorted as a frozen odalisque in an art museum. This exoticized view of the oriental woman, as critics such as Fatima Mernissi write, has turned even the well-known Scheherazade—a political leader who saved her kingdom—into a belly dancer.[10] Although as Mohja Kahf details, the West initially viewed Muslim women in the Golden Age of Islam as powerful political players and queens—not as objects, slavelike odalisques, not as oppressed, voiceless women—this obsession with the sexually permissive slave or the sexually repressed woman has

increasingly become the stereotype, used as bellicose justification for invasion and for policing.[11] These sexual icons emerged in colonization, based
in extremes: one is either a sexual temptress (like Eve) or an innocent virgin
(like Mary).[12]

Resisting these religious icons, these Western extremisms, Haydar inter-
rupts this sexualized fetish, such as the temptress/exotic dancer, drawing
attention instead to modern colonial empires that have targeted women.
Using a political rallying cry, she instructs others not to make assumptions
about her body. "What's your hair look like?" the rapper speaks back to the
camera. "Bet your hair look nice!" Rolling a litany of needling assaults, she
raps out, "How long your hair is?" These colonizing attacks continue. Does
that scarf "make you sweat?" "Ain't that scarf too tight?" And she's responding, not as a star with backup singers, but as a group, a rap star and her rap
dancers, a multiracial solidarity of US Muslims. So this is not merely a protest against oppression but a political action, producing a movement—what
Judith Butler terms a call to assemble.[13] So this is not about dancing as the
object of the male gaze in a fetish-based fantasy[14]; it is, rather, a rapping of
resistance, part of a continuous history, as in antiracism and gender outcry
of Black Muslim women's protests, protesting in solidarity against sexual
fetishes of colonization.[15]

This rap icon is not only reinventing racializations but even further resisting war propaganda. Muslimness is a racial category, Junaid Rana posits,
since garb, accent, and skin have been read as markers in a global racism
that envisions individuals and countries as part of a single place—a Muslim
world.[16] The scarf is marking a wide range of public identities, and less than
half of these next-gen activists choose this signature. Much more than a piece
of clothing, the scarf, this politicized marker, claims solidarity, in response to
the everyday violence that US Muslims experience during this never-ending
war on terror.[17] This stance has been described by Haydar as a greater sisterhood of US Muslim women. "I know Muslim women who started wearing a
hijab because they want to be in solidarity with their sisters," says Haydar in
her interview with Jennifer Chowdhury for *Marie Claire* magazine.[18] These
political affiliations and group identifications are very different from claiming citizenship in a singular ethnicity, for instance, as a Syrian American.
Within her primary call of resistance against white hegemony, Haydar tells
Chowdhury, these online songs unify, opening up pleasure within collectivities, a powerful bond through rapping as well as through wrapping scarves.
These digital icons refute sexual empires of fetishism.

The dismantling of this empire requires that these activists reclaim their
bodies, for imperialism assumes the right to know what women should

look like, the right to invade private spaces, to ask personal questions. One of the ways in which Haydar shatters this orientalist gaze at her body is by means of a powerful gesture of protest: she rubs her pregnant belly. For it is her body, her sexuality, her choice, not to be questioned by others. And it's her baby, not to be bought and sold, or named by others. Rapping out that others have no right to interrogate her body, her appearance—her bright red lipstick, her hot-pink scarf—her song tells others to get their hands off of her body, in effect, to stay out of her hair, out of her personal choices, even while foregrounding her right to touch her own body and her kin.

Gazing with agency at the camera, they are strong subjects, their pinks, prints, stripes, folds, colors—all glamorous inscriptions of power—reinforcing their individuality and diversity. Wrapping my hijab is a statement of the variety of comportments and presentations that refuse singular ideas of Muslim womanhood, refute any single idea about their scarves. No wonder, then, that she has been interviewed by women's fashion magazines with as much interest as *Vogue* paid to supermodel Halima Aden, the first hijab-wearing model to ever cover *Vogue*.[19] But in contrast to the ways that fashion has been adopting these women's scarves and styles, these activists continue to speak of their political designs.

On one level, in her video *Hijabi (Wrap My Hijab)*, Haydar's rapping video is part of her own anticolonial movement. And this includes a national positioning, as she recruits her rap group, with her multiracial dancers, and her digital rapping honoring Black leaders, speaking of singers like Mahalia Jackson and celebrating Mosdef's "Flowers 4U" in her blog. She also interviews with Tsafi Saar, April 21, 2017, and touches on her own search for identity in the US and on her return to her ancestral lands in Syria.[20] This historical trajectory of music created by US Muslims, as Hisham Aidi theorizes in *Rebel Music*, locates the space of struggle within a greater trajectory: the historic involvement of Muslims within anticolonial resistance.[21] In her digital videos, Haydar has situated herself within intersections of antiracism and anticolonialism—as a trans/national feminist.

As shown in previous chapters, these celebrities call out the exoticized object, as they reconstruct icons of the politicized subject: iconographies with distinctly Black Lives Matter solidarities. In the same way, Haydar's rap video *Hijabi* refashions her iconic style and models ideas of her own Arab American background within the context of Muslimness and of Blackness. In her 2017 interview with Saar, for instance, Haydar said that on her social media site, she invited several Black women who are US Muslims to join her on the video,[22] showcasing numerous forms of wrapping their scarves, including an African style, the so-called *hoodjab* scarf that wraps one's hair with a bun in back.[23] So the multiple styles of the scarf—a panoply of political and personal, cultural and religiously diversified fashions, in effect, "designing citizens"[24]—have all been woven into a political style associated with Black Muslim and Arab American hip-hop.[25] Although only two of the women wrap their scarves in the style of the African diaspora—the brown scarf wrapped back, the tan woven up higher—the multiple means of wrapping their scarves suggest the complex ways that these designs have become part of a design with Blackness as part of its pattern.[26] Unlike imperialisms, which have no place for Blackness in the landscape of the Muslim world, this rap icon offers a clear affirmation of Black Muslim lives, in effect highlighting racial identities of Muslims.[27] As these sites spread in networks, these racialized iconographies are still part of unresolved conversations.

But in this digital dance, this performance with its critiques of policing bodies as part of sexual politics, wrapping and rapping are not only actions but also locations of a new racialized script and gendered collectivities. For veiling is also a speech act, as J. L. Austin would have it, a contract of belonging.[28] The individual identity of the first person, the I, performs amid a larger group of racially and ethnically diverse women activists. But in this instance, they rap while unwrapping the imperial logics surrounding the identities of Muslim women. For this act of veiling lays claim to an identity, to belonging within a cross-racial bond. In this performative, "I wrap" reminds us as well of Austin's claim that the marriage contract is enacted by saying "I do." But this is much more than a private bond; this is a much larger performative of a virtual community. Not merely words, these statements reclaim racial citizenship for US Muslims, so it's not only an act but also an action. By investing in their action of wrapping their fashionable scarves, these women embody their beliefs, their gender, their politics in a mutual resistance against sexualization and racism. For so many women, Haydar tells Chowdhury, "a hijab . . . is so many different things."[29] These multiplicities, wrapping and rapping performances of solidarity, are refusals of the nation's organizing logic.

In contrast to the mythical nation and its views of the fractured identities of the Syrian who is American, the American who is Syrian, Haydar's video is a political performative not only rooted in the radical equalities of gender, race, class, foundational to prophetic teachings in Islam but also, for this light-skinned rapper, constructed out of multiracial citizenships, seeking justice for the marginalized. It will be helpful, then, to situate her virtual solidarity within a racial context, for in the United States, identifications of Arab Americans have long been in flux. Although in 1790 the US Constitution included only free white persons in citizenship,[30] this included Lebanese, often classified as white, although whiteness was usually tied to a location, privileging Europe.

In 1893, however, all immigrants who spoke Arabic were lumped together as greater Syrians, classified as other Asians, but they were often viewed suspiciously—as having an in-between status—since they identified themselves primarily by means of their own village or religion.[31] These immigrants did not adhere to the practices of white supremacy aligning against Blacks.[32] So it was a "second-class citizenship status" that was given (and often taken from) them.[33] This marginalization continued during the Jim Crow era, which legalized racial segregation in the United States. Amidst this "racialization of ambiguity," to use Nadine Naber's term, there have been enormous stigma and violence—a Syrian lynching, for instance, in 1929—and the census continues to name them only as marginalized whites.[34] In response to this uneasy racialization, Haydar's inscription of Black Muslim allegiance, an alternative archive, exorcises histories, stripping away hidden racisms.

Clearly, then, Haydar's rap video frames her nationalism in Black alterity. This digital strategy refutes the stereotype of Muslim women as foreign threats, since their style of music, their racial identities, and their American accents provide an irrevocable claim of belonging. It comes as no surprise, then, to discover that Haydar is not the only one confronting the camera in her speech "My Hijab, My Choice," for just over her shoulder hangs a poster of her hero, the Black Muslim activist Malcolm X.[35] With thirty-one thousand views, her interview with *Fusion* has become part of a network of "social and symbolic links," where common interests create attachment—what Stefano Allievi terms virtual communities.[36] In this case hers is a vision of radical female power set against the backdrop of Black Muslim power. But here, for Haydar and her inscription of iconography, she refuses the harem motif, even as she redefines her alliance and her sexuality. Here the site of the struggle is Blackness.

This singer confronts racism by rapping what it is to be in a multiracial solidarity of Muslimness. But in rapping in a range of groups across nations, her contestation also marks trans/national iconographies. Naming a number of groups—Sufis, Sunnis, Shi'ites, Sudanese, Iraqis, Canadians, Palestinians, and Americans alike—Haydar pushes all these groups of women to protest white supremacy. And she mentions Indonesia, the country with the largest number of Muslims, as a challenge to imperialisms that conflate Islam and the Middle East. Problematizing stereotypes of Arabs being more Muslim than Blacks, this rapping resists the divide-and-conquer mentality introduced by European colonialism, a system that has long thrived on racist hierarchies.[37]

So how does her superstar rap icon perform resistance? Because fighting against the violence within and beyond the borders requires resisting these sexualizations, her rap rally performs collective solidarities and physical embodiment. Even her pregnant body becomes a site of contestation, evident in many comments from people in the digital world. She should not be "rubbing her belly," because it's too suggestive, *too sexual*. Responding in her TED Talk, she looks straight at the camera, mischievously, redirecting assumptions. "How do you think I got pregnant to begin with?"[38] But this is just the start, for at the pinnacle of her performance, in her demonstration of her own agency over her body and her baby, she exhibits her ultimate protest gesture. From under her shirt, she pulls out a jacket—a *political prop*. For she had already delivered her baby *before* the rap video. This digital mimicry of staging pregnancy confronts the ways her body has been fetishized in a country whose courts threaten to take away women's power over their reproductive choices. What is her protest movement? Not a natural inclination to rub her pregnant belly, this gesture was a *political act*. Her rap video, her political performance, is a reclamation of embodied power.

In showing her own control and her rap action of stripping away the illusion of pregnancy, she demonstrates how, as an activist, she is withstanding the dual assault of those who attempt to control and exoticize her, simultaneously imprisoning her in a cage, then assuming she requires rescue. Rejecting this fetishized spectacle, these women, these rap icons, take down the house, dancing and singing, interrogating the daily onslaughts of street attacks. "Keep swagging my hijabis!" they sing to us while on the stairs, only to disappear in a crosscut, leaving us alone with our mystical guide. Re-claiming feminist icons, now instructing us from her living room, Mona Haydar has become our female imam—or in her words, a "Muslim chaplain"—sitting sternly in front of a wall tapestry alive with gold calligraphy, a divine blessing. Imaginatively reconstructing sexuality and power within her star icon of herself as a *shaykha* religious authority —all of this befitting her master's degree in ethics from a seminary and her work as a chaplain at New York University—Haydar invites us into an antiracism training that refuses sexualized assaults, an icon of sexual and religious authority.

## CELEBRITY RECEPTION: DIGITAL TRAPS

The origin of these protest icons springs from her trans/national activism, and from her awareness that other rappers receive glory and fanfare while she receives death threats and constant digital surveillance. White supremacists either do not know that she exists, or they target her on the internet. "White supremacists," she says, "don't like people like me."[39] And there are men who send messages asking if she is married. If she doesn't respond, they start threatening her. And if she does respond, they ask if she is content in her marriage, suggesting she would be happier with them instead! Like the well-known threats and sexual innuendoes that political icons like Ilhan Omar have faced, this rap icon and her Black Muslim sisterhood have faced the very real lived experiences of racism. In her many online interviews, she talks about how others have tried to twist her power into one of two distortions: sexualization or victimhood. She lists all the numerous comments on her rap video *Hijabi (Wrap My Hijab)*, including those of white supremacists who assume that they know her religion better than she does. About her scarf, they state: "It's not like you have a choice, do you?" And if she's following the "rules of Islam," then "why do you want to grab attention?" As for her rap protest—well, that's really a "cry for help," isn't it? Even more overt racism is accompanied by obscenities. "Go back to Trashcanistan!" for instance, with comments that her "kind" has sex with animals. This racism is perverse and exoticized, *sexual fetishizations*.

In resistance, this rap icon positions her own online trans/national claims. While Haydar's video positions politicized identity for a Black sisterhood, her website's blog also embraces other protests, such as democratic uprisings in Syria and in Egypt and in Tunisia: "With the current state of the world . . . it seems that the world is imploding and exploding all at the same time. And I am doing the same in solidarity."[40] This unity, of course, is in her protesting those rulers placed on their thrones by *white imperialists*. It is a solidarity that claims not a Syrian legacy but, rather, a cause—a rejection of white supremacy, rallying against colonialism, in trans/national feminism. It is within this history of resistance that she positions herself, framing the dual claims of her heritage and her activism as a citizen in the United States. Placing this entry amidst multiple blogs on Black Muslim power—as in entries on Malcolm X—her blog consistently promotes antiracism and decolonization, an *anticolonial* rap in digital media.

Despite her critical antiracist work as a famous rap star in these digital networks, Haydar as an individual cannot embody the full range of Black, white, Asian American, South Asian American, mixed race and other identities of US Muslims. And within Muslim communities there are often racialized hierarchies. So even while considering how protest honors the political work by Black Americans, is this a Black Arab solidarity, as many claim, an intersection, or even— as Michelle Hartman, quoting Theri Pickens, questions—a replacement paradigm, where Arab Americans have simply become "'the new Black?'"[41] Even as she's a politically conscious rapper, to use Tricia Rose's words, reflecting grassroots movements,[42] her iconic presence as the

sole authority—the Muslim chaplain—stirs resentment, given how digitalization selects few icons. An online blogger complains that these music videos
are going viral even though she's not the "first hijabi to speak out about
matters pertaining to Muslim women." Another online blog asks if Haydar's
fame is partly an issue of colorism, a "fair skinned Arab?" Where's the "viral
love" for Black Muslim rappers—like Alia Sharrief, like Poetic Pilgrimage?
this blogger continues. "Why aren't they having their videos go viral up and
down my timeline?"[43] As a site of contestation, then, her rap sets to music
Su'ad Khabeer's analysis of American trends, wherein "Blackness and Muslimness merge to challenge and reconstitute US racial hierarchies."[44] At the
same time, misperceptions of Arab Americans as the true Muslims are part
of a legacy of what this scholar calls a de-legitimation—an anti-Blackness
even in Muslim communities.[45] This scholar calls for ways to "disrupt narratives of division among Arab, Asian and Black US Americans," ways to build
cross-racial solidarity.[46] Given her studies in Morocco, on Arab Moroccan
rap and Black Gnawa music, this scholar also identifies with splitting, for
she is Black and Latinx.[47]

Significantly, in a cross-racial solidarity with another lead singer and
Latinx icon, Jackie Cruz, Haydar sings about sexism in *Dog*.[48] Racking up
over three million hits, her YouTube rap videos like *Dog*, like *Hijab*, further
reimagine a virtual sisterhood of women. Even as the continual crisis of
news spins its ideas of Muslimness in sexual fetishizations of Arabness, in a
video viewed by over three million viewers, her words call out that any men
who sexualize her and Cruz are "dogs." In these digitalizations, "bodies have
become archives," as Wendy Chun writes, and these icons have been mapping
groups in online networks;[49] in this case, increasing imagined (and not-yet)
cross-racial solidarities. What is critical, then, in following digital activists,
such as this chapter's next activist, Blair Imani, who challenges structures of
power as part of her own resistance aesthetic, is a digital icon, offering us a
much-needed multiplicity of voices as part of de-imperializing sexualities.

## DE-IMPERIALIZING SEXUALITIES:
## A BLACK BISEXUAL MUSLIM ROSIE THE RIVETER

During the COVID-19 pandemic, wearing her pride mask, Blair Imani points
upward and looks to the heavens. Following her iconic look of pride here,
her icon includes her message. "Allah created LGBTQIA+ Folks."[50] As she
teaches about the Tulsa Massacre and proclaims the importance of Ramadan,
there is a digital post of her online icon as part of her identity: "I'm Black.

Bisexual. Muslim." Her pride icon is a public protest and a positioning of her online activism. Which provokes constant questions, as to how she can be both Muslim and bisexual. In response, she reposts her pride pics, her riveter icons, her calls for accountability. Over thirty thousand like her post. In her pride icon, her questioning expression—her arched brow, pursed lips, side-long glance—is one of resistance. And this image of resistance is framed in her iconic pose of a Lady Liberty: her red scarf and white blazer, her makeup stylizing patriotism with eyeshadow that has re-created the US flag on each lid. And she captions her star image "Wednesday mood." This is my face, she says, "when someone calls me *Anti-American* for spending my entire career trying to make this country live up to the promises of liberty and justice for all." In her use of Lady Liberty poses as well as the iconic 1940s Rosie the Riveter, this digital activist, using her skills as a "queer historian,"[51] has been reclaiming national belonging, reframing intersectional sexualities. Following her lead, then, her claims require a historical reconstruction of racial icons.

Of all the icons in this book, one of the most famous images in an era of world wars was the riveter, which has become a feminist icon, so let's start with its history. The figure of Rosie the Riveter was created in a song written by Redd Evans and John Jacob Loeb in 1942. Rosie became famous in Norman Rockwell's illustration of a working-class Irish American woman, imagined as single, posted on the May 29 cover of the *Saturday Evening Post* in 1943. But in 1948, Black protesters were holding not an image of Rosie the Riveter but signs for "NO Defense Contracts For—Anti-Negro Employers," as Penny Coleman researches, in front of the Glenn Martin plant and in earlier marches, given discrimination in hiring practices.[52] So this riveter icon is part of a history, an era of war and of discrimination. And this icon of a white riveter continues to be a contested site. Imani's bisexual iconography selects a type of Rosie image—from J. Howard Miller, in 1942, a poster placed on factory walls for a few weeks, much later idolized by the women's movement, in 1982. It has been highly criticized for its limited presentation of feminism as a working white woman. Reinventing this icon, Imani's post has two parts: the image is of Imani in the classic pose of muscled power imagined by Miller, although her captions shift from war propaganda into her own language: not "we can do this" but an invitation for other Black women and women of color and LGBTQ+ Muslims, "WE GOT THIS!"

Thus, Blairsie the Riveter challenges white icons and racialized sexual codes. Posting her cosplay of the riveter icon, Imani details how women, especially whites, were encouraged to join the workforce during the war. But Black women, she says, had long been part of the workforce, not only during the war, but well and long before, given the unrelenting horrors of slavery, followed by sharecropping, then minimally paid domestic labor jobs. So these images of single, white working-class women, making heroic choices for their country belied the many tens of thousands of Black women, facing discrimination in their jobs, and trying to balance childcare and earning a needed income.[53] Although almost nineteen million women worked during the Second World War, afterward most were forced into lower-paying jobs or laid off, expected, like a romanticized dream, to return home.[54] So it was propaganda, Imani points out, that celebrated women only in connection to the industry of war.

Reconstructing riveters as icons challenges how national history imagines those who labor in the nation. And in mass media as in textbooks, images of intersectional sexualities are limited. Housing opportunities and vocational possibilities and promotions are often reserved for straight citizens—even selecting certain types of gay or lesbian citizens who are seen as white. And these terms of economics (and their white iconographies) were frequent in the policies of the Second World War. Since these government structures assisted white veterans and showcased white war effort, Imani's frequent postings of Rosie the Riveter in her own image is a *re-visionary history*. Claiming status as a working member of society, naming her own multiplicities, reinventing herself as Blairsie the Riveter, in her post, Imani discusses the misconceptions of race, gender, sexualities, and labor, and repositions this working icon as bisexual.

She configures another riveter, too, when she posts her grandmother's picture. In her strategies of iconography, as in her "Smarter in Seconds" video on intersectionality, educating on Kimberlé Crenshaw's term,[55] she returns to the 1940s, detailing how her grandmother had worked at Lockheed Martin, an aircraft manufacturer, in this era of riveters. There was not only a racial wage gap but also a gendered racial wage gap, she notes, since her grandmother was making less than white men, white women, and Black men. Given that many Black women have had to work weekly jobs and often take second jobs to make it, Imani points out how Black women have had to work harder than their white counterparts. Repositioning historical icons, she recalibrates the importance of the racial-gender wage gap in her own radical roots.

And why do we still need to return to this icon? As it turns out, not only did this propaganda of riveters in World War II omit images of Black working women, but it showcased racist treatment of Black women, as Maureen Honey states.[56] The only figures of Black labor within white advertising were based on stereotypes of slaves, from the Jim Crow era to the end of the war, usually bound with red headscarves, such as the nursemaid Mammy, whom Margaret Mitchell and then Hattie McDaniel immortalized in Hollywood's

*Gone with the Wind* in 1940. This racist icon of the "asexual domestic care-giver" did much to erase the brutal economic history of slavery and its rape and sexual assaults.[57] Based on a minstrel song about Old Aunt Jemima, the pancake mix and similar commercial products appropriated this figure in the twentieth century—a kind of "commodity fetish," a cookie jar that erased sexual violence and demeaned the work of Black women.[58]

So it comes as no surprise, then, that Imani sends her work schedule alongside her fashionable photo to mass media, reframing her work and her iconicity as a bisexual Black Muslim digital activist. In a 2020 *New York Times* feature, there's a shot of Imani in a smashing mustard-color dress and matching felt hat, topped off by an all-caps bold title, "LIKE A BOSS"—all conveying stylish authority.[59] But the origin of the term *The Boss* refers to the pop icon Diana Ross, as well as the title of one of her albums—the Black female boss revising codes of the white boss-man and redefining her power as part of her sexuality, further defined as a sexual icon in the trans community.[60] Although this phrase is used by Slim Thug's rapping about coming into money and, thus, power on the streets, it's also a statement about her digital activism as a form of labor. In all of these, then, this icon is a recoding of race and power and labor and bi/transsexuality—which is no less than an iconic revolt. Recoding scripts of sexualities amid race and religion in her own online icon, Imani describes her workweek, featuring her prayers and her LGBTQ+ activism.

Unfortunately, the digital world can barely keep up with Imani. Either unwilling or unable to engage with the complex work of this bisexual Black Muslim who's challenging the prevalent narratives of racism, homophobia, and Islamophobia, the *NYT*'s three-paragraph overview focuses on her work in confronting structural racism. While this is important, of course, her intersectional sexuality is not present in the summary, but only in the details given by Imani herself. The daily log of events, with its potential to subvert stereotypes, could have been more powerful if the press had selected a framework that also addressed the ways that LGBTQ+ Muslims are erased. Although the focus is on the Black historian, who is the "boss"—important work to be sure—there is a refusal to acknowledge her own identification. "I'm Black. Bisexual. Muslim." Three paragraphs leave little room for the fullness of her self-identification, for the complexity of her political work, her development of her pride icon.

But, arguably, part of her activism is in claiming her own powerful fashion, adjusting her eye shadow and makeup to match her scarf—what she calls her "monochrome look"—as part of how she gets "glam" for her interview with Ibram X. Kendi on antiracism. She also insists that her digital activism is not unpaid, and that she carefully selects which fashions and brands she promotes. Always active, she asks a photographer to do the shots for a brand partnership post in a campaign for reforestation. Imaginative as always, she's climbing a tree in her lavender suede platform shoes, part of her rainbow aesthetic—without segregation of labor and her intersectional identity here. While she says she loves her morning Fajr prayer and her evenings "talking to Allah," returning to bed she's checking on her videos to post on Instagram for Intersex Awareness Day. Alongside the iconic photo of the digital activist, her work diary reclaims sexual identities and spiritual complexities and celebrity work as part of her Black female labor.

Situating herself in a greater economic history, her digital image of the Black riveter reconfigures commercialized white feminism and, in other posts, details the legacy of slavery and of Black labor. One of her tactics is to be clear about the economic debt racked up by slavery. In her history video on Juneteenth,[61] for instance, she talks about the end of chattel slavery, when US soldiers took over Texas and finally announced, a month after the end of the Civil War, that its slaves were, in fact, free. And in her posting on the Tulsa Massacre, she also invites her father to speak with her, part of her strategy of heteroglossic virtualities. And her Auntie Imani speaks of the destruction of their businesses, churches, and hospitals in Tulsa, and videos of other activists join in describing how three hundred Black people were killed. Her father and her aunt support her as an affirming stance. Adjusted for inflation, says Papa Imani in a close-up in the end, there was $31 million in property loss. So her pride in history—reclaiming events and her authority as a historian—embraces her family history and embraces, too, their including (not rejecting) her multiplicities. This inclusion of her family members authorizes her history in a complex tapestry woven out of past and present claims; it is a strategy of online iconicity—a heteroglossic virtuality of historical trauma and contemporary love.

Using her riveter icon, Imani also posts on how her work is funded. The riveter's speech bubble announces that she's hiring an assistant in LA, inviting yet another paid position to join the team, again clarifying that digital activism is a form of paid labor. Funding to make it as a bisexual Black Muslim activist is a form of resistance in our society. To pay for her work, she gathers grassroots support in a number of ways—Patreon, Venmo, or GoFundMe—to pay the technical team that helps to create her videos. And as has been true for white commercialization and its dominant market, paid partnerships on her site also support her labor in the digital world—advertising a box of multicolored Skittles candies, for instance, wearing a rainbow scarf with bold swaths of color. Well aware of the ethical complexities of funding, Imani lists the reasons she has selected these paid partnerships. She supports Skittles, she says, because the company funds LGBTQ+ artists during Pride Month. When you swipe its matrix-like QR code, you're introduced to these artists and their pride murals. Like her work schedule on the *NYT*, like Facebook, like any other media outlet, her own digital activism also needs the support of advertisements. But unlike the cornucopia of products in print and the everyday racism in comments, embedded in search engines, in targeted algorithms, in a corporate platform—all branding racial oppression, as Safiya Umoja Nobel and others have shown[62]—each of Blair Imani's brands reinforces her iconic intersectional stance.

Still, even while promoting brands for others, Imani also works toward "personal values, media values, and brands," as Michael Goodman puts it, so that what she cares about becomes a currency, which he argues can resist the state.[63] But her star power does not mean that she has sold out. Imani's Black riveter and social justice icon is marketing resistance, just as clearly as *Vogue* marketed its white fashion icons in the postwar period. Consider also that most superbloggers of fashion and corporate fashion owners remain overwhelmingly white, as Minh-Ha Pham shows; only a small minority are people of color.[64]

Then the internet demands constant labor with no limit on work hours. Since most cannot make a living, they can easily be exploited by corporations, their sites buried as expensive search engines continue corporate images of whiteness.[65] Even more problematically, in these online workplaces, the response is not colorblind, so their digital sites have to do more work to be given equal opportunities, and also more identity work to navigate stereotypes.[66] At times feeling isolated, these bloggers may cut down on the emotional investment in their virtual sites, in turn eliding some of their racialized identity.[67] Even as diverse female bodies sends the message that these corporations care, she continues, in the process many posts "fetishize feminine smallness," glamorizing unhealthy body weights while challenging the dominant whiteness of fashion, in forms of "exploitation and empowerment."[68]

In contrast to this framing of femininities, even as many of Imani's digital posts and videos highlight her bright makeup, her heteroglossic icons and pride counterposes, her strategies are also evident when she refuses these postures. She has a few videos about skin care and acne, where she wears no makeup, showing her own skin blemishes and talking about the causes of acne, such as hormonal changes and allergies. Her iconic strategy of recoding racialized bodies, which are often encoded as either threatening or as demurely beautiful, appears in such intimate close-ups.

Nor is her protest stance, even if funded by corporations, the same as the sexually exoticized or diminished stance of the fashion blog. It is a power pose—eyes directed at the camera, face forward. As in her video *Black Trans Lives Matter*, she posts a multiplicity of power poses, arms akimbo. Starting with this powerfully posed sequence, she then adds other LGBTQ+ activists of color with their own power poses. Establishing a "queer hybrid self-fashioning," these distinct outfits show diverse aspects, even modes, that refuse to fetishize one's body, and create a certain ordering of identity in costume and performance—what José Esteban Muñoz views as a process that constantly remakes the self.[69] Demanding recognition, this video refuses a singular image of Black bi/trans identities, and with almost twenty thousand likes, this powerful and fashionable video accomplishes political work.

The icon is distinctly sexy. She even restages her Rosie the Riveter look, posing with her red scarf, not with a flexed arm but with pursed lips, blowing a kiss to the audience—"a little bisexual smolder for you."[70] Calling on her own sexual identities and her right to choose what she wears, she poses in four frames—covering with a scarf, then in subsequent frames, unwrapping it, so that we see her serious expression as she stares down the camera. Reinventing the codes of queering Muslim sexualities, you can see her dressed as a *Star Trek* icon just as often as you will see her wrapped in a pride flag.[71] Using the flag to signpost her work, she adds iconographic photos, rainbow signage, as her resistance aesthetic. Even the lush purple border that frames her video, adding warmth and vibrancy to her clothing, is part of her power pose—an iconic impact. Posing with a bright red scarf, she announces, "Intersex people are just as common as . . . Redheads!" After all, she adds, they're 2 percent of the human population. In short, even in teaching intersexuality, Imani's poise and pride aesthetic are part of her iconic star power.

In some ways these icons—as in superheroes or superstars—fit with Muñoz's idea of identifying with one's heroes, as a kind of role model and then moving past these icons.[72] But this is not a coping "disidentification," for her icon is a protester. And her protest gestures demonstrate political acts, following Juana María Rodríguez,[73] challenging codes of straight behavior, her online icon also shows gender as a selected design.[74] Not unlike the sexual/spiritual authority of Haydar, in her carefully sculpted resistance aesthetic—bright red lipstick and meticulously framed pride-colored aesthetic—the focus gives authority to Imani as the center of the video's attention. And her instructions are detailed and helpful. Just a click away, her frozen portraits become pride videos, such as an eighteen-second clip, wherein she reminds us, "Before asking for pronouns, make sure to offer yours first." And she complicates understandings, asking her viewers to understand that "Pride isn't just for 'OUT' LGBTQ+ People." In her caption she affirms that Pride Month is for all of us, which includes those who have decided not to publicly share their sexualities with others. So her icon is one of many voices in the streets with pride.

In refashioning Americana motifs, she posts for #BiSexualVisibilityDay in her jean jacket and bright lipstick, hair tied back, a red scarf recalling earlier Riveter poses, calling in anyone who identifies under the bisexual+ umbrella, urging them to sound off in comments below. There are 339 replies. Discussing their own coming-out or praising Imani as their favorite Bi-icon, other activists of color add their voices, as in her videos on bisexuality, which many guests join. Four different voices, four distinct ethnic groups, all fighting "bisexual erasure." "Bisexual is an identity, not a behavior, not a phase." So, in resisting white supremacy's devaluation of Black labor, critiquing straight normativities, she is redefining the entire concept of labor; and, Marlon Bailey adds, to challenge these sexual codes and categories is part of "queer cultural labor."[75] As in Blairsie the Riveter, this icon as a spectacle of deliberate design, speaking alongside heteroglossic voices—such as Black, Latinx, Native American, US Muslim—performs a smoldering affirmation of countercultural codes.

## TRANS/NATIONAL FEMINISMS: COMING OUT AS DIGITAL ACTIVISTS

Understanding these star icons and their intersectionality requires careful histories. In the case of Blair Imani, her belief in interracial solidarity and her prayers for divine compassion have long fueled her public protests against police brutality and hate crimes. Already in 2015, she started working with local mosques to fight for both Black lives and the rights and safety of Muslims in the United States—especially for Razan Abu-Salha; her husband, Yusor; and her sister, Deah Barakat, three college students who were shot in their condo, inside their *home*. Nevertheless, federal agents were convinced by the shooter's story, that he was upset about parking; they did not accuse Craig Hicks of a hate crime. That same year, working with allies in mosques and reading the Qur'an led to her conversion. And then, a year later, when the police killed Alton Sterling, a thirty-seven-year-old Black man, she again took to the streets, in Baton Rouge, now wearing her veil, and she saw an armored vehicle run over the body of a young woman.[76] She watched as an officer grabbed a photographer and slammed him to the ground. The police banged another man's head into the concrete; yet another protester, a white woman thrown down, was told that she was a "traitor." "These aren't even your people," they said. The SWAT team drew weapons on the nonviolent protesters. Seeing the violence, Imani knelt down to pray, reaching for the divine in her whispers of the *takbir*.

Then, they came after Imani. "'Really give it to her,'" the officer muttered.[77] Hearing this, she started screaming. Later, at the police station, she was in tears, shaking as one officer removed her scarf, after which the booking officer intervened, so she could retie it. Then she was humiliated by being strip-searched along with other protesters, who kept talking to her and supporting her as she wept. A day later, after her release, when she heard police sirens, she started trembling. Afraid to leave her home, she was unable to return to the streets. This was when this public activist took to the streets in her own way, activism in online media. In her digital fight against police brutality, she bears witness to the compassion of multiracial protesters. She prays that these movements of compassion will be the "driving force to change the world, InshAllah #BlackLivesMatter." As her digital archive records her trauma, she reclaims her agency in her faith and her politics; for in the midst of the most brutal harm, her digitalization sounds out notes of activism and whispers of healing as a form of power and as a movement joining in the call to prayer.

Continuing her resistance in digital spaces, Imani took a deep breath and agreed to talk about safe spaces with Tucker Carlson on Fox News. Given that so-called counter-terrorism policies have heightened surveillance, she said, safe spaces are areas for conversation and support. "Doesn't it seem like all this 'identity politics' about race, or about Muslims, or about LGBTQ," Carlson lambasted her, end up "somehow all sounding the same" and "end up converging?" Which is when Blair Imani, unintentionally, came out on national news. "Some of us, like myself, exist in all of these communities," she protested. "I am a Black Queer Muslim." Interrupting, the conservative host attacked her, saying that she was not here to represent those communities. Well, actually, she said, she was: she was a Muslim and, additionally, a Black Queer person. But when Carlson dismissed any identities except that of American, Imani clarified, "I'm Black first." "But primarily you are an American," the talk host retorted. "We all are . . . first and foremost. You are an American!"[78] Implying, of course, along with fem-nationalists, that any other identity must surely be anti-American.

During this interview, her phone buzzed with death threats from the audience. And these cyberattacks continued, deadly minefields laid by global racisms.[79] But the majority targeted Muslims, suggesting that US Muslims be shipped out of the country, that there should be no mosques allowed. Also, there was the jingoistic suggestion that since Muslims would be killed in other countries, they should count themselves lucky to find freedom in America: Muslims must be rescued and brought to the United States. Yet another online assault stereotyped Muslims as homophobic.[80] Since coming out she has been ostracized and lost prospects, Imani says, but being an out and proud Muslim is a "blessing that every closeted person of faith deserves to experience." The threats (and the support) she received after that moment, she continues, completely changed her life. Having dealt with intense responses and publicity, one of her key lessons, she says, is that one must be prepared for the backlash. And, unfortunately, the political spectrum of assaults, ranging from assumptions about sexuality and religious identities to white supremacism to neoliberal imperialism, is more than ready to oblige, all questioning how it is possible that she can be, simultaneously, Muslim and Black, bisexual and American.

The resulting video of Imani's fighting back went to 480,000 followers in a tweet, de-imperializing these colonial feminisms. But this digital resistance has taken on a multiplicity of forms for multiple groups. Refusing to be in community with any Muslims who are cyberbullying and dehumanizing "other human beings generally and other Muslims specifically," she calls out her faith in a post in which she stands in front of a mural with wings.[81] Posed like an iconic angel, Imani's ten-foot turquoise wingspread encircles her on the graffiti wall. "Trying to maintain an angelic demeanor in the midst of demonic behavior from bullies," reads the caption. In her political naming, she states her faith claim: "I'm a Muslim." Calling out the attacks, she uses the language of prayer and theology, assuring her audience that "Allah can handle" any final judgments of behavior without the help of internet trolls. Although there is never a time when others should engage in bullying, she adds that Ramadan is perhaps the worst time to be hateful toward other Muslims. This sacred time is for reflection, acts of service, prayer, and fasting, she concludes, fending off attacks with faith. Her strategies here show the challenges to gatekeeping and heteropatriarchy within the Muslim American community.

In contrast, when it comes to the attacks of white supremacists, she lets her followers, who understand the nuances of the system, take the lead. So that when someone whose relatives came through Ellis Island with "four sponsors and a job lined up" asks, "How is it fair that people who have not done the same diligence be allowed to sneak in?" she reposts his comment with a caption urging her followers to call their elected officials about immigration. So her digital activism has backup within a larger virtual community. If she decides to respond, then she does not add it to her feed. Directly messaging harassing and curious speakers, instead of engaging in public response, is an important boundary, she says, since patriarchal systems have enforced the idea that people who are not white and male and straight need to explain themselves. "This is a fallacy," she declares. "Homophobia and Islamophobia are so pervasive in society," she adds, resulting in a digital avalanche demanding that she explain her very existence. It's not anyone else's business how she dresses.[82] And these assaults erase her own pleasures of dressing and performance—her own spaces of "hetero-sexy" affirmation.[83] Exhausted by the same questions, however, she finally posted a FAQ sheet, although, she emphasizes, none of these answers are owed to the public. Simultaneously gatekeeping, her work traces the "pleasures *and* difficulties of moving between multiple, layered identities"—what Clare Croft calls "queer dance."[84] And in this instance, these are parallel projects that address sexual orientation in a complex dance of digital activism—antiracism in a tango with de-imperialism.

Unfortunately, many groups view her as the "token Muslim queer," which is not at all true, states Imani. And in her online presence, she suggests how LGBTQ+ and Muslimness is not just in our country, it has long been a historical presence. Her TEDx Boulder Talk, "Queer and Muslim: Nothing to Reconcile," with almost thirty-seven million views, presses against this tokenism.[85] She details how Western colonization introduced Victorian ideas of sexuality into the Islamic world.[86] In the original encounters with the West, she says, documents record Muslims as being much more sexually flexible—often bisexual. So the idea that Muslims are uniquely homophobic is not grounded in history. It's propaganda. But during the Victorian era, reliant on codes of civilized identities in sexual practices, there was a criminalization of non-Europeans. So the condemnation of LGBTQ+ in Muslim regions was a result of colonization. And as a result, Imani argues, the puritanical and oppressive interpretations of the Qur'an originated in the Western world. In contrast, in countries that were not directly colonized, there is much more acceptance of intersectional sexualities. More importantly, she insists, in the Qur'an, there is "no condemnation of same-gender loving relationships." As she states her position, she can already imagine the online pushback, the multiple questions. So she takes on a second voice, a rather humorous, high-pitched Elmo voice in anticipation of the public response, helping to keep things in perspective. "But Blair," she quips, "what about Sodom and Gomorrah?" Laughingly acknowledging that many in the audience may not know this story or heard it wrong, she then details how these towns were known for their sexual violence, including incest and rape. So the story's not a condemnation of loving relationships between the same gender but a condemnation of sexual assault and trauma. Her exegesis shows the ways in which sexualities have been part of a framework of power—her de-imperialization of sexualities, a trans/national feminism.

De-imperializing sexualities as a digital activist requires specific strategies—heteroglossic icons of resistance. Identifying as a "queer historian," she
also posts her own iconography on a gigantic screen above her TED Talk,
where she is wrapped in a rainbow flag with her iconic makeup. Challenging
these codes and norms, activists use symbols as part of reclaiming their rights
and their bodies and their place in the nation—inclusive of their sexuality
in ways that may be "outside the normative protocols of nationalism and
within them," as Roderick Ferguson indicates.[87] And in a direct message,
Imani was asked how she deals with the daily assaults from people who have
closed their minds to various perspectives.[88] Imani responds that she has a
voicing strategy: the "Elmo Method." She reads these painful barbs out loud
in her Elmo voice. This "definitely defuses any animosity or malice," she says.
It also makes her laugh. Adding one more message, she says, "Works every
time." Her posting has received almost eleven thousand likes. Many of her
followers—smarties, she calls them—comment on how important this vocal
approach is to the haters.

Furthermore, she uses her own image and her own story—including
voices of her parents—to create digital intimacies. These details of her life,
as Gayatri Gopinath argues, are not of nationalism, with all its violence and
politics; instead she reclaims intimacies, the layers beneath the national.[89]
She talks about her childhood in a liberal Christian family, which did not
restrict her sexual orientation. Even at the young age of eight, she was at-
tracted to both genders, which was very hard to sort through when the Disney princesses married only princes or, equally confusing, says Imani, when
princesses married beasts. So she felt that she had to suppress that part of
herself. But then, when she came out to her mother, announcing that she was
a lesbian, her mother responded, "Oh, no, no, no, honey . . . You are bisexual."
At that point, she finally had language for her identity. Understanding her
identity, in 2015, when she converted to Islam as a "Queer Muslim," she felt
loved and accepted because she was created this way, and "Allah makes no
mistakes." And that was when she changed her name from Brown, as she
writes in her memoir, a name descended from her slave ancestry, to her selected name, Imani—faith in Arabic—thus, entering into a "beautiful religion
with immense cultural, racial, and spiritual diversity."[90] Her pride icon has
power, emerging in histories of faith.

In all of these ways, then—in recording and recoding these icons of sexualities, trans/national racializations, and political manifestations—Haydar's as
well as Imani's digital activism offers a new way to encode the history of the
US. As Celine Parenas Shimizu writes, presenting one's own "race-positive
sexuality" reclaims the intersections of the racialized body and sexualized

identities.[91] What this chapter has argued, then, is that these heteroglossic icons of the digital world have been restructuring problematic histories, embedded in white icon-o-spheres, signaling critical forms of de-imperializing sexual empires. For, as Sara Ahmed writes, the formation of collective bodies in normativity has been policing both sexual orientation and orientalism.[92] Thus, it is essential to make room for these heteroglossic histories—Imani's historical queering and Haydar's iconic sexual reclaiming—and their online icons. Digitally staging themselves, they imagine a revolution—especially given the ways imperial maps have charted histories. Returning to Mona Haydar, then, her decision to rub her belly claims her own body, even as her wrapping and rapping make claims for multiracial citizens. And Imani demonstrates the need for more room for Black Muslim LGBTQ+ histories in her own political refashioning. These activists have drawn attention to the work of their productions, in control over maternal labor, in clear colors of pride, reconceiving radical feminism with its iconic movements and its orientations of digital activism.

# Chapter 4

# GRASSROOTS ICONS

## Facebook Resistance

> If you could hold a large march, you could also change the
> narrative, threaten disruption, or bring about electoral or
> institutional change. And now, digital technologies were
> profoundly altering the relationship between movement
> capacities and their signals.
> —ZEYNEP TUFEKCI, *TWITTER AND TEAR GAS*

Although celebrities such as rappers and sport stars receive more fame, what's missing is attention to the public and digital activists, like Pacific Northwest activist Aneelah Afzali, who have organized immigration rights and BLM events. For it is their grassroots vision that has shaped public platforms—their photos, their red-white-and-blue figures, their superhero icons and political branding as in Afzali's Facebook page—imagining change in digital communities. Growing up in the US, Afzali remembers being bullied as a kid. "We're going to blow your country back to the Stone Ages!" But this threat only added to her sense of constant anxiety. She could not remember Afghanistan, her birthplace. Her only place of memory, her country, and her home is the United States. In the wake of these painful encounters, Afzali's digital media with her branding of superheroes, part of her vision of belonging, not unlike the journey of solidarity in Ms. Marvel, is all part of her political stance. Her superhero figures support radical feminists—rooted in images of Malcolm X, imagining new interracial solidarities. In this chapter, then, we will navigate these websites of Afzali's digital icons, mapping her strategies in social media, to ask why such online icons matter in grassroots activism, and to explore the tensions that exist between these celebrated icons and the streets.

Aneelah Afzali, Director of the American Muslim Empowerment Network. Photograph by Abbie Austin. Reproduced with permission.

## WHY DO THESE ONLINE ICONS MATTER?

Icons—as well-known images—are used not only as part of political brand-ing but also as part of an ethical stance that invites protesters to join in. Rooting her network of protest in Black Consciousness, one of the most prominent images on Afzali's Facebook page is that of Malcolm X. Against the backdrop of this icon on Facebook, she details her antiracist philosophy, profoundly influenced by his teachings. "If you stick a knife in my back 9-inches and pull it out 6-inches, that's not progress. If you pull it all the way out, that's not progress," continues Malcolm's quote on her full-screen poster on Facebook.[1] "The progress comes from healing the wound that the blow made." Her iconic posting situates images of herself—her protest gear, T-shirts, red-white-and-blue banners, and superhero images—alongside

Malcolm X. This strategy—a kind of radical superheroism that honors the role of Black Muslims and their protests—is associated with her own ethical stance and her recognition of large-scale injuries against US Muslims. These icons on Facebook are part of Afzali's larger calling for multiracial bonds, for invitations to take to the streets, for a gathering of American Muslims— echoing her own proud claim to citizenship. Rejecting the traumatic taunts of her youth, these digital icons lay claim to her belonging as an American Muslim—a racial script of pride, a sign of collective power.

In 1990, when Afzali was in seventh grade, her father received a traffic ticket. She told him to fight it. It was "racial profiling," Afzali insisted. But he was just going to pay the ticket and move on. "No, no," she protested. "It's a matter of justice, Dad." At the hearing, the thirteen-year-old girl stood up to interpret for her father.

"Are you a lawyer?" the judge asked.

"No," she responded.

"If you are not a lawyer, you need to sit back down," said the judge.

It was at this point that Afzali wanted to become a lawyer, to become part of that secret society. But it seemed like an elite club, an impossibility. Even college felt like a faraway dream, graduate school even more remote. Still, she loved mock trial at her high school, she handled all the paperwork for her parents' various businesses, and she managed all the forms for her older sister's divorce. She even played a lawyer in a high-school play. But as the first in her family to attend college, she was anxious. "As a refugee, as an immigrant, as a woman of color, I couldn't consult others, because people who looked like me never went to law school." Equally painful was the oft-repeated insinuation that students like her were at Harvard for reasons other than merit. And when she started her legal career in 2003, she still felt like she didn't belong, further fueling her self-doubts. Surprised that she was "so articulate," she was complimented, as a junior partner in the firm, on how *intelligently* she spoke. All of which only heightened her sense of being an imposter. While racist assaults have shaped her ideas and icons, she also tries to forget these traumatic memories, many accompanied by threats and potential violence. "Honestly," she says, "I have tried to keep them out of my mind to survive."

Her icons are symbols of belonging, fueled by her own story. Born in Kabul in 1977, Afzali and her family fled during the Soviet invasion. Refugees in Germany, they were then sponsored by her grandparents—her father's family—in the United States, an approval process that led to three more years of displacement. Afzali has often been called on for her expertise in immigration issues, part of her work as director of the empowerment network, hired full-time by the Muslim Association of Puget Sound, a hub of activity for nearly seven thousand people. She holds many public and virtual rallies, such as "The Muslim Ban: Three Years On."[2] And before these rallies, she publicizes goals and motivates communities. Her Facebook and its hashtags urge on great numbers of people at relatively short notice. Working in interracial alliances, with Latinx and Black leaders, like Bianca Davis-Lovelace, protesting the Seattle police killing of thirty-year-old Charleena Lyles, Afzali calls on us to hit the streets. "Take Action, and You're an Ally!" After calling the police about a burglary, Charleena was shot seven times in front of her children: her eleven-year-old boy and his two younger sisters, one with Down syndrome. This urgent protest against police violence, Afzali explains, is personal for her because of own experiences of racism and her resistance to violent military and police action. And she leads protests in front of Northwest Detention Center in Tacoma, where immigrant families are imprisoned, fathers and mothers rounded up as they walk their children to preschools. After these protests her accompanying snapshot shows up on her Facebook page and website as well as on the site of her virtual community of almost five thousand. And in these icons—both of Malcolm X and her own photo, types of protest icons—she evinces solidarities.

On June 10, 2019, for example, there is a photo on her Facebook page of female activists from various racial and religious backgrounds in refugee camps in Mexico. Underneath is a smaller photo of Afzali herself, holding a protest sign featuring a very green Statue of Liberty, whose thought bubble asks, "Was I unclear?"[3] The poster's colors pick up on Afzali's purple T-shirt, whose insignia makes another claim: "Moses & Mary & Jesus & Muhammed. All Refugees." Reframing these figures of religion, Afzali urges her public to welcome immigrants. Although there is a vulnerability here—she stands alone—there is a framework of two women: Lady Liberty, the symbol of liberation in the United States, and this activist, a symbol of protest. These dual icons stand together, eliciting awareness, evoking a powerful national aura.

And in her online icon, her photo of her body, of her banner, for instance, her stance, as part of the banner's patriotic hues of being proud, calls for a new form of journalism as another site of being powerful. Holding her banner, thus, "American Muslim, Proud and Powerful" at the Women's March, Afzali is surrounded by posters of a Muslim woman veiled in an American flag. Not a rescue mission, as object of the Women's March, but a leader with vision of the US. It is a site of patriotism and of power, an iconic photo, that reinscribes racial scripts and mainstream news. "Before we had to rely on mainstream media oftentimes to be able to have this kind of reach," she said. Now she can do that directly, without having to rely on mass media that may or may not cover her stories, her issues, her needs. "We are now empowered to do that directly ourselves."[4] In fact, "every single one of us now is empowered to be a journalist." We have a Facebook page, and "that's often the best way to organize some of our events, especially when we're working with a lot of other groups and organizations. It's critical. I honestly don't think you can do effective advocacy right now without using social media." It is a kind of citizen journalism on these protests. But there is a layering of images—of national icons, of national power—as well as of ideas and of times listed for the next protest. As in the Black Power Movement, these digital icons mirror power.

These online icons are rooted in her ethics and in her politics and in her faith—not a blind patriotism. Her turn toward radical feminism was part of a longer journey, which, for Afzali, began in law school. Although born a Muslim and raised with Islamic values—such as education, hard work, compassion, mercy—she grew up in a divided family. Her mother was devout, but her father was a "Ramadan Muslim," celebrating holidays but praying without regularity. So as a child, she gravitated towards what was easier. But things changed when she saw a passage from the Qur'an that had been posted at Harvard Law School, "God is talking to us, oh those who believe, to stand firmly for justice," inspiring her own journey. She recalled this verse years later in 2012, after reading the Qur'an from cover to cover during Ramadan. Every other Ramadan, she would read about half of the Qur'an, after which, until the following year, the book would close, placed on the shelf. When she read all of the Qur'an, it just shook her to the core. And thus began the political activism that was very much part of her spiritual transformation, her own healing, and her commitment to that which Islam emphasizes, a life of service, which took the form of public and digital activism. She wanted to use her gifts and skills toward the greater good, leading toward her work with immigrants and as an activist, which is what "Islam teaches us to do."

While Muslim women wear scarves for a variety of reasons—for culture, tradition, religion, politics, identity—about half of the Muslim women in the US wear it, half don't, she reflected. It is not "what you wear, but how you act." So when Afzali started wearing her scarf, her pride in her newly found identity was a key reason. More broadly, however, she was also responding to the radical feminism that she found in Islam. She sought solidarity and political activism with others of her faith. "Why would I not want to exhibit that?" she said. In the same way you'd wear the jersey of the home team that you're proud of? Or placing a sticker on your car in support of BLM? She wanted to stand in solidarity—an antiracist and de-imperializing stance. As with her scarf and her posters and her posts, it is a self-positioning—a protest icon, posting in thousands of feeds, in videos in protests, in multiracial solidarities.

In contrast to the celebrity images, like a rap star, Afzali's cover photo is somber, wistful, reflecting and performing her protest. Her activist image, her own photograph, suggests her political power. This online image is her protest aesthetic, an emblem of her organization. And these images are grounded in Black pride and in Islamic feminism. In this case study, she's in no way a token presence, for Afzali's story is also part of an important movement of digital action within circles of women throughout the US, given that over 70 percent of US Muslim women have supported Black Lives Matter.[5] This solidarity expands into an iconography, then into her organization. Her images, her grassroots icons include the time of the next rally.

Commenting on, liking, and following Afzali, her Facebook followers have turned the activist into a kind of political icon, a digital activism shared on social media with others. For this is more than a few hundred followers on a social media account. How others narrate and situate images of themselves in social media, of course, is both innovative and personal, part of a larger narrative that responds to Facebook's "What's on your mind?" These icons are not only of the lone individual. For Afzali's postings, amid her network and protest workshops, support numerous platforms, as shown in the next chapter. Posting onto their own platforms, what further and crucially circulates, then, is not just Afzali but a larger band of sisters, a larger promotion of protest as a way to change structures and to rewrite a history that finally includes their voices. Not limited to immigration issues, her group participated in the End Mass Incarceration: Day of Action in front of the capitol building in Olympia, Washington. Fighting across racial boundaries, she also supported the Indigenous Peoples Day at the Daybreak Star Indian Cultural Center in Seattle. And during the pandemic, Afzali organized food and vaccine drives, and distributed masks for essential workers all over the city. This is digital activism at work. These icons become visual points of consciousness, protest identities.

But then her presence is amplified by others, actual and digital, within a larger collectivity. Her more than four thousand fans on Facebook clearly adore her. "We love you, Aneelah!" writes one. And as the rest of this book delineates, this figure of the protester is also part of a national trend. When Afzali went to speak at a BLM protest, for instance, she posted it on her Facebook page. "Thank you for representing us," another woman in her network commented, building an even larger sense of interracial solidarity in US Muslim radical feminism. Not an individual speaker but a representative of protest—like the celebrated figure of Kamala Khan—her icons in

red-white-and-blue work as a kind of digitalization, calling for more protesters. So, in these activist icons, what is established is a certain grandeur of the
political figure, itself a type of political documentation. Within our digital era,
it is a malleable process that creates and then re-creates a kaleidoscopic army
of identities: over time, these images are supplemented, or even replaced,
reordered to inspire others to create news media by citizens.[6]

These posts, I would argue, are part of a larger *protest aesthetic*. For there
are a variety of ways to construct an identity on Facebook. In her many
profile portraits, her icons and her interracial solidarities are suggested:
another photo of two leaders, religious icons: Reverend Davis-Lovelace,
a Black pastor, who wears her white pastoral robe and works with Reach
Community Programs; and Afzali, who wears her white T-shirt, sporting the
striking icon of a flag-wrapped Muslim woman, "We the People Are Greater
than Fear." As in her online icon, a protest image tinged in red-white-and-
blue, her images are grounded in the physical world—her panels of women,
her visits to mosques for non-Muslims, her question-and-answer forums,
and, above all, a persuasive, eloquent voice, trained in law school, that has
launched protests in various communities. And these protests have taken
on yet another digital body on websites, lists, Zoom panels, invitations to
Facebook events—a figure with an emergent, even *greater public*. Even as
these networks are gatekeeping,[7] these digital platforms organize thinking, suggesting ways to stage pictures, ways to report the news, ways to tell
stories—a strategy of online iconicity.

Not the same as a celebrity's presence, this is a neighborhood watch, beyond all borders, to keep each other safe. Her Facebook activism—publicizing
her fundraiser, supporting refugee camps—states, "WE WILL PROTECT
EACH OTHER." Not unlike her icon, an image of the Statue of Liberty
embraces a Muslim immigrant. When Afzali joins a solidarity group bringing awareness of a refugee camp in Mexico, her green T-shirt reminds us,
"Jesus was a Refugee." "What really struck me," she says, "is that in the camps,
so many didn't know that people in the US welcomed them." Her images
have become a modern avatar of liberty—a living, breathing, 2.0 version
of Lady Liberty's clarion call. Afzali's ubiquitous presence on the web, then,
is born out of her concern for others—part of a greater solidarity, what
Zizi Papacharissi calls the "networked self."[8] In response to the pandemic,
Afzali has shifted to even more digital forums and online rallies, to chats on
Facebook Live, info-videos on YouTube, Twitter/X postings of #Facts Over
Fear, grassroots funding online, updates on Instagram, panels posted on her
American Muslim Empowerment Network website—even as she continues
to pound the streets, megaphone and banner in hand, in powerful antiracist

and de-imperializing stances—her digital icons mapping her organization of the streets.

These choices not only emerge from the images taken, as kinds of protest performances but also craft heteroglossic feminism in the digital world. Nor are these images of the single activist. Others view her image, even as she views and adds those of other fellow American Muslims. So it is a kind of self-sculpting. Social sculpting, even. And it is the argument here that it is a part of a *larger* movement—a physically located, street-centric, political performance, a radical iconography even, pulsating in the digital world.

## DIGITAL ACTIVISM : POTENTIAL AND PROBLEMS

Grassroots sites are also attacked. What is her strategy? She mobilizes solidarities among her nearly five thousand followers on Facebook. "I'm sure I will see the typical xenophobic, Islamophobic, or other non-compassionate responses in the comments section of this op-ed," she writes.[9] She draws attention to the digital assaults that this extra digital attention inevitably brings with it. "I appreciate in advance any of you adding positive comments (as I won't be responding to any)." She clearly frames her own political position, refusing to get trapped, refusing to go on the defensive, refusing to answer the usual insults, hidden as questions. Sometimes the question may appear neutral. "Can you tell me about women's rights in Islam?" At other times, it is openly hostile. "Is it true that women are oppressed by Islam?" But both questions assume that women are oppressed by their own beliefs, hiding their aggressive assumption that women of color are voiceless. As a critical tactic, she calls on interracial allies to use their cultural capital—their organizational backing, their resistance groups, their faith communities, their professional vocations, and, for many, their white privilege—to fight back when hate groups gather, whether at her mosque, her public podium, or her digital media.

Most troubling, the superhero icon of protest, as Afzali's strategy, is not recognized in the press. What we see is that the superhero as subject is twisted into the object. When Afzali submitted her protest in an op-ed column to the *Seattle Times*, for instance, her eloquent essay was published. Her idea of superheroes suggests that the newly invited refugees from Afghanistan will be our future superheroes—the ones coming to the US to save us. Unfortunately, the press added some of its own touches, its own politics. Most prominently, the press added a captioned photo, reframing the disastrous war and occupation within a photo of a group of forlorn-looking schoolgirls in Afghanistan. Added too was a caption on the twenty years of progress in girls' education in Afghanistan, a propaganda move. All this with a headline—"The Superpower I Call Home Cannot Abandon the Afghan 'Supergirls' of My Homeland"—which was not her own.[10] Just as the photo (and its caption) thwarts her meaning, the headline misconstrues her words.

At the same time, Afzali's strategy, her radical framing of icons, which I am calling superheroism, rises above the frame of these stereotypes. Offering a way for us all, she points to the need to follow the next generation of activists in the streets, the critical voices of herself and her fellow activists. The problem, Afzali says, especially during a time when hate crimes have been rising, is that Muslim women must start speaking out more in public venues. Viewing these rising hatreds as part of a massive industry within media, in five videos she has filmed resistance on YouTube, such as animated images of herself to inform the public of the facts (not just fear). Elaborating her liberation philosophy in an interview with me on June 30, 2021,[11] she said that the trouble within resistance movements is that many in society, thanks to mainstream media, do not even understand that there have been injuries. The problem, she added, pulling from a quote from Malcolm X, is that "they haven't begun to pull the knife out. They won't even admit the knife is there."[12] So, this next section asks the reader to sort through these ethics and superhero icons—Afzali's public protest with its creative forms of radical feminism and its digital activism—and on a more troubling level, it follows the way in which the newspaper's headline threatens to thwart her meaning, her ideas of superheroism, appropriating her words, their photo weaponizing her image. Using this lens of radical feminism, it's time to find the knife.

In the *Times* her op-ed focuses not on the success of the US occupation but on the disaster of the war and resulting betrayal. "Even as our country betrayed the Afghan people, we—the American people—should not. Instead, may we be the superpower that demands better and helps save many Afghan supergirls (and superboys). Specifically we can pressure the President and Congress to ensure the safe evacuation of our Afghan allies and friends." Notice how her subjects (as the superheroes to save us all) differ from the spectacular headline. Let's contrast her quote with the newspaper's choice of headline, especially the italicized words: "The *Superpower I Call Home* Cannot Abandon the *Afghan* 'Supergirls' of *My Homeland*." What's the problem? Like the taunts of her childhood, *her homeland*, even though she has never visited that country, is still and *always imagined* as Afghanistan. This after spending her entire life dedicated to greater justice, including her law degree, her decades of work in the US. But the headline refuses her identity as a citizen. "The Superpower I Call Home" is a body of white folk—this *superpower*, like some comic superman image, an image of whiteness. The headline strips her of her identity, situating her as a foreigner, like a visitor, who calls her homestay a home. This headline assumes that she is not a citizen of the United States, but rather *Afghanistan* is her *Homeland*. Typical of stereotypes, once again she is forced to become a foreigner—this despite her claims to Seattle, her home. Together with a headline that indicates that she is a foreigner, naming her homeland as Afghanistan, mass media strips her of racialized citizenship. Thus weaponized, the headline further suggests that the (white) superpower must rescue foreign girls, like Afzali, repeating the painfully misbegotten trope of the white savior—no less than a jingoistic justification of the war. This despite how she has spent much of her column condemning the longest war in US history.

Secondly, her photos on Facebook show her nieces as superheroes. But look at how her column is accompanied by a photo of a group of nameless girls, all wearing scarves, from Afghanistan. It looks like a charity photo or something from an NGO. True, this image is doing important political work, calling citizens to contact their representatives to open the doors of immigration. And only a fool would argue that girls' education is not an essential need. But what is missing in this image and its press caption—"Girls walk upstairs as they enter a school before class in Kabul, Afghanistan, Sept. 12, 2021. There are fears the Taliban will restrict the educational gains made by women and girls the past 20 years"[13]— what's missing is the way that the US occupation has exacerbated political corruption and extremism among Afghanistan's interest groups and has murdered countless civilians in drone attacks. In contrast to Afzali's underscoring the "many abuses by American and allied forces in the twenty-year occupation," the media's caption memorializes the war as *twenty years of success* in women's education.

Clearly, then, this captioned image plays toward propaganda. This press photo of a group of small girls wearing scarves is a blurred image. We can't really see their faces. And this image plays toward the propaganda that we must rescue girls from their own religion. There is no indication of US involvement, exasperating the violence and the proliferation of extremist groups. But what if the photo depicted masses fleeing Kabul? Or what if the *Times* wrote a front-page profile of Afzali, including her full-scale photograph? It could be one of her many photographs on her digital sites, where she, holding her microphone, speaking to her hometown audience of Seattle, calls her country to account for its crimes. Not a propaganda image—an embodiment of protest. But this blurred spectacle by the press, the detached image of these girls on the stairs, erases Afzali's position. "I abhor the trillions of our tax dollars that lined the pockets of US defense contractors," she writes.

"They are the real beneficiaries of our war, along with corrupt warlords we supported, not the Afghan people."

Thirdly, Afzali's praise of "supergirls (and superboys)" as those who will save us all—as future citizens of the US, leading us all in an ethical path for our nation—is lost in this headline. Instead, this jingoism of saving only the girls—do not "abandon the *Afghan* 'Supergirls'"—is yet another implicit endorsement of US military violence and occupation. Most troubling, it undercuts the protest of Afzali, rejecting the grassroots activist, refusing her status as superhero in the streets. Having been relegated to the status of a foreigner, she becomes an object of rescue. This in contrast to her op-ed, where she is the subject, demanding change. This problematic ethnocentrism, unaware of its own knife—a form of white supremacy—implies foreign Brown women must be rescued, as scholars have long argued, a racist colonizing complex in much of media.[14] In stark contrast, Afzali's strategy, her column's trope of "supergirls" and "superboys," as rightfully at home in our nation, welcomes these future stars, holding the US accountable for its twenty-year "debacle" of violence and corruption.

Let's look closer at her op-ed, tracing this lawyer's activism as well as her awareness of the world of immigration law. Afzali must simultaneously document the violence of the extremists that have come to power alongside the violence of the US war that has helped them get there. In fact, to press for visas for her cousins who are in Kabul, she must document the injuries they have experienced. As a graduate of law school, she carefully tells their stories as a way to press for their claims and, more largely, the claims of many other families—a position of greater solidarity. Over the past ten years, working endlessly into the night as a lawyer and as an activist in solidarity with countless US citizens who have relatives in many countries, including Afghanistan, she has compiled a list of local harms, which are essential in publicizing her cases and in her legal filings of immigration forms. Unfortunately, these harms are inevitably misinterpreted by mass media—yet another virtual knifing—since the press rarely distinguishes extremism and the merciful teachings of the Qur'an, thus confusing fanaticism (Taliban) with her own faith in Islam. Afzali, however, resists these stereotypes, explaining these injuries within structural harm. Detailing how these harms must be addressed as part of "accountability" for US actions, evident in the "mistakes, lies, corruption and abuses that characterized the 20-years in Afghanistan," she, as a legal expert, backs her claims with evidence from Craig Whitlock's recent *The Afghan Papers*.[15]

Superheroism is a strategy. And it is a collective calling toward rights. In her op-ed, then, she documents the trauma, while including the US in the *structural damage*. For example, her family member who had an interview for a special immigrant visa cancelled because of the Taliban takeover and now faces the threat of execution for having worked for a US agency. Still, she must tell these painful stories of harm, detailing how her aunt was beaten when the Taliban first came to power, "hit so forcefully that to this day, she still suffers physical, mental and emotional injuries. She can't even see the Taliban or hear the word 'Talib' without shaking in fear." And she documents how her uncle was "rounded up with his entire neighborhood, interrogated and beaten, while forced to watch as the Taliban gruesomely tortured and killed others during their prior rule." He is still partially paralyzed after being beaten. Afzali's strategy seeks to clarify structural blame for the suffering, a larger framework of public protest, the superheroes in the streets keeping the US accountable.

Using her own vulnerabilities as part of her claim to citizenship, she discusses feeling traumatized, together with fellow Afghan Americans, for citizenship is a social contract. When it is not honored, citizens have the right to protest, to demand and deserve and receive recognition and rights. As a lawyer, Afzali further blames her country for the confusing number of forms and bureaucratic processes and a tangle of red tape that seems to leave "no real options for many to escape inevitable harm." Her simultaneous claim of harm as based on the policies of the United States, her insistence on her rights as a US citizen, and her clear list of changes in legal processes are always placed into a larger solidarity of rights, based on accountability. Her idea of superheroism is not about the war hero but is based in our collective claims as citizens.

Superheroes in the streets, a philosophical positioning, assumes a supportive structure against foes. And these strategies of resistance are constantly deployed in public digital stages/pages/feeds. When we led an activist-training workshop together, Telling Our Stories, Afzali counseled the thirty women from her American Muslim Empowerment Network that they must recognize political mud-slinging immediately. Some questions assume violence, such as "Do all Muslims practice jihad?" Other questions pretend an interest in shariah law, implicitly accusing Muslims of rejecting democracy. In digital activism as on the street, sometimes these topics are relayed with a neutral tone, but in other instances, they are accusatory, Afzali said at the workshop. Either way, they can cause defensiveness, creating a negative impression of American Islam. Once again, "you're stuck." Afzali's strategy is not to go on the defensive, but rather, to express herself openly, cordially, and frankly. And, just as importantly, to lead the conversation on her cultural citizenship with intelligence and interracial awareness, a radical feminist response.

Rather than the very limited defensive maneuvers in digital activism, it is a rhetorical maneuver that Moya Bailey celebrates as productive, generating new direction.[16] Generative moves of superheroism calls forth collectivities, builds radical online icons, redefining their own citizenry as US Muslims.

## DIGITALIZING SUPERHERO ICONS:
## GRASSROOTS ANTI-IMPERIALISM

Her online icons have been encouraging US Muslim women to join the Black Lives Matter movements. But what is often overlooked are the ways that these resistance movements, to use Afzali's words, get *stuck in the mud*. Why? Because how this country spends its money, withdrawing it internally, lavishing it externally, is a trans/national mire. As she draws attention to the war in Afghanistan, one of the greatest debacles in our history, to quote Afzali, irresponsible and callous, one of the greatest betrayals of all times, where no less than three administrations have been covering up their failures, she once again took to the streets. As she often does, raising awareness of immigration policies, this time she's calling for historical accountability for the longest war in US history, calling for reparations for those fleeing its borders. So it is in this that we see her use of superheroes as digital icons. Her digital activism with online icons of superheroes draw attention to our doors closed to those we have harmed, including in Afghanistan. Standing with her microphone on the platform by Westgate Mall, Afzali raises awareness, speaking to a massive group of protesters. While her many supporters repost her speech in video clips on social media, her own Facebook photo records this public protest.

In her digital activism as well, she posts close-up photos of her cousin's children as part of her Facebook. Her cousin has two little daughters in Kabul, aged two and six, who have matching shirts that appeal to the greater idea of justice and of superheroes. They say, "I'm SUUUPER GIRL!" With their yellow and white T-shirts, the six-year-old is posing, and the cute two-year-old, brimming with curiosity and energy, is lifting up her fabric mask. The littlest one, says her cousin, is a bit on the wild side—a little *shokh*, as they say in Dari. These T-shirts deserve more attention, because the stenciled sketch on the shirt is of a young girl, surrounded by painted stars of power. The superhero as a form of girl power is a global symbol. But it is also doing subversive work. This performative agency of being heroic is emphasized by the caption on the T-shirt, emphasizing the individualism of a *supergirl*. No longer objectified victims, these girls have super-potential. And on

Afzali's website, these photos are sitting next to a collective call toward political action, a collaborative effort of opening borders and restoring justice.
Spreading the call for grassroots funding and activist petitioning, tweeting
these images of superheroes, this digitalization is a form of digital activism.
#SaveAfghanistan #SaveAfghanLives #saveafghans #SaveChildren: this is
not a call to save girls from their religion! No. This single image of digital
activism calls on the superhero trope to mobilize political change. And given
the disaster that we have created, these superheroes (with parts of their faces
inked) wear masks for their own safety in digital media. Calling us into her
family—her intimacies with her cousin's children—we attend more closely
to her radical superheroism.

Afzali's call for recognition of the next generation of US superheroes is
a strategy, a brilliant tactic. Both her op-ed and her digital activism have a
past-present-future emphasis on activism: the future superheroes, the heroes
in the US will be Muslims brought to this country to help save *us*, as part of a
measure of accountability and restorative justice. And in her digital activism,
she navigates the responses that she keeps on her feed, as multiple people
respond, reposting her op-ed in the *Seattle Times*, significantly, increasing
her national aura of authority. For instance, the civil rights activist group for
American Muslims (CAIR) begins its post with this quote from her: "Even
as our country betrayed the Afghan people, we—the people—should not."
Starting with the *betrayal* of the US government, this digital reproduction
draws on this legal expert's list of concrete measures to pressure Congress to
ensure a safe evacuation, facilitating visas and refugee admissions. Similarly,
her street protest calls for refugee relief while simultaneously condemning
the violent US actions.

It is critical to see how Afzali depicts her own protest in digital activism.
Her strategy is not as a token hero but in a multiplicity of voices and icons—
what I am calling digital heteroglossia. In her online forum, sponsored by her
empowerment network, her protest on the crisis in Afghanistan, September 23, 2021, lives on, immortalized on her activist page on Facebook. These
digitalizations of different voices, different embodiments, different experiences, symphonies of complexities, of racialized citizenship, of political
solidarities are arrangements of heteroglossic virtualities, not a superstar
icon, but pluralized protesters in the streets and in online media.

Superheroism is an online mechanism, but this radical strategy has its
roots in the streets. Watch how her metaphors of rescue, her superheroes in
the streets, refuse propaganda of rescuing Muslim women from their own
beliefs. These superheroes are clear that they are fighting antiracist and anti-
imperial battles. In her public protest, then, Afzali is clearly aware that the

endless war on terror has caused racist assaults in the US and, beyond these borders, has slain thousands and displaced nearly forty million. This dual awareness emerges as she, powerfully standing on the platform in Seattle's Westlake Mall, emphasizes her stance against occupation, clarifying the situation with an analogy. If someone has occupied your house, it is understandable that they should leave, she calls out. But if they have burnt down your house, she continues, they need to repair it. In her analogies she reaches out to her audience, calling them to rethink their identities, their politics, their heroics, in the most personal of terms. And although she is very clear that it is time for the United States to leave in the wake of its disastrous occupation, she is equally clear that the manner and haste of this evacuation have betrayed those who have assisted the US and the country as a whole.

Superheroism must rebuild sentimental citizenship. For resistance movements to avoid getting stuck, both public protest and digital activism must envision sociopolitical harm. The challenge is in the way that stories of harm have been used. Telling stories of pain is to leave one extremely vulnerable, so she's always aware that these stories might not only mobilize political change but also mobilize discrimination, once again inviting stock stereotypes of oppressed Muslim women. As a strategy, then, in her Facebook post, she communicates her own pain with a sliced heart emoji and #heartbroken, even as she thanks all those who have reached out and called and prayed and supported her with kind messages. Her digital post shows a thank-you card replete with flowers. "I will forever be grateful for your help." It is a past-present-future injunction, at once gratitude and a political call to action.

Giving a special shout-out to the political representatives who have tried to get her relatives out of Kabul, she commends our *collective efforts* even as their rescue may be impossible during this abruptly closing window of opportunity. Personalizing this solidarity, she writes that she'll never forget how her online community and political supporters have tried to assist her family. She also records her own turmoil. She needs to stop writing now, she adds, because she is a "hot mess of tears." As seventy-eight people send their hopes and prayers and hugs, these individuals are seen in the small circles of their selfies, faces of support, a sentimental/political connection, a virtual community. Notice the nuanced navigation of public/digital activists like Afzali in her public protests, her ethical re-sounding of national sentiments. It is a "colossal moral, military, and political failure with dire consequences and geopolitical ramifications we do not yet fully realize." Her platform, calling for accountability, expediting and assisting immigration, mobilizing multiplicities of superheroes, is a vision of *restorative* justice.

## RADICAL SUPERHEROISM: A DIGITAL STRATEGY

Even the frequent and seemingly casual greeting "Where are you from?"— is a conversational landmine. In an interview on April 4, 2019, I asked Afzali about her strategies around this alienation, given all her work with multira- cial groups. "I don't mind the question," she responded. "But it's the follow-up question, where people don't accept your answer," that is problematic. When she answers, "Seattle," people inevitably follow up with, "No, where are you *really* from?" There is this tacit assumption that because you are Brown, then you *must* be from somewhere else. Afzali has no problem with curiosity, but the question still disturbs her. Comparatively, questions based on ignorance, the lighter microaggressions—"Do you like tacos?" for instance—are "not worth getting worked up about." So "I try not to let it bother me," she adds. But perhaps this is a defense mechanism in itself, she says pensively. Still, even as she has become inured to such assaults, "what hurts," she says, is when even "allies don't get it." Not even the *Seattle Times*, a relatively liberal newspaper, accepted her answer to the question "Where are you from?" They did not place her in Seattle. Not even in the US. Instead, they impersonated her voice, evicting her (in their headline) from her own nation.

The uncertainty about the intent of these questions is a key issue in these attacks. Microaggressions are traumatic because they are often unexpected, from friend and foe alike, and because their intent is often unclear. While seeming like an attempt to cross cultural boundaries—what's it like, being a woman and a *Muslim*?—the assumptions that undergird these questions are oppressive, problematizing relationships, harming the target. Given their cumulative impact and frequency, Afzali's ability to cope with these daily insults or assaults, to survive and to succeed in the US, requires constant vigilance, a constant navigation. In response, she encourages women not to repeat the insult, no matter what the intent of the (friendly or hostile) as- sailant, but rather to rise above these daily assaults, in public and in digital activism, in speaking out, in ideals, in group icons, reimagining themselves in terms of larger solidarities.

Given these (online/public) oppressions, Afzali is clear about strategy in digital activism and on the streets. "Don't waste time" reinforcing the talk- ing points of your opponents, she says. "Our opponents have us constantly talking about what Islam is *not*. And we never get a chance to say, what *is*." Avoiding defensive responses and postures and tones is key training, which she used during the 2019 activist-training workshop. More often than not, the inevitable question "Where are you from?" leads to deeper assumptions about women and Islam, which she tries to tackle directly. Although she coaches the women on how to respond to misinformation in digital activism and in street assaults, she warns that continuing on this track leads to constant, mind-numbing repetition. "Psychologically, that's not healthy," she adds. Studies on the psychological stress of these assaults, have, in fact, documented how these demoralizing attacks, including certain types of questions, can break down one's self-confidence.[17]

So what generative superheroism does Afzali use to subvert these political landmines? Radical feminism. Since, historically, colonization has splintered groups, fragmenting racialized and religious identities, her liberatory framework situates itself in a different era. It is a radical return, as well as a feminist rendering, recalling the Golden Age of Islam. In the activist workshop Telling Our Stories, she tells the women that it is the intent of Islam to empower all people, especially anyone who has faced oppression—and not only women, but any marginalized group. In fact, she continues, Islam established a number of women's rights without parallel at the time or for generations thereafter: the right to own property, centuries before the Western world even debated the possibility, the right to participate in civic affairs, the right to education, the right to custody, the right to marry and divorce, all of which have been transformative within Islamic societies.[18] So extraordinary were these social changes, says Afzali, that the critics of the Prophet Muhammad complained that he was too much of a feminist. Yet it is these stories of the empowerment of women *through* Islam that need to be told, she says. And her empowerment group, as shown in the following chapter, uses digital/public activism to teach this radical feminism: a powerful rendering of women's rights in Islamic teaching, its stories inspiring our own society to change and to work toward transformation, joining these feminists, mapping their virtual revolts, positioning new icons in online media.

Even as celebrities face pressures of corporations and of limited representations, grassroots activists must navigate their online icons as part of their political branding, as a strategy of calling others to the streets, as an invitation, suggesting that above and beyond individuals, the super, is a virtual collectivity, in bonds of organizations—both public and digital. In this case study, Afzali's strategies invoke radical forms of superheroism in her national claims—a self-positioning, in her superhero icons, in her Lady Liberty images, in her public and her digital activism. And since her public actions and digital protest are often interconnected to her solidarity group of interracial women—the American Muslim Empowerment Network—and in collaboration with many other groups, such as BLM, more context is needed on her network of women, their stories and their digital icons, explored in the next chapter. As such, this chapter concentrates, then, on a particular leader and her iconographies in order to consider how her empowerment group has situated their identities within their organizations, revivals, protests, and artistic or social media. Given that Islam in the US consists of diverse Muslim communities, and that it is impossible to talk about American Islam without focusing on specific individuals and case studies,[19] grassroots leaders and their digital networks need to be studied, for both are critical. As such, the following chapter theorizes the distinct ways in which these dynamics of public protests and digital icons, this superheroism in the technological age, is at work. We must lean into these protest histories in order to unfurl new banners and understand these structural changes being called for, noticing the virtual revolutions in filming and in posting these digital videos—their solidarity icons—their radical aesthetic more clearly.

Chapter 5

# SOLIDARITY ICONS

## A Virtual Revolution

A word for the "real but abstract" incorporeality of the body is the virtual.
—BRIAN MASSUMI, *PARABLES FOR THE VIRTUAL*

Only tracking the trail of digitalization, as in the trail of the tweets, without regard to the motivations and politics of celebrity activists becomes part of an apolitical mode, a technological fetishization. But there is a challenge here, since these celebrities—given their vast influence, their vast number of hits—receive most of the notice. True, they often use their visibility and social media to shed light on injustice and influence how we engage in political action.[1] But the problem is that the individual superstar, as an icon, cannot possibly represent the complex identities of US Muslims. As they post their celebrity images, their strategies of superheroism are not those of activists, who post their images along with their group images, their solidarity icons. There is a tension here, since individual stories of the celebrities seem more important than those of grassroots activists, and their emphasis on the individual overshadows the important work that these groups, as interracial collectives, have to do as well. So these groups have a distinct purpose in filming and posting and positioning images—distinct strategies of online iconicity—in the digital world. In contrast, then, to our previous accounts of famous icons, this chapter analyzes how US Muslim women in a workshop for activists, Telling Our Stories, facilitated by Aneelah Afzali and myself, respond to each other and navigate their public and virtual protest identities.

Moving beyond the most famous activists—the sport activist, the rap star—this chapter attends to the importance of the individual activist, and the equal importance of starting with individuals in order to move toward solidarities. Because what is also challenging is the tension between these activists, as they begin to speak of their heteroglossic identities and specific pressures on their identities and as they work together in workshops, in panels, and in protests. This work considers how such workshops turn individual stories into group effort. And it further theorizes the relationship between grassroots individuals and their internet activism, their individual images and their film presence as a group, produced in group photos, YouTube clips, and Instagram videos. In terms of strategies, in their responses as individuals, as well as in snapping photos of the events, in reposting their videos, circulating online, in their claims of activism they are pressing against the idea of the famous activist as a lone individual, choosing instead to digitalize not only themselves but also and especially their solidarities. For Dina, for Mennah, for Uma, and others, their activism as individuals is the opening salvo of a virtual revolution. Tracing their stories in this chapter suggests, more broadly, their national narratives, their placement of the individual "I" of the activist within their claims of collective belonging. And, as a way to refuse technological fetishization, which tracks only famous icons, this work considers how their stories have been integrated into the unfolding of their digital selves, in the meshing of their protest icons and the filming of their collective group image, a classic case of the whole being greater than the sum of its parts.

This is the story, then, of how the individual contributes to a collective, a case study of protest and its digital trail. Wandering in with their kids, sitting with their notebooks, recording with their phones in various workshop sessions, a diverse group of about thirty US Muslim women were asked to talk about a transformative moment that led them to become activists and then to consider how their stories might be handled by the media, heightening awareness of their virtual identities. They began with the stories that they wanted to tell—stories of harassment as well as stories of becoming activists—acknowledging racism and injustice, building their ideas of women activists as part of a greater solidarity. As a strategy of radical superheroism, their director, Aneelah, was inviting them to reclaim their identities—as proud US Muslims. At the first session, she showed them a video of women, each of whose stories end with the claim "I am an *American* Muslim." At later sessions, they were filmed as well. And their public events, such as their panel at Seattle Pacific University, were also filmed and edited for Aneelah's research archives and web resources. These filmed icons, showing their solidarity, are a kind of political work. But, once again, their protests do not happen because these women have Twitter/X accounts, and their resistance, given their ongoing activism and their use of many forms of political communication, is in no way new. But the scope and pace of digital activism as well as their online strategies—as in their digitalization of solidarities—constitute critical work that needs more attention. And their stories are not disconnected from those

Nashwa Zafar, Suad Farole, Miyase Katircioglu, Nura Abdi, Amenah Stewart, Theresa Crecelius, Shama Farag, Author, Rokaih Vansot, Dina Al-Bassyiouni, Aneelah Afzali. Group photo from workshop. Photograph by Abbie Austin. Reproduced with permission.

of other groups, like the civil rights coalition of US Muslims (CAIR), which is also virtually present in social media as collective icons in Instagram images, in Facebook pages, and even in group shots, posted on shared websites.

But how do individuals choose to include their own protest identities as part of these online icons of solidarities? What are their individual strategies of digitalizing, of placing the individual "I" within a collective online icon? After Dina Al-Bassyiouni's story below, for example, of choosing to become an activist, Aneelah gave her feedback, providing her with a sense of how her (virtual) selves might be perceived during this period of rising bans in immigration. And then she was filmed, twice, so she could see herself and her presentations. Essentially, these activists were mirroring their political identities by giving each other feedback, then filming themselves, then reposting those clips. My argument is that these online protests reflect individual choices, but they are also *codes*—what Richard Schechner calls part of a role in a script[2]—political performances in search of an audience, seeking, as Janelle Reinelt and Shirin Rai argue, to change expectations of laws and policies.[3] Thus, this workshop opened space for their stories and histories, building trust and interracial awareness, snapping group photos, posting in websites and in Facebook, and in filming YouTube clips—leaning into protest icons of themselves while visualizing their group in photos in the streets and in the digital world.

## DIGITALIZING THE "NEW ME": DINA AL-BASSYIOUMI

As mentioned, Aneelah wanted, as a main component of the solidarity workshop, each woman to talk about a transformative moment when she decided to become an activist. Afterward, she gave specific feedback—a virtual screening, if you will—about the poise, the voice of each participant, and especially how largely white audiences would view their stories. So how does this influence internet activism? When individuals choose to tell their stories or post their images, their protest images and their group icons have a common purpose—in this case, pressing against the stereotypes of mass media. For Dina Al-Bassyiouni, her transformative moment came after moving to a new high school in a new city. Confronting microaggressions, she decided to wear the headscarf and to be more politically involved, as a symbol of a "new life" and a "new me."[4] But then there are the unexpected questions. When people ask her where she's from, she answers, "Redmond." "Before that?" "Maryland." "But before that?" She doesn't answer, plays a bit, until they ask the right question. "Where are your grandparents from?" Her grandparents live in Egypt. Even more painfully, her teachers, placing their hands on her shoulder, attempting to rescue her from her cultural straitjacket, ask, "Are you forced to wear that?" Microattacks like these can have negative effects that harm mental and physical health, as seen in studies of greater stress levels.[5] And then there is, always, the implicit assumption that there is no individuality, that Dina serves as the spokesperson for an entire population. Despite these frequent attacks, there is a "paucity in psychological literature regarding religious discrimination."[6] Further missing is the response to these attacks, as in her decision to join this group, as part of public support, as part of political mobilization, and as part of a virtual image of the group, posting her own image and group images as a kind of national icon, an image of civic authority and political influence—their virtualities filmed, photographed, and recorded.

Having to speak on behalf of 1.3 billion people and thousands of years of history and millions of interpretations always came as a shock. "Why can Muslim men have four wives?" her classmates would ask. "I don't know," she said. Since this is not a common practice, nor is it agreed upon, nor is it legal in most countries, Dina had never thought of it. "How can you be Muslim, if you don't know that?" Stereotypes were used as attacks against her. Noticing her new scarf, students further demanded, "How can you be religious, but not know about your religion?" She felt like she had to defend her faith and identity. The insults and assaults were damaging, as research on microaggressions suggests, hostile messages, these attacks have, over time, an impact that can be many times "more harmful than a single hate crime."[7] But what these studies do not detail is that these questions elide the possibility of more-meaningful questions. What Dina wanted to be asked was what new movies she liked. "What fashion did she like?" The questions that other high school girls routinely and casually ask each other. As Dina leans into her own sense of style and personality, she seeks approval and negotiations, not questions that suggest singularity, exclusion, and exoticism. What is less attended to in the research are the reasons that these insults are so extraordinarily challenging to respond to. Answering such questions, but showing that they are offended, recipients are often judged as overly sensitive.[8] In crisis Dina found herself writing out all the questions about Islam and starting to look for her own answers. She began reading religious books alongside the Qur'an, seeking not only answers but, by finding mentors in this group, seeking out her own unique identity as a teenager, protesting as part of her path, soliciting new alliances, and posting new claims in protest.

All of which turned into an intergenerational search, since the answers that had worked for her mother were not detailed enough to help her survive the hostilities of a high school in the US. While her parents had taught her about Islam, the teenager needed her own journey. So Dina finally turned to other religious leaders, the imams and leaders in her community, and to other religious texts alongside the Qur'an, and finally to the streets, to grassroots leaders like Aneelah—a panoply of iconic figures. Drafting her own answers, crafting her virtual identities, in the streets and in digital activism, Dina joined the protest.

The film of Dina's speech unfolded in several stages. For homework, the participants wrote their stories in journals, then shared their stories in pairs, and then gave each other feedback on a moment, a call to activism, an experience of transformation. After Aneelah's feedback, each took another turn at filming, turning this film clip, their revision, along with other women's stories, into a collective presence. In this process the virtual self becomes more polished after listening to other women's speeches. Thus it was that Dina shifted her story into a more collective frame, including, in her next telling, a sense of her virtual self.

What kind of virtual screening happened in the workshop? Responding to her story, Aneelah suggested that the long narrative of the challenges with her parents might be read not as normal pushback of teens stretching their wings, but rather misread, as a story about the trouble with Muslim parents. It was suggested that she instead discuss her own experiences in high school and her work in groups. As sessions progressed, Dina found her own path as she urged the group to consider their words in relation to the multiplicity of perspectives on Islam, including, for instance, more voices of unveiled Muslims, since she didn't want them to feel invisible. So, just as Dina modified her own story, presenting a more politicized virtuality, she also sought out ways to uplift other Muslim women. Islam is not based on a "single experience," Dina said; even within the mosque (and within families), "we forget that there is more than one way to practice Islam." For the filming, then, her eyes sparkling with a trace of gold eye shadow, this virtual performance leaves her initial anxiety behind. She posts her own protest images and group photos as a digital activist.

In her photos of protest and links to other youth in their Instagram sites, such as #MAPS/youth, Dina carries images of her protesting self and of her community of resistance. These virtual communities and their digital activism are one of many sets of mirrors. Given the multiplicities of identities, there is no single mirror in which we are, like Narcissus, transfixed. Instead, we carry our several images with us, these virtual images of our appearance, picturing ourselves as we interact with others; so these changing sensations of self are tangible as well. Our ideas of the virtual world include ourselves— our touch, our taste, sounds around us, reactions to us, all of which inform our sense of our identities within structures, as Brian Massumi argues, our own virtual images of ourselves alongside images of the digital world, one of many ways that we can hold onto our sense of our own image.[9]

But these digital imaginings (and public roles) are also performed within communities, bound to others as part of a greater whole, both physical and virtual. During Ramadan, even after eating her last meal at 3:00 a.m., fasting all day, attending school until evening, Dina posts on an upcoming event, drives through traffic to her mosque to host an interfaith gathering, then reposts video clips of the women's panel and of her table. Despite her hectic schedule, including a dentistry program at the University of Washington that runs from 7:30 a.m. to 5:00 p.m., Dina also dedicates herself to a high school group. Given her own traumatic teenage years, she sympathizes, she says, with these students, often challenged by public stereotypes, the pressures of social media, and the resulting problems of mental illness. Devoted, Dina also works with the youth group at her mosque every Friday, without fail, inviting them into a public and digital community of support, in her own images of activism, in her own postings of the women's coalition, her images and group photos, her strategies of positioning collective icons, suggesting her own and her community's resiliencies as a group.

## DIGITAL ICONS: POSTING INDIVIDUAL
## AND GROUP ICONS IN SOLIDARITY

These icons reflect a small slice of her political vision, her strategies in digital activism, asking us to further ask, on the one hand, how individuals begin to position themselves in groups as part of an online affinity. And on the other hand, how individuals use their own images and their group images—what I am calling solidarity icons—as part of their own strategies of radical collective iconographies. This work suggests that the strategies of the individual and the tactics of the group, despite their distinctions, reflect kinds of liberation strategies. First of all, these individual stories are all aimed at a common goal. The clips filmed each participant, and the process filmed their many voices. Which produced, for some of these activists, a sense of the "we" as a strategy in a radical collective superheroism, a sense of self in the midst of many others. As they reconstructed their presentations, bearing in mind a longer film, by the end of the workshops, by the end of the panels, by the end of the mosque visit, they had a common goal as they produced a collective presence, their virtual production, to be shown to other women in future workshops, screened by other spectators, and posted on Aneelah's website. And these solidarities within videography further demonstrate the importance of healing as part of the support.

Since the most common type of post on social media is of an individual in the everyday moments and special occasions of their lives, these icons of individuals are situated amidst solidarity, in a photo of a group, a group panel, a group at a protest. Their personal posts have become part of a solidarity. In postings, for instance, of their houses and mosques, even swing sets in parks, by activists like Mennah, Uma, Theresa, and Shama, there is a widespread reclaiming of place. Since these activists have been posting online icons, in their postings of themselves and of each other many position the "I" and the "we" in icons as part of larger communities, disrupting icons of the individual as a celebrity, calling others to become activists, hitting the virtual streets. So, as we learn from Mennah El-Gammal, follow her story, trace her digital activism, let's further consider how her online icons of the individual are also reposted as solidarities.

## MIRRORING AND FILMING POLITICAL SELVES:
## PROTEST ICONS, MENNAH EL-GAMMAL

Walking on campus at her university, Mennah El-Gammal was verbally assaulted: "Sand [n-word]!" This explosive slur, directed at her as an Arab American, is understandable only within the specific language and context of racialized violence in the US, a nation that has, from its origins, racially targeted, jailed, beaten, shot, and lynched Black and Brown alike. This assault, one of many in her community, created a crisis for Mennah El-Gammal: it was the transformative moment when she decided to become an activist. And in the midst of Black Lives Matter, her desire was to join with other American Muslims, taking to the streets as part of groups. In the public forum of the "Mosque Visit," Mennah began by talking about her love of kickboxing, a piece of her identity, before relating her traumatic memories. "It's a great way to relieve stress after class," she says, moving her hands in rapid blows, emphasized by the flowing sleeves of her leopard-print blouse. But at the heart of her talk is the story of her choice to wear a scarf, worn not only after a series of racist remarks but also as part of her protest against the hate crimes that have increased "42 percent in Washington," she adds, including a four hundred percent increase in Seattle alone.

So after many experiences of being called off of the plane and surveilled within airports, Mennah speaks against the racial/religious targeting involving government agencies, such as the FBI and US Border and Customs, which has increased 60 percent.[10] "People are not going to accept me, even if I don't look Muslim," she thought. For Mennah, this was a turning point. As a young adult, she decided to wear the headscarf so people could *see* that she was Muslim.[11] Even as her public protest is part of a visible signature, at the same time she also develops her digital activism as part of her political stance. And as she tells her story as part of a panel of US Muslim women activists, her story is one of many, part of the work of coalitions to hear one another. And in their multiracial panel, there is a filming of their stories as part of a collective digital presence. Unlike the work and presence of the individual celebrity, as this panel is filmed and the photos are posted, there is the suggestion of a virtual collectivity. Joining together in networks, in massive movements, in interracial solidarities, this public defiance is a trans/national trend.[12]

In her narrative of becoming an activist and in her story of activism, there is a collective solidarity being claimed. During her speech, narrating her protest action, pursuing a minor in human rights, taking to the political streets, Mennah was one of two students who fought for a Washington state bill to guarantee accommodations for religious groups in postsecondary education, such as extra time to take exams during the fasting of Ramadan. After two years of work on time allowances in education for all religious holidays, supported by the civil liberties group for US Muslims, Mennah reports that the bill became law. "This solidarity should give us hope," she declares, "uplift others in the struggle." Raising money on Facebook for Muslim prisoners, her virtual path includes her own form of protest against mass incarceration in the US. On Facebook her own icon, as an individual post, is part of a strategy—a radical feminism and economic activism—in political arenas of education and mass incarceration.

In this way, digital icons and virtual identities in protest groups are very much part of the politics of the streets. Given that many (grand)mothers are attacked on the streets because of their decision to wear their favorite purple scarf, in stores as well as on college campuses, many twenty-something activists are responding by taking back the streets in their protests and in their headscarves as an act of political defiance. Imagine it this way: it is a strategy to call out the racist bullies. "Pick on someone your own size! Leave my (grand)mother alone! You want to make trouble. Then, make trouble with ALL of us. Bring it!" Within the digital world, our performance of identity takes place on a stage as well—on a digital platform that we share with those protesters who have come before us, leaving us with choices, both critical and creative. In looking at protest, both on the stage and on the digital platform, there is an embodiment of self that we imagine, more than the sum of our parts—in effect, a *virtual self* that responds to our sense of society. In our choices we are not just standing on a stage, and in our selections we are not just taking selfies; more often than not, we are *re-creating ourselves.* And this chapter considers what these virtual selves and protest performances might look like for these women, for these activists. How do their icons project a virtual coalition? Calling out racism in the streets, joining in groups, and posting in online sites have been stepping stones on the path toward political affinities. And the online icons and film virtualities are quite different from those of famous sport stars or rap stars as activists. As we follow these virtualities—in filming and in posting—in this case study of a group, their online icons and their public affinities are critical to understanding how an individual's public protest can also create trails within its digitalization.

## VIRTUALITY'S MULTIPLICITIES: UMA ACHOUR

Of course, not all protests involve putting on a headscarf. "For me, as a non-hijabi, I haven't really faced Islamophobia," says Uma Achour, a twenty-something. Still, even though she hasn't been attacked, as an Arab American she still faces push back on her racial identity. In New York, when people found out she was Muslim, people would ask, "How can you live without doing this or that?" Uma has grown accustomed to weighing such questions with their hidden agendas on a specific scale. "If they're on the right intellectual level to hear about Islam, then I'll waste time on that. If not, if the person is just being ignorant and hateful for no reason, then I just don't bother." But there was another form of Islamophobia—a second type—that she confronted when her mother, who wears a veil, visited her from Morocco, in an incident that triggered her own transformation. "People were staring at her. And I felt it. The way that they were looking at her, or would try to bump into her or something, that hurt me," she says. "That struck me," she adds, touching her heart. "I couldn't do anything about it." Her sense of the other—of the others watching her mother in the streets—is central to her sense of a virtual audience.[13]

As is especially evident in these stories, our five senses offer a way of understanding. The way others looked at her mother, who wears a veil, was painful for Uma as well, a pain gripping her heart. This was doubly painful because her mother did not always pick up on the discrimination, while Uma, as an American, long used to its coded racism and refusals, from the media, from the streets, felt the hidden blows. These incidents motivated her to speak, to tell her story, to join this group, to go online, to do something about the injury to her mother, essential to her very sense of self, thus entering into politicization, into solidarities across thresholds of physicality and of digitalization. As she thinks of the many attacks on her mother, the pointed remarks, the spiky insults, she is still unable to call herself an American Muslim. Perhaps she is thinking of the many faces that have not made room for her, since they could not accept her mother. And it is injuries like these, even to others, that bring a heightened awareness, an anxious vigilance, which has been reported in surveys of US Muslims.[14] But this is also a catalytic point, for her protest in the streets and in the digital world rejects this virtual censorship.

In these political voicings, these protests have made us increasingly aware of bodies and movements and digitalizations as a "political affect," writes John Protevi, suggesting that we are navigating our world not only by imagining it but by *feeling* what we might be able to accomplish.[15] Since politics intertwines with both our minds and our bodies, are there forms of thinking that rise from "digital bodies and civic events?"[16] Bodies and actions and protests intertwine with digitalities to influence and inform awareness. Revising the "invisibility"[17] of Muslims, in interracial terms and in trans/national refusals of policing of borders, these women have shaped their own protests, built their own online constructions, sent their own messages, posted their own clips, arranged their own visual icons. Adding to critical work on these women's movements, this book asks how experiences of protesting together, how the emotive images on our placards, how the artistic modes of our sentiments, and how even our Snap-chatted expressions can influence how we feel about ourselves and our world. Changing our ideas of politics, broadening our field of vision can influence how we think about these movements in ways that are physically felt, emotionally laden, and digitally expressed, etched in memories and psyches. This kind of work in digital networks and grassroots groups suggests strategies that support political identities rooted not in the state and its laws but in communal bonds and in online posts, recentering protest icons in trans/national practices.

## PASSING INTO THE VIRTUAL REVOLT: FETIYA OMER

Although some white audiences would consider the speakers on the panels to be mostly Arab American—despite their various experiences in the US and their hetero-ancestral roots in Egypt, Morocco, Iraq, Turkey, Pakistan, Malaysia, Afghanistan, Iran—these carefully constructed panels included a Black and a white female speaker as well, purposefully suggesting the multiracial diversity of US Muslims. Fetiya, for instance, a Black Muslim from Ethiopia who moved to the US at the age of eighteen, says that she did not wear hijab for thirty-eight years. Even after 9/11 she was "under the radar. Nobody knew who I was." She had graduated from high school, headed off to college, without experiencing hate crimes. And once she got into business, people knew Fetiya as a person, "as just me," so there was no need for her to explain herself. But then she stammers for the first time, looking around at her audience apologetically. So, "I . . . I . . . I passed," she whispers, her face pressed against a scarf the color of autumn leaves, billowing in the front of her suit coat. And it is true: in the US she could pass, on the streets, not as a Muslim committed to Islam but as a woman who is Black. Awareness of racial identities in the streets and in digital media is a kind of double conscious digitalization.[18]

Ironically, while passing has often been reserved for whiteness, with its concordant privileges, Fetiya suggests that she is passing as a Black woman, freed from the insults leveled at Muslims. This important concept of *passing*—passing in ways that are not coded in whiteness—is not nearly as researched as it should be and is an especially fraught issue for those (like Fetiya) who nevertheless finally chose to wear a scarf. Still, in her case she passed for the dominant group—not dominant in racial identity, but rather in the Judeo-Christian-secular tradition, which gave her "more privilege than those who do not (or who cannot) pass."[19] However, recent research also suggests that when someone like Fetiya passes, the experience of microaggression might be even more frequent, because others, assuming that a person is not Muslim, "unknowingly communicate negative messages about Islam."[20]

Of course, the word "passing," which recollects a racialized history, is a particularly interesting choice for a Black woman born and raised in Ethiopia. Significantly, using this word in a new context, Fetiya adds that after 9/11, "I passed through that, a few years ago," remembering the history of assaults on US Muslims. So it was just two years ago that Fetiya wore her scarf, in part to serve as a role model for her ten-year-old daughter, teaching her to value social justice. Even though she does not feel directly targeted, for she still claims her Ethiopian identity, she wants to raise a child who is a "strong *American* Muslim." And as a mother, she adds, "I want to make sure that I am also equipped." Now, although Fetiya has noticed few changes at work, since so many already knew of her faith and didn't have to question, when she meets strangers, she has to explain herself to people who position her variously, like a social Rubik's cube, in terms of her "foreign-ness," in terms of her Blackness, or even in terms of her religion.

But the problem, she says, is that "I didn't have the skills to explain what my religion was." Wondering how to obtain these skills, she then joined Aneelah's workshop. So in the midst of these pressures, there can also be a series of images as part of solidarities—icons of protest and photos of commonplace activities, as well as group shots, leaning together, of Fetiya holding her daughter's hand, and of others lifting BLM signs, and of smiles in their frames—and, thus, there is a measure of comfort in these virtualities. And that is how, given her newfound political status as a public figure, we hear her story and her identities—as a Black activist, recognizing her icons and her strategies in all these ways, providing her own daughter with a model of virtual power.

## VIRTUAL REVOLUTIONS IN WHITENESS: THERESA CRECELIUS

For all these women these practices of telling their stories is a form of politics, since this was also part of a digital practice of creating a film and posting their group events and images. However, even as the choice to veil is a slender piece of these politics, it is important to note, as Aneelah has stated, that only half the US Muslim women in the US choose to veil, and there are many instances where women of many racial backgrounds consider taking off the veil for their own public safety. Not only Black Muslims have to account for their religious identities on the street, but white Muslims as well. Converting to Islam after 9/11, Theresa Crecelius felt it was the right fit for her, and selected the headscarf, long before she met her husband, whose parents were born in Afghanistan. So her transformative moment was based not on her decision to veil but rather in response to her family's court case. As she tells her story, this activist also faces a number of questions on racial identities. But even after all these years, she is still entertained when people ask where *she* is from. Inviting them to guess, none can quite imagine that she was born not in India but in Idaho. Many Muslims don't understand that she is a convert. When they find out, they are surprised. And then Theresa asks about why this conversion is surprising, unearthing some of the lack of acceptance around her. At the same time, non-Muslims are grappling with why Theresa has chosen to wear a scarf. In response Theresa flips the question, asking them where *they* are from. With preppy clothes out of American Eagle—her striped shirt and slacks, and a navy-blue scarf—she smiles, admitting, rather humorously, that she sometimes keeps stringing people along, just to help them understand their own questions. But then their confusion escalates when they look at her kids. So she continues to explain, saying that her husband is Afghan American. Rather painfully, these inquiries continue. Eventually, her husband rescues her, having grasped these racist codes, having spent his own childhood in Portland. She feels his gentle nudge. Just "tell them that you're white," he whispers.

The moment of Theresa's transformation was not in response to these daily insults, or even in her conversion, which she felt to be a natural extension of her childhood faith, but rather another event, following a phone call, years after she had met her husband. Ringing her early in the morning, her sister-in-law said that Theresa's recently retired father-in-law, Jameel Kamran, originally from Afghanistan, had had an accident on his farm in Washington County in Idaho. "Could they come soon?" Driving in the car, her family with her, she wondered, why wouldn't the family speak of the accident? Had Jameel, a capable engineer, been hurt while building a farmhouse for his younger son? While harvesting their orchard? As they walked toward the farm, they were embraced by her mother-in-law, weeping, as others spoke haltingly of Jameel. Around lunchtime he had gone outside for his prayers. But he was not alone. To help with the farm, they had hired a white man, a name found on Craigslist. While kneeling, his forehead on the ground in his devotion to God, Jameel was killed. The white man came, hitting him over the head with a shovel. When Jameel didn't return for lunch, his family went looking for him. Instead, they found the worker, who was using Jameel's phone. Confronting him, the family stared, horrified, as the man's boots kicked at the straw where he had buried the body.

For Theresa, this was her moment, the point when she became an activist—not the moment when she decided to wear her scarf but in response to this murder, when she seriously considered taking it off. It had always been her choice; she just didn't want to make her children a target. Six months pregnant, her three-year-old son still cradled in her arms, Teresa was anxious for the welfare of her unborn child and toddler. But this moment was a transformation, she says, "because in Islam, when you witness an injustice," she continues, "then you are required to do something about it." Watching the casket being carried away, still deciding about her public stance—her decision to *continue* to veil, and her family's decision in the court case—she was proud of her family, for they had pleaded for a more lenient sentence for Jameel's killer. After plea bargaining and refusing the charges of murder, the verdict was manslaughter, which was less time in prison—twenty years—because in Islam, she says, "we believe that forgiveness is better." Her activism, naming injustice and her family's response, posting online, deciding as well *not* to remove the veil, were also choices *not* to live in fear, to follow her belief, to be forgiving, to seek goodness in all people. Thus, Theresa has continued to wear the veil as her public political statement. From this site of trauma her public and digital activism rises—her fundraiser on Facebook, for instance, for those fleeing Afghanistan after the twenty-year war with the United States. Speaking out in a panel, she calls audiences to action, into cross-racial coalitions. Her protest rings clear, not just her family's decision in the court case and her decision to keep her scarf but her words, her intonation, her online posts, her group photos, and, as a member of the panel, even her stillness. "If you hear hate-rhetoric against Muslims, if you see something that isn't right . . ." She pauses. Within its space, you can almost see the man with the shovel. "Then, *say something.*"

## A MOTHER'S VIRTUAL REVOLT: SHAMA FARAG

These stories of individuals and their group narration of the transformative moments when they became activists, as well as their filming of panels and their postings of their protest icons in the digital world, can also be part of their healing. As Shama and Nashwa, in the next section, move from their individual stories into collective identifications, so too their digital images intertwine in their intergenerational bonds. It comes as no surprise, then, that these public and online icons are more than liberatory strategies, as guides in structural change, since these activists address claims of self and of healing.

"You have to speak the language of the people that you are living with," Shama Farag begins, peering at us through her red glasses. "You will not have that," she says, "if you are not getting yourself out more." Having spoken at a church, a synagogue, even her son's school, she still feels like "there is something I'm lacking. So I'm here to learn about it." Shama's uncertainty is not just about speaking, but about dealing with the public. Having learned that she was born in Egypt, some expect her to show up on a camel, she scoffs, adjusting her bright purple headscarf. Others say that they've always wanted to see the pyramids. Or that they are sorry about the political unrest in Cairo. But the mundane questions of daily life, about food, or school, or parenting, continue to elude her. And, in fact, parenting in the United States created her own crisis of identity, pushing her toward cross-racial solidarities in a political movement, marching, even with her sons, in protests in support of Black Lives Matter and Palestinian rights.

After first moving to Seattle, her youngest son was struggling at school, but when she went to talk with his teachers, they spoke less of classwork and more of her parenting, making pointed inquiries that seemed to target her as a Muslim. Feeling judged, her anxiety grew. And then at the park, when her son would fling himself on the ground and scream, mothers cast insinuating glances her way. Playing out a virtual filming of herself, she pictures a Muslim woman with a headscarf who can't control her child. Although her son can memorize entire scenes from a movie, he couldn't answer simple questions, like, "Who are you playing with?" So she headed to a speech therapist at a hospital, where she noticed an older man trying to control his fifteen-year-old son. Upset by the appointment, the boy was yelling loudly. When she talked to his father, he said that his son had autism. Looking at her son, her heart sank in despair. Returning to the hospital to make a different appointment, she heard her own son's diagnosis. Also autism. Overcome by tears at the workshop, she paused before continuing. Her worries were now doubled. Her fear for her son coupled with the fear of being in public, haunted by the threat of stereotyping, as seen in the case of Shama, disturbs mental health and interferes with the ability to function.[21] Given the physicality of this angst, Shama herself ended up in the hospital, wondering if she had breast cancer. It turned out to be stress. Despite the alarming rise in the numbers of cases involving Islamophobia, there is surprisingly little written about the impact of racism on Muslims.[22] And the repercussions of such ongoing discrimination are not only physical, including health issues such as insomnia and heart disease, but also mental, involving anxiety, depression, or damage to one's sense of identity.[23]

But what needs more press, as well, is how women facing these assaults have turned toward their own feminisms, their own radical beliefs, their own political revivals. Shama knew that she had to change her life. "This was my transformation moment," she says. "I knew that I had to deal with this with more courage." She felt called to embrace the situation, focusing on her love of her son. And her father's love. What most helped her to accept this situation, she remembers, was his parenting and his teachings that Muslims should do good and hope for good. But every time her son reacted in public, she saw herself twice over: both as a mother and as a Muslim. "Why doesn't your son talk?" people would ask her. "Is it because he's bilingual?" Or when her son would rub his arms, they'd assume that it was a cultural tradition. Or when he would misbehave, they'd connect his behavior to the supposedly stultifying traditions of Muslim families. There was a judgment, as if she didn't raise him well. In these moments, she had to reclaim her faith, the very faith by which she was misjudged. "When I lack courage," she whispers during a coffee break, "I can almost feel my father's hands on my shoulders, encouraging me towards goodness, praying for me, even though he has passed away." This remembrance of his love and the greater good, like the tradition of Islam from time immemorial, has passed from father to daughter, from mother to son, from one activist to another, and now to her virtual audience. And in her activism on Instagram, her photos of her own protest, holding her placard, she includes in her frame her two sons, holding their own signs of resistance.

Shama's virtual identity has many layers. Aneelah urged her to be careful with stereotypes, like they expect me to come with a camel. Humor is great, she said, but it can reinforce conventional views like these. Others suggested less graphic detail about her breast examination. But because Shama has long imagined how others have viewed her as a Muslim mother, her most public response, published on her website with her name and her icon, is a recently published book, on Amazon. Starting with an autistic child, Shama Farag's *I'm Different . . . I'm Special* celebrates a diversity of abilities and religious backgrounds. On the cover a mother pushes her child on the swing, a scene that reimagines her own traumatic experiences at the park. On the first page, a young boy looks up from his puzzle and says, "I'm great at puzzles, but might not be a hugger. That's why I'm special." And it is not her only book that is sold on Amazon. There's *Egyptian Cooking Made Easy*; she finds cooking and baking are excellent getaways to relieve her anxiety. Traveling further into these networks, these protest icons—their pictures, their captions, their protest products—are not only battling street assaults, for these images of themselves, their families, and their children are also forms of coping, and even of healing.

In tracing these online icons of protest, for Shama, there's also her children's story about refugees from Syria, trying to integrate into a home with a family in the US. And then there's her own Arabic novel, *Kermalak*, along with YouTube sites that explain the festivities of Eid to children, as well as a testimonial "I am a Muslim" on SoundCloud, and a blog that details her transition to the US. Not only does Shama's Amazon site stress her faith and her writing talents and her coping mechanisms, but her book's dedication to her two sons, Mohamed and Eyed, hovers above a quote: "Open your heart and see the good in others." Returning to the icon of the Muslim woman in the park, pushing her son on the swing, its last page echoes her father's words and reflects her own political revival. "My faith taught me to smile, to greet others, and to say salaam for peace and love! That's why I'm special." Her virtual identity, then, is also a collective revolution, placing individual icons of a mother amid other multiracial icons in her book. Cherishing her faith, nurturing her children, remembering her father, and longing for a more inclusive citizenship, Shama continues to speak out in the face of racism in the parks and classrooms of this country.

Thus it is that the harshest of physicalities have been reviewed in the group. At the same time, their stories are framed—as icons of a *protesting self*. As with the strike to the heart felt by Uma, so too Shama feels her stress, holds onto the swings near her son, watches the mothers stare. But these postures, these moments, also leave personal and *virtual* impressions. A type of vision of herself based in her responses.[24] Like the surprise that hitches in Fetiya's chest when she sees her mother being denigrated, like the pain in Shama when she's being judged, there is a visual image next to the pain. But equally striking is the group's reclaiming of activism. These activists have been speaking to each other and reposting and repositioning their self-images. In this way, these images and feelings have been situated as part of a group. As in the case of Shama, there are imagined roles to play, a virtuality of selves, which can be further performed for one's society, not only in the memory of a fatherly embrace but also unfolding as protest within pages of Amazon, in screens of Snapchats, even of SoundClouds and Instagram selfies of marches with placards alongside her sons. For this writer of blogs and speaker of stories, Shama is calling forth a multiplicity of identities, and in this case, a protest movement, virtual trails, beating with a daughter's memory, a mother's heart.

## VIRTUAL REVOLUTIONS OF A GO-CART PRINCESS:
## NASHWA ZAFAR

These protesters seek healing not just of the individual but of the group, whether the collectivities are intergenerational, interracial, religious, ethically cause-driven, or, in the case of Nashwa Zafar, regional. "I'm from Texas," she says, by way of greeting her companions. Although her parents are Pakistani immigrants, Nashwa is born here, claiming her own regional identity as part of her slogan of "we the people," so much so that her own story, as it takes shape in a number of filmings, is about her identity as a Texas Muslim. As Nashwa tells it, her awakening took place at an event at the University of Texas when an activist, clearly another US Muslim woman, got up on the stage and greeted the crowd with a "Salaam, y'all!" For Nashwa, this was a catalytic moment. "My head exploded!" she recalls. Adopting this statement as her motto, she ran with it. This woman—she doesn't even remember her name—made it "100 percent okay to be a Texan and a Muslim." It was the dawning of her national identity as an activist, and, in public claims and in online postings, as an American Muslim.

The group loved Nashwa's story. But please, they begged, in anticipation of the next filming, "tell us more!" So Nashwa took another shot at it, this time speaking of Ramadan, which is like Lent, she says, with its time of fasting and reflection, when "Muslims practice self-control and gratitude" towards their families and communities—a time to "rejuvenate themselves" spiritually. But growing up an hour's drive from the nearest mosque, without any sign of a minaret, they had to make their own Texan traditions. So they would go to a very exclusive, international restaurant, she jokes. "IHOP!" Open twenty-four hours a day, IHOP serves breakfast at three, four, five o'clock, in the wee hours before sunrise. Soon, the staff became concerned, she says. "So many Muslim people kept showing up at these weird hours." "Why are so many of you here?" they asked. "It's three in the morning." But once Nashwa and her community explained the month of Ramadan—why they were all chugging water, for instance, hydrating before another hot summer day, since fasting excludes water as well—there was a growing understanding between the management and workers and Muslim community. "But they just couldn't accommodate the number of people that came in!" Nashwa says, laughing, her eyes wide, as she leans forward in her T-shirt, jeans, and forest-green scarf. Soon they had jugs of water lined on tables. Hiring more staff for the early-morning shift, they also began to keep track of the shifts in the lunar calendar that marked each year's Ramadan.

Unlike the pressures on celebrities to represent all Muslims in the United States, there is liberation in setting down one's roots in a region. Embellishing her stories of Texas even more for the students at the university panel, Nashwa began to speak of her own childhood. At school, they did a pledge of allegiance. Twice. First to the flag of the United States, then to that of the Lone Star State. Discussing what it was like to grow up in Dallas, she refuses to play the role of an outsider. "I grew up as a Texan," she says. Fondly recalling her double pledge, Nashwa says, "we just have a lot of pride." Nashwa's affectionate "we," the first-person plural, says it all. Either way, then, Nashwa stands out and proud of it: first in Texas as a Muslim, now in Seattle as a Texan. And her postings online and her Facebook icon continue to position herself as a Lone Star activist.

Moving beyond her initial filming at the workshop, she told the students another Texas tale, once again situating her icon, her regional identity, as part of a collective iconography while filming the public panel, alongside Black, Iranian American, Arab American, white, and mixed-race activists—all US Muslim women. Because Nashwa does not know her extended family very well, she explains that the Muslims in her mosque at Dallas, with all their different traditions, became as close as family. She remembers when she was a kid, praying on the floor of the mosque, a converted laundromat; or Sunday school, sitting on a plastic tablecloth, eating cheap cheese pizza, popular food for all youth groups. This adopted family became her culture, her tradition—not the same as her relatives in Pakistan, whom she scarcely knew. But they also followed Islamic traditions, wherein the Prophet says to put on new clothes and gather with friends and family for prayers. So her aunt would send packages from Pakistan. Their outfits were not simple, she says, drolly. Coming from Southwest Asia, they're "blinged out"—glitter and gems with "all the sequins one can imagine." Because her mother refused to cook, since Eid festivities were her vacation too, they would have a buffet brunch, which meant that Nashwa had to get some bread. Destined to do the bagel run, she headed to Einstein's in full bling. Soon these Southwest Asian, Islamic, Texan traditions zoomed together like brightly colored bumper cars. When a little girl called out, "Daddy, is that a princess?" Nashwa loved the question. "Yes, yes, yes," she replied. The "bagel princess has arrived!" Later, her family decided to go go-carting. But right away her aunt called, insisting that she not change into boring people clothing. So, tucking their glittering skirts into the go-cart, they enjoyed themselves, laughing loudly, the go-carting princesses of Texas. And it is this glittering gem of a photo (and workshop video) that continues on her social media and on Afzali's website as a feminist icon of trans/national identities, scripting its way into individual and collective sites of this digital activism.

Nashwa's reclamation of her selves—as a Texan/Texas Muslim, as well as her new iconography on public stages and on platforms in online media—is a political stance. Especially in a climate in which the media suggests that to be Muslim is to be un-American, being Muslim and being Texan reminds us of the importance of both Islamic and constitutional law, claims Nashwa. In Islam, it is clear, Nashwa states, that in whatever country one lives, people must abide by those rules: render unto "Caesar that which is Caesar's." But the Constitution also grants us the right to practice our religion, she says, and if she follows those rights, asking for the "minimal decency given to Americans," then she is following the law and being a follower of Islam. As for me, Nashwa concludes, "I'm grateful to be here as a Proud American Muslim." This solidarity icon is what radical superheroism looks like. Interrupting white nationalism, it is an individual performative, a radical activism, and part of a greater movement of digital activists, posting group photos and filming icons, heteroglossic resistance.

Expanding upon her regional narrative—simultaneously rooted in radical feminism and in women's practices with online icons—the national holiday is, likewise, reimagined. Ramadan involves serving the poor, and since Muslims are called to charity in Texas, Nashwa passed out food to the homeless and visited the elderly, allowing her to develop new expertise, she claims, in bingo. Which thoroughly confused many of the older Texans. "Why are these Muslims here?" they'd ask. "Doing good," she replied. It is not only for Ramadan but for the "good of all society," she added. After serving the poor and fasting during Ramadan, the feasts and festivities of Eid would begin, once again resulting in a joyful collision of traditions. Since her younger sister loved American movies with the Christmas lights, Nashwa decorated with lights and ornaments. But not an Eid tree, because that's "just weird," she says, laughing. And wrapping presents and placing them in front of the fireplace is also strange, she says, because in Texas there is no need for *more heat*. That fireplace: "It's all decor." Nashwa's charming stories delight her audience—stringing lights, eating pancakes, chugging water, playing bingo, riding go-carts in princess dresses, exercising constitutional law, celebrating religious freedom. Ending her story, winking at us, Nashwa calls out, "*Salaam, y'all.*" Her video presence as the activist from Texas is replayed and reproduced in online forums, where the screening of the bagel princess is visualized on a soundtrack in which the audiences applaud and the other panel members join in, as an ensemble of appreciation rolls together in a screening of protest identities.

Unlike the famous images of celebrities, what we have here is a dual role, for the individual activist and their group pictures create digital media with personal icons of activists and for further imaginings of interracial bonds and coalitions. And these online icons have been posting in film clips, close-ups of individuals, long shots of the group. In terms of the staging of platforms in the online world, we select an image from among many possibilities. In a sense this image is part of a look or a vibe that we are presenting. When we select images of protest, whether images of those we admire or photos of ourselves—holding an image, say, or a placard on the streets, a banner, or in the midst of a massive group, as online icons reclaiming the streets—these images are among many in this historic era of protests. Replicating the protest figure, the massive number of these icons generates a heroic aura. Fixed in place, these photographs of a historic event or a public protest are considered real, even though they are marked by angles, by selections, by poses. These practices of protest, then, have become part of the collective postures of a group, one of many sites of memory, as well as of collective identities. And we can think of protesting as one of many possible ways that we imagine ourselves in motion. Virtual selves. Individual images. Collective icons.

In these digital icons, these *counter*publics stand out against the typical, all-too-familiar stereotypes of the press, often focused on women (un)veiling, stripped of their intentions, their communities, and their own digital doubles. In this workshop these ideas of activism and the radical collectivities of this protest group and its virtualities resist how famous celebrities, marked as tokens, are interpreted as exceptions, unlike other Muslim women. Like photographs of ourselves collected in a scrapbook over time, a series of life events—sometimes alone, at turns with family and friends, even in the larger settings of plazas or streets—we are always aware of the camera, the other who has taken the shot, who is watching us.[25] Inevitably, there is a vision of ourselves as part of a larger relationship: the "I—me" (a sense of inner self and its articulation); the "I—you" (a sense of self in the midst of society).[26] The strategies of this workshop have brought more awareness of these solidarities. And in the midst of this work, there are stances of the digital activist, not only in the group photo and in the filming as a strategy of radical superheroism but also in a virtual image and its role in the revolution against racism—one of many voices rising, one of many protest photos reposting.

Unlike earlier accounts of star icons—the famous image of the celebrity as activist—this chapter considers how individuals have located themselves in public protests and in filming, in telling their stories, and then in filming again, and again, increasingly aware of their common bonds and the need for cross-racial solidarity. This case study of their workshop and panel and their digitalizations has told the stories of Uma's mother, of Theresa and her father-in-law, of Shama's children, of Nashwa's Texas upbringing, and more. But it has also been about their conversations, about discovering companions, about a group of friends who came to trust one another, and who had the courage to look the camera in the eye, and then to share their stories with the world. No longer the tale of Wonder Woman, or a lone protester leading the charge, these are the stories of street activists like Dina, Mennah, Uma, and their friends, claiming their icons and laying claim to their national identities as a group, as part of a digital and experiential solidarity of US Muslim women. Their online group photos, like radical superheroes, are projected into their digital activism, providing us with a model for restructuring politics, reinventing activism, and de-imperializing histories. Rising phoenix-like from the ashes of the past, theirs is a radical feminism that has taken the protests to the streets and their digital communities alike. It is a virtual revolution.

# DIGITALIZING WONDER WOMEN

The power of algorithms ... [and] digital decisions reinforce
oppressive social relationships and enact new modes of racial
profiling, which I have termed *technological redlining*.
—SAFIYA UMOJA NOBLE, *ALGORITHMS OF OPPRESSION*

A Google search for "Ilhan Omar," one of the two congresswomen in the history of the US who are US Muslims, leads not only to reports of her political agency but also to malicious sexualization and villainization. But if the search term is changed to "Ilhan Omar" and "Muslim," even more slander inundates the screen. If we type the word "Muslim" in Google images, a set of images appears. But which images? What we see are usually figures of the female protester on the streets—their images blurred by media's lens, their faces covered, their voices muffled. These results follow formulas written by tech companies. What we see are clustered images from previous searches, often iconic images selected by the majority of users. This leads to a kind of "technological redlining," Safiya Umoja Noble writes, racial profiling via algorithms, its impact clearly oppressive.[1] Fighting back, online activism has mobilized new signs and images—as in Congresswoman Omar's icon of the superhero alongside her own images. In tracing their use of national icons—what I am calling their strategies of *digital superheroism*—such critical territorializations continue to stand on unstable platforms whose "publish-then-filter" methods permit racist attacks in comments, allowing problematic content to remain.[2] Since research on the web is not going away, these battles will continue. In contrast to these online sites, *Superheroes in the Streets* provides a more radical search engine, following a core group of important activists, all US Muslim women, who are inventing products that have been refashioning racialized icons as part of their public protests and their digital pathways. Having traced these digital presences of superheroes, of star athletes, of rap stars, and of grassroots activists alike, each of its chapters analyzes the ways in which these online icons participate in structural critiques of racialization, militarization, digitalization. Throughout this work, this new mode—as a kind of paradigm shift—this lens of digital superheroism calls the reader to decipher the distance between mass media's images of the female protester, invariably buried behind a veil of modern propaganda, and the altered iconographies of activists and their innovative sites, refashioning power in icons, revisioning new heteroglossic virtualities, promoting these online icons with their liberating histories, their *online superheroes* portrayed as protesters in the streets.

Strategically deployed in digital activism as part of public sites of controversy, these protest icons—superheroes, for example, rap stars and sports stars, flag-wrapped models and political heroines—also change how we view historical meaning. To begin with, these images, these racial icons, have been used as weapons, as Nicole Fleetwood argues in her important work on Black icons, in widespread demonstrations in the civil rights movement after the murder of Emmett Till, and of recent marches after the murder of Trayvon Martin.[3] Although these racial icons reflect the ongoing vulnerability of people of color, what's often missing, she continues, are icons of women of color.[4] It is the problem that Audre Lorde calls the "mythical norm," which shows patterns of power but also is forgetting various kinds of oppression.[5]

This historic era with its unprecedented numbers of protesters has offered more understandings of antiracist measures. But every crowd of protesters is made up of individuals and includes new multiracial groups. So what's still needed is more research on these unique individuals, their heteroglossic voices, and their solidarities. Tracing the public protests of these activists and their digital icons—part of an emotive archive, as Ann Cvetkovich puts it[6]—is important research in these antiracist movements. Targeted by police and street assaults and cyberbullying and by government policies such as immigration laws after 9/11, next-gen activists, according to Sunaina Maira, are a crucial part of this archive, their many cultural histories long overlooked by scholars.[7] Their creative activism is also in digitalization, recoding icons of what is heroic or memorable in their placards and in online postings. As shown throughout this work, this digital activism—posting a racialized superhero, the alter-ego of a riveter, or one's own organization on the streets; holding signs, at public protests, then posting group photos with banners and with signs of territorial selfies, is not just of racialized icons and a picture, circulating on the streets and in online networks. These aspects are part of a countercultural iconography of the female protester, reinventing the codes of icons and their ideologies and their structures of power. Rising from awareness of racializations and militarization, this radical feminism—more in line with the Black consciousness movement of Malcolm X, as well as the Qur'anic feminism of the Prophet's wife Aisha, herself a famous poet, scholar, and military general—offers a wider critique of US power, of inclusive trans/national feminisms, and, just as critically, a model of cross-racial alliance for lasting change.

## WHY NEW SUPERHEROES? DIGITAL RESISTANCE AGAINST STRUCTURAL FORGETTING

But why are so many of these protest signs that are posted by digital activists entwined with these national icons, such as superheroes? In this book I show that many of the public and digital signs have used the superhero and superstar icons to reinvent scripts of racialized citizenship and reimagining structures of power. Resisting villainization and fetishization of mainstream media and online searches, these racialized icons shift the idea of what a hero looks like and what systems of injustice they must fight, for these iconic structures are critical revisions of history as well. For instance, for the editor Sana Amanat and her famous superhero flying across the screen of *The Marvels*, and for the US Olympic athlete Ibtihaj Muhammad and her iconic sabre-swinging new Barbie doll, their star power resists the trope of the white savior in the news, as *they rescue us*, bringing needed political attention to injustices. Thus, it is critical to consider the ways in which the superhero icon and the celebrity and the collective icon are all doing kinds of cultural and political work, even as these icons are in tension with each other.

Many have been drawn to these icons in their creative and digital forms, and this allure, this affinity with the superstar and the superhero, is part of a reinvention of racialized scripts, as well as a remaking in the digital world of online bodies and their "social space."[8] Of course, the way that public gatherings of bodies become part of even greater currents, as John Protevi writes, enhances an emotional wave of politics, their superhero icon and these superstars, all part of a series of data, weaving and emerging in new combinations.[9] Navigating amid images that came before, these racial icons take their place within a larger family portrait of national icons; even as these racialized icons are also met with contestation. It is the very purpose of these feminist icons to stir up this common emotion, these sites of memory, wherein a sense of our national identity is presented.[10] But in this digital age, the battle over who is in the public space and who is recognized is evident in these racial icons, for superheroes are sites of identity.

Equally important, one of the most forgotten time periods of racial injustice is the era following the Second World War, an era devoted to the white superheroes of the forties and fifties. Thus, superheroes were born in a war era, and on the cusp of this war, W. E. B. Du Bois wrote of a Black nation that was buried within the nation, of a time when the calls for justice continued to fall on "deaf ears." Even as three-fourths of our community were disenfranchised, he wrote, there was no talk of reform.[11] Ironically, this was the very time when social reforms for white people were enacted by President Roosevelt's New Deal, as the historian Ira Katznelson has shown.[12] During the war and into the postwar era, however, even though over 1.2 million Black Americans and tens of thousands of other ethnic Americans (for example, fifteen thousand Arab Americans) served in the war, the heroes of the war effort were represented as white, and the systems of benefits and work were likewise whitewashed. Legislation regarding welfare, work, and war benefited whites, this historian continues, so that people of color became even more disadvantaged during and after the Second World War.[13] The government further failed to recognize their heroism in battle, although seven Black recipients of the Distinguished Service Cross were finally honored—a half century later, in 1997. And Black and Brown women were certainly not envisioned as part of the labor force in iconographies of white riveters. So these war heroes, fighting Nazis and commies alike—from the shield-thrusting Captain America to the lasso-throwing Wonder Woman, who also served as a nurse on the battlefield—these heroes, replayed on the screens of the American imagination, came to represent what was absolutely good. And absolutely white.

Not only did the mass media fail to include Black veterans in its films and paean to war, the government failed to provide them with funding for housing. Because the federal government prohibited banks from lending to people of color (which was unconstitutional), many were unable to apply for government-guaranteed mortgages to purchase houses, since they knew that the Veterans Administration would reject them on "account of their race."[14] This allowed redlining to flourish: hundreds of racially explicit laws, regulations, and government practices worked to form a national pattern of "urban ghettos, surrounded by white suburbs."[15] In fact, these public perceptions with their white superheroes normalized economic codes, obscuring government policies that continue to be overtly racist and imperialist. Richard Rothstein further documents how Black veterans then did not gain wealth from home equity appreciation as did white veterans, and how their grand/children could then not inherit that wealth as did the grand/children of white veterans.[16] And with less inherited wealth came fewer opportunities. Even today, for instance, they are often more financially burdened than their "white peers" to afford expensive universities. In effect, this myth of the white superhero fuels the fantasy that the racial wage gap is a question of individual initiative, not structural racism. Exclusively fighting Nazis and Communists, these heroes bridge time periods, erasing these *intentional* government practices. In the meanwhile the public perception was that racism was the result of a few bad apples, and that it just happened—what Rothstein calls de facto segregation—as opposed to de jure oppression by the state.[17] In fact, as critical race theorist Charles Lawrence argues, defining racism as an intentional act by a *single* person (a lone villain) who intends harm and discrimination remains the fantasy of the courts and the public.[18] Because the political structures in the United States have become part of that *fantasy*, like the white superheroes who continue to popularize and defend it, these whitewashed myths continue—as if the individual policeman, for instance, like DC's Joker, is the only problem, not the racist structures embedded in court systems, in the laws, and in policing itself.

It is essential, then, to revision these online iconographies, especially since these ever-popular icons feed into an empire of forgetting. It took over a hundred years for racist icons (such as Mammy or Uncle Tom), promoting ideas of willing slave labor, to be refashioned in commercials well after the postwar period.[19] In fact, it was not until 2021 that Quaker Oats finally rebranded its icon Aunt Jemima and renamed its brand, reluctantly nullifying the marriage of "white racism" with this "cult of domesticity."[20] Thus, it is no accident that new Black and Brown riveters are entering into this digital era, joining these racial icons of superheroes. With the red scarf of the riveter as well as her pride icons, Blair Imani's blog and digital activism further remake online iconography as part of her claims of labor as a "Black. Bisexual. Muslim." In prior images of riveters, these women wore headscarves, their hair tied back. Essentially remodeling war propaganda and white icons, Blairsie the Riveter has been refashioning poses and posts and politics—her Islamic feminism, her Black digital labor, her reinvention of her resistance aesthetic in her hetero-sexy styles and inclusion of LGBTQ+ Muslims.

Even as the new superhero sweeps in to the rescue, transforming Kamala Khan into a flexible advocate for herself, and, as a superhero, helping others in the streets, this is more than an empty representation, since it decodes structures of power and national forms of exclusion. Reposted on thousands of feeds across the country, Kamala is no ordinary superhero, for she is an activist, refusing anti-immigration bans and racist attacks, taking to the streets, her journey accompanied by multiracial guides. And it is her radical feminism, rooted in Islam with its concern for the dispossessed, that provides the foundation of her political activism. In her origin story, her parents and the imam always spoke of a greater good, just as the Prophet Mohammad had defended the orphaned and the widow. And Kamala needs to protect those who cannot defend themselves, even if it means placing herself at risk. What this American hero discovers is that goodness is not who you are, much less what you look like, but what you *do*. In creating this character, the editor and the writer, Sana Amanat and G. Willow Wilson, respectively, are themselves activists in interracial solidarity with US Muslim women, creating this long-running and popular comic series, also a television series. Emblemized by this latest activist Kamala, subsequent protest productions, such as Saladin Ahmed's *Magnificent Ms. Marvel*, such as Bisha K. Ali's miniseries, have been restructuring postwar trends and unmasking racist divisions of power, reimagining these intimacies in the streets of New Jersey.

Almost inevitably, websites have erupted targeting the editor and the writer, both US Muslims. There has been rising fury that they have created this brown-skinned teen alongside her teammate in an upcoming film, Monica Rambeau, the Black female superhero who nearly stole the show in *WandaVision*. And this backlash is online, rising to the top of Google searches, yet another structural form of discrimination. For those who know the activist's name, the keywords "Sana Amanat" require only six hits before the racist and Islamophobic sites emerge: some so toxic that Bing has removed some material from this search. When the writer G. Willow Wilson was asked to consider taking on Kamala Khan, she thought, "You will have to hire an intern just to open all the hate mail."[21] Even earlier, when she was writing other comics, the digital racists targeted her online, accusing her of being a socialist, a radical Muslim, and a homosexual, attacking American values. So, for the writer, this is neither a story about a model minority nor one about multicultural inclusion. It is, rather, a story about a female hero who is part of a generation that has been misunderstood and maligned. How this young generation has been attacked, the writer states, has influenced her own virtual identity:

> I noticed at the beginning, if I got into it with a troll, it would inevitably cascade into the timeline of fans and readers who would either try to jump in and defend the book or try to speak rationally with this person or people who were not interested in having a rational conversation. And that really disturbed me. I did not want that blowback to cause major distress to readers and, in that vein, that did change how I behave online. I don't shy away from talking about important issues, but I know what key terms the trolls might be searching and I avoid those terms. I talk about things in a different way that won't pop up in

their little searches. . . . It's not a huge part of my life but there is sort of a protocol I've had to adopt.[22]

Like the oppressive hits and trolling bloggers with their digital surveillance, who have upset the habits of this online writer, so too the scrutiny and harassment and anxiety of surveillance are part of the superhero's life. The newest Ms. Marvel's first attempt at heroics goes painfully wrong. When she is shot, the police come to the scene, after which Kamala worries that the NSA will wiretap her mosque. Unlike other heroes, celebrated for their good deeds, when she works toward the good, she's also worried about racism, that she will be misjudged by the police. Thus, her anxieties about not being one of the white wonder women escalate into structural assaults by the police, politics, and politicians alike.

In video gaming as well, these racial icons of justice continue to be digitally redlined. For instance, in contrast to the superhero of the series, Kamala, who listens to the sage advice of her father, the only advice of the Avengers, in the video game, is not to get killed. No journey of compassion, this is a frightening game in which mainly white heroes, representing the United States, save the world. But what's missing is the rallying mantra "Get up, Kamala!" Not just teen talk, these words seek out strength in the original story, seeking collective good by dismantling the immigration office and further systems of power to "defend people who can't defend themselves." These are the thought bubbles of a political movement, a rallying cry, a rousing radicalism, wherein this superhero relies not in a blind faith in current structures but in Islam. "Islam is central to her identity," says the author, and the ethical roots of the religion show, for good deeds are a part of faith, part of her "DNA."[23] Unhappily, in the chain of protest products, especially the video game, part of the messenger RNA that translates the code is missing. In Kamala Khan's gaming world, it's up to white superheroes to save her and to save the day. No hint of the racism and the militarization of the comic-book world. No cultural references. Her memories, like those of her predecessor, have been erased.

These structures of oppression are circulating on the internet, Sara Wachter-Boettcher observes. The problem is not just the technology. It is the assumption that the information—coded in neutral language as data that is being used to create and run these programs—is neutral.[24] Even in the miniseries of Ms. Marvel, as another instance, the screen writer Bisha K. Ali had to shut down her online accounts, after being hit with over five thousand tweets[25] in response to this series, even as she has now opened, and must work to actively monitor, her Twitter/X world. Just as these companies and other social media platforms are hiring outside companies to monitor disputes and contestation over content, there is also the problem of censorship and selection of materials. In contrast, instead of censoring, what this work has suggested is a reading lens and a decoding practice, as part of critical thinking, a double-conscious digitalism, affirming the radically reworlding and deimperializing visions of these next-gen activists.

Moreover, even as racist algorithms target these activists, resistance is building in small *counter*publics, linking icons to rework aesthetic codes, as Roman Gerodimos writes. When you make your code of ethics and stylistic choices the subject of negotiation, you open yourself to the community, "allowing both parties to be changed."[26] That means including your self-portrait, your family, and your personal media, along with your political tastes, in these multiple images, these heteroglossic captions, these specificities of gendered media. It is these reterritorialized imaginations that have been refashioning racial scripts and sexual codes. In each of these chapters, feminist icons—Kamala Khan, Ibtihaj Muhammad, Blair Imani, Mona Haydar, Aneelah Afzali, and others—are powerful mechanisms that reconfigure our current war propaganda and labor ideas and visions of political structures. For these activists, starting with an icon of power and then adding a feed of one's own self-portrait and the intimacy of life, is to shift these ideologies of racism and of labor and of heteronormativity into a more dynamic feed of online potential, full of heteroglossic virtualities, an empowering movement that builds as thousands repost images. That said, this concluding chapter considers yet one more of these icons—one of the most popular posters in this historic era of protests, a Muslim woman wearing a US flag—a decoding of these strategies of superheroism, in order to see how it has been circulated, contested, (mis)understood, activated in digital media, and thus becomes a key icon associated with US Muslim women. How does this online icon fit within the context of antiracism and de-imperialization?

## DIGITAL SUPERHEROISM: DECODING POST(ER)S IN EMPIRE

Hanging on walls, held up in placards, circulating on feeds, one of the most widely recognized icons in this historic era of protests is a poster of a US Muslim woman veiled in a flag. She has become a symbol of antiracist protests, a revolt against a racist president, and an icon of the Women's March. Along with her sister prints of Black and Latinx women, a triptych titled "WE THE PEOPLE," subtitled are greater than fear, this icon was printed

Nashwa Zafar, "Mosque Visit: American Muslim Women Speak Out." Muslim Association of Puget Sound. Photo by Abbie Austin. Reproduced with permission.

with Shepard Fairey's trademark swathes of red, white, and blue—a staging of national belonging. What happens when we use this icon as a case study of superheroism and its double-conscious digitalization? What happens when we deploy a radical mode that analyzes the poster made by this famous artist? As Mahmood Mamdani argues, racial regimes are not the same for all, and it is possible to "deracialize without decolonizing."[27] So how is the activist icon a site of racialization as well as of empire? In order to answer these questions, let's return to this icon and the original creators of this image, the photographer Ridwan Adwani and the activist Munira Ahmed.

Although the *Washington Post* and the *New York Times*, even *USA Today*, were quick to celebrate the protest poster of this US Muslim woman, wearing a flag as a scarf, it has become, in this era of digitalization, a contested sign. Yet there has been no attempt to sort out this contestation, the collision of views, the negotiation on the streets and in the digital world over this image. The lens of superheroism, however, will provide us with a tool for analyzing both the potential for creating an aura of national belonging as an antiracist measure, allowing for more inclusion and security on the streets, as well as the problems of the patriotic image in a jingoistic age.

To start with, it is important to recognize that icons change meaning over time. Although the original image was a photograph, this iconic photo is still a selected gaze, a politicized perspective. In the original, the photo of Munira Ahmed, wearing a US flag on her head as a scarf, is part of a series of images taken after 9/11. The image is captioned, "I AM AN AMERICAN." In turn, the poster makes further changes to the iconic photo. In the poster, artist Shepard Fairey redesigns this photograph to be washed with red, white, and blue coloring. Drawn to the image of the American flag, Fairey harks back to Norman Rockwell's *The Four Freedoms* of the Second World War,[28] transforming heroic images of the war into racialized icons. No longer does a working-class white woman with her riveter lead the way. Today we follow in the footsteps of three new Ladies of Liberty—one Black, one Latinx, one US Muslim—providing us with a greater hope for a multiracial national trajectory that includes US Muslims—what I see as an antiracist gesture, but not necessarily a de-imperializing one.

But even as mass media spread these images, even as these racialized icons have been reposted and retweeted and Facetimed in thousands of posts and poses by next-gen activists carrying their posters in marches, knowing that these signs are part of their particular histories, it is critical to ask where the image originated. Following the radical mode of superheroism, let's return to the activists—the photographer Ridwan Adhami, who took several photos of Ahmed, in a project that began in 2007. Actually, it started as an "unpaid modeling gig," Ahmed said. Adhami was doing a shoot for *Illume*, a magazine in the Bay Area, focused on Muslims in the US.[29] Meeting at a lunch spot, they discussed the project and had lunch just blocks from the site for the first photo shoot, the New York Stock Exchange. Right away, she felt that Adhami was a visionary.

For Ahmed, the massive replication of this image, one of the most iconic images in this era of historic protests, is almost unimaginable. The changing meanings, the genealogies of this protest sign, began even earlier than this project in 2007, since she has such strong memories of being targeted in the backlash of 9/11.[30] As a New Yorker, born and raised in Queens, Ahmed vividly recalls being in first-period class, listening to the weeping of friends who had lost parents, killed in the Twin Tower attacks. Since many Bangladeshi Americans who were working in the towers died, or as part of the rescue attempt, her own community was impacted. Shortly afterward, her neighborhood was targeted with assaults against elderly US Muslim women—hate crimes and attacks on Muslims in New York City that have not stopped, even hitting mainstream presses as recently as the summer of 2021.[31] Ingesting this collective trauma, she redefines courage in this time of ongoing wars, reimagining not the soldiers in combat as much as courageous women in the US wearing a hijab. In the midst of this trauma, Ahmed feels exhausted, because she has to constantly remind others she is both American and Muslim.[32] During this time, there are attacks against mothers and grandmothers in her neighborhood who themselves choose to wear their scarves.

After watching the smoke billow in his skylight in 2001, Ridwan Adhami was just as traumatized. The terror of this destruction and the anxiety of the missing and the dead in his city became amplified by the newspaper's line-up of US Muslim men associated with prisoners and terrorists. Wanting to show his own response to the loss of 9/11, he asked Munira Ahmed if she would stand near the Trade Center and the destroyed Twin Towers, framing her with an actual flag draped around her head. So, his simple image, "I am an American," the bright-eyed Ahmed staring back, rejected mass media and its masculinities of empire. Shooting in the aftermath of 9/11, this next-gen activist simultaneously watched attacks on Southwest Asia and the Middle East, and then was getting targeted as a US Muslim citizen. So it was an assertion of his own political position and his national identity, since these politicized others were not just out there but also at home where they were attacked. "We're here," he said. "We're Muslim." And, "We are New Yorkers. . . . We belong here."

When he first posted it, Ahmed's photograph flowed through digitally active networks of US Muslims—a series of blog sites in a virtual community of healing and support. It was a countercultural production for those who identified with the image. Whenever there were microaggressions regarding his supposedly anti-American politics, he responded by reposting the image, which, in turn, became more deeply rooted, shared with others and posted again. As this young artist felt attacked by others, swept up in the collective blame for the collapse of the Twin Towers, he was motivated to join the growing protest movement out of a need to resist the rise in anti-Muslim sentiment. The photographer discussed how his resistance aesthetic, with its ethical calling of what he *should* create or what he *shouldn't do*, had been informed by his own heritage as a Syrian American and as a US Muslim. At the same time, he said in a 2017 TED Talk, these iconic postings of this resistance icon, with its resonance with hip-hop culture, provide a sense of historicized solidarity.[33] Describing how this image went "viral before viral was a thing," the photographer suggests the iconic image has taken on "second and third lives" in its decade-long evolution.[34]

Eventually, however, Adhami came to the photograph with a measure of melancholy. Weary of insisting, "I'm American," he said, he was "over the image." That the nation inevitably positions the "racial other as always Other" and absent to the heart of the nation creates a haunting emptiness, an "uncomfortable swallowing" of loss—what Anne Anlin Cheng calls the "melancholy of race."[35] This submersion of self to survive eventually leads to new forms of resistance, no longer wrapped in current national discourses, a critique of the modernity of colonization and its new narrative of empire, a subversive refusal, what Ranjana Khanna calls a "colonial melancholy"—a haunting loss, a refusal of assimilation, a type of decolonization.[36] Returning again and again, the reproduction of this icon has become an ingestion, a haunting critique of how US Muslims have been treated.

Still, for Adhami, in the wake of the traumatic election of President Trump, this image became "relevant and once again necessary." When approached by the organization Amplifier, he agreed that this image could be remade to protest the election of a racist administration—a poster that would be designed by artist Shepard Fairey. But Fairey wanted to include images of several communities that had been harassed and excluded, excoriated by the fear-driven rhetoric that was completely un-American. He wanted this symbol to remind us of the freedom of religion as a founding principle in the United States, part of a long-standing tradition of welcoming people. Thus it was that his iconic photo became one of three images of protest against the inauguration and in support of the Women's March. Then these iconic posters were reprinted in the *New York Times* and other newspapers, so people could use these full-page images as protest posters. "It's unfortunate that there are still people who feel America is about excluding people of different origin," Adhami said, agreeing with this protest campaign. This is not what America is about. These inscriptions of the self in digital postings, continually retweeted during the past two decades, commemorating the loss of ideals, has erupted into protest. What has been "inassimilable," a kind of *political melancholy*, writes Khanna, has now become "interruptive and present."[37]

But let's turn away from these mainstream presses and protests that celebrated these posters to the independently funded *Middle East Eye*, a digital medium, where investigative journalist Molly McCluskey captures conflicting perspectives on this iconic poster, especially as activist Ghazala Irshad argues that the problem is that the poster reinforces mass media's conception that all women who are Muslim wear a scarf, when it is a choice.[38] What's more, this patriotic image erases the US military's wars in the Middle East and North Africa, as well as the surveillance and legislation and random arrests of Muslims in the past few decades. "I don't want to wave the flag around all the time," she says, refusing any blind patriotism. "I'm against the war, but I'm still an American." Her racialized citizenship refuses policies of discrimination, and she questions whether we must carry a poster of a Muslim woman wearing a flag as a hijab to "prove that we're Muslim and American." The political fashioning matters for fashion blogger Hoda Katebi, as she asks how she can hold up a poster of a Muslim woman draped in the US flag, chanting about solidarities, even as "drones carrying the same flag" killed her family in Yemen, with no comment from the feminist movement.[39] For still others, this icon presents the conditions for *good* Muslims, echoing concerns by Mahmood Mamdani, and as voiced by Shehabuddin, over the constant policing of Muslim citizens, who are required to show their patriotism without any criticism of the way the government wars were killing Muslims overseas, covering up the fact that anti-Muslim racism is widespread.[40] These pressures to enact patriotism, as further traced by Carol Fadda, channeled toward "docile citizenship" and "consumer citizenship," a constant pressure, a national performative—a crisis of identity.[41]

In the *Middle East Eye* article—even as its captions suggest that this protest poster "stirs debate" among US Muslims—what's still needed is a framework for these icons of antiracism *and* de-imperialism. What's missing, leading toward more ambivalence, is that this poster with its patriotic hues fails to critique the eight modern wars and ongoing violence. Also what is missing is how racialized identities are at stake, for the veiled image of the poster is functioning like a "second skin" of political identity.[42] At the march, carrying her poster, Safia Mahjebin, who decided to wear the scarf, considers its racialization. All people, she says, have to wear their identity on their bodies.[43] Given that those who select the scarf are much more likely to face racism and abuse, she argues that this poster signifies strength in the midst of "vulnerability."

Although the alternative press of the *Middle East Eye* shows controversy, what is not unpacked is how this image has been endorsed as part of an antiracism activism that affirms the belonging and safety of US Muslims. Safia Mahjebin, herself a member of this early virtual community of digital activists, remembers being entranced by the original photo of Munira Ahmed. Very strongly, she views Fairey's patriotic image of Ahmed as a symbol of belonging. She still remembers the ways in which the original, iconographic photo first circulated in virtual communities of American Muslims. And now it is a national icon. She saw it as a demand to recognize their racialized citizenship and rights and existence on the streets. So when the iconic poster was raised aloft by the hands of thousands on the streets, she had a physical response, literal "goose bumps," a new political emotion that she had never felt toward this picture before, despite having seen it online.[44] For her, this powerful icon in the hands of thousands replaced the "callousness" of conservatives and the detached "placidness" of their counterparts. "Seeing it again in this new context and in new circumstances, makes me reappreciate it," she told the independent journalist. While agreeing that the image captures only a single image of Muslim women, in the context of the women's marches in 2017, she felt that the use of the flag as a scarf was necessary—was, indeed, the most recognizable symbol for US Muslims.

Still, the icon has a range of meanings, various ways that it has been decoded. Yet another next-gen activist in this march commented that it was "surreal" as well as "humbling" to see this image as a national response to the immigration ban.[45] In *Sisters in the Mirror*, Elora Shehabuddin agrees that, during this massive protest, Fairey's poster was very recognizable.[46] She notices that many appreciated the intent of both artist and of the "participants who carried the poster to send a message about a more inclusive United States and a broader definition of US feminism that now embraces Muslims." Many women reported feeling welcomed, like Saira Toor, part of the Muslim Women's Alliance in Chicago, "amazed by the outpouring of support and love." So the image of resistance has been positioned in terms ranging from immigration support to an inclusive and radical feminism.

But this marketing campaign of "We the People" is also troubling. The image has "raised concerns," as Shehabuddin writes, because Fairey whitened Munira Ahmed's complexion: "white standards of beauty," adorned with red lipstick.[47] Unlike the whitened skin and glossy glamour and patriotic swathes of the poster carried by millions in the women's marches, Munira Ahmed's gaze on the photographer in her photo in the post-9/11 landscape in New York is more intimate, more realistic. Her own image is of a Bangladeshi American, one who does not veil in everyday practices, shows her own skin tone, her own individualism, her own racialized claim of belonging. So, in many ways, Shepard Fairey's design of the poster of the women's march wields an assimilationist's view of postracial America, which is extremely problematic.

A prime example of such assimilationist propaganda is the seemingly innocuous, even celebratory, short video *Munira Ahmed Marches for Women's Rights*.[48] The video of Fairey's poster (a series of still images with captions) offers its own misreading. Although the screen states that Ahmed marches for women's rights and equality, many toxic stereotypes of Muslims suggest that they march for women's rights because of their abusive husbands and a religion that is somehow more abusive than others. The next slide shows that "she's a Muslim American," but with no indication of her racialized experience as a New Yorker. And then we learn that the protesters picked up her sign in order to send a message. The final slide, juxtaposing her photograph and the poster, exclaims, "And what a message this is!" But there is *no sign* of what the message could be. It is sensational and vacuous. Badly produced. And reproduced with 157,000 viewers on Facebook. It's a whitened print poster that erases any sense of histories.

Controlling history through a whitewashed icon is a form of forgetting, an erasure of the past. The assumption, Catherine Ramirez argues, is that assimilation successfully eradicates history, even as it strips away heritage and personal identities.[49] But assimilating citizens is a problematic construct, because many groups are not seen as fitting in—because of visual codes of racial differences and legal policies of racist exclusions—so that assimilation is less about absorbing practices than maintaining inequality.[50] The myth is that in the US, Muslims, Black, and Latinx alike are "unable or unwilling to integrate fully," their practices viewed as not civilized, suggesting that borders are not just about imagining a nation but also about control and power.[51] The price of citizenship, Ramirez contends, can be a continuous *trial*, demanding an exclusion of cultural practices, consistently recycling Anglo-American icons, whitewashed and cisgendered.

Contrast this rolling, vacuous digitalization to the grass-rooted digitalization of Munira Ahmed's own Facebook page, which includes a photo of the front and back covers of the January 22, 2017, *Washington Post*—on the back, a paid ad by Amplifier to be used at the Women's March to protest the election of Trump. Although Fairey's patriotic image of "We the People" dominates her own photos, the crossed-out headlines announcing the election of a president who brought with him the Muslim ban make her own position clear.[52] Showing her own interactions in these shifting waters of icons, she has reposted images of the official, whitened image of the poster alongside one of her latest photos, wearing not an American flag but a hoodie, an icon of the Black Lives Matter movement. Instead of an intervention in the war economy, her poster/photo duality with its hooded sweatshirt is markedly antiracist, joining explicitly cross-racial coalitions against police violence—her own textured picture, of course—refuses to be washed out.

Circulating these images, quite a few Muslim bloggers would often tag her in the comments, saying, "Look where this photo popped up."[53] So this icon is a site of negotiation and contestation, and its imagery is still in flux. In her original photo, her image stands against the attacks Muslims were experiencing, refusing the charge of *anti-American*. In the Fairey poster, the icon resisted the Muslim bans. And the popularity of the poster, according to Ahmed, is that it shows her as a Muslim and an American. "You can proudly be both," she says.[54] A more recent image as a racial icon in a hoodie, a symbol of Black Lives Matter, situated after seventeen-year-old Trayvon Martin's killing, further enhances racial bonds. There is a clarification here. For her icon is neither assimilative nor blind nationalism, wrapped in a flag. It is, rather, a proud claim of racialized citizenship. So the poster has become part of a collision of meanings and negotiations, intended as antiracist, failing to represent de-imperialization, and even reframed in cross-racial alliances—all these negotiating longing, varied in its virtual communities and responses.

And how are these *counter*publics using these signs? Consider, for instance, Amani Al-Khatahtbeh, author of *Muslim Girl: A Coming of Age*, widely recognized as the most famous blogger and digital activist, founder and editor-in-chief of an online magazine for Muslim women.[55] There are 112,000 followers on her site, which shows a close-up photo of herself hugging the iconic poster of the woman using a US flag as a scarf. She's not holding Fairey's poster aloft but embracing it, holding the placard near a profile of her face with its serious expression. This whitened poster of political belonging is simultaneously juxtaposed to and joined by her own image, her claim, her own message, her own heteroglossic virtuality. So she's not just an icon of the Women's March. This online icon is renamed, receiving over 937 likes in return—in actions of political intimacy.

Given that these multilayered icons of national affiliation are much more than handheld signs and purchasable products and Insta-poses and stories, these new images have been remodeling racialization in all kinds of poses and captions, demanding attention to the online *messaging*. These new fields of longing and reception in the popular imagination also invite us to attend to the ever-varied reception of these images on iPhones, alongside the collective sentiment of varied audiences, not only of publics but of *counter*publics. These images are being duplicated, then copied and copied and copied again on posters, T-shirts, cups, and marching placards alike, reposted on Instagram and Facebook, then turned into political buttons for a shirt.

The messaging accompanying these circulating icons is critical. For instance, two of the organizers of the Women's March, Linda Sarsour and Zahra Billoo, both US Muslims, were asked to step down because of their own public support of the Palestinians, disenfranchised in a massive land grab in 1948, implemented by the United Nations, then dominated by Europe and supported by the United States.[56] Just as ironically, even those marching for women's rights, holding multicultural signage, splinter when posters critique our military policies, and endless blank checks continue to fund imperialism. Once again, there is an antiracist stance that refuses de-imperialization.

Unfortunately, the complexities of the resistance aesthetic are usually lost in Fairey's iconic poster that adorns countless dorm rooms throughout the country. Commercialization, however, has also been replicating this icon with equal enthusiasm. Indeed, there are three new Lady Liberties, and there are free downloads and copies for the walls of schools.[57] For just $13.56, you can purchase Fairey's popular red-white-and-blue images—part of a printed series of Black, Latinx, and American Muslim—frequently held aloft as placards during marches. Or sipping coffee from a mug, you can support this idea of "We the People," for just over fifteen bucks. On the other hand, these sentimental objects are a means not only of marketing but of marking inclusion. These protest productions are reposted in the digital world and in dorm rooms in ways that are personalized by the digital/public activists and claimed within their virtual communities. So the sign carries a range of political implications, marking safe spaces on the streets that are antiracist (not deimperialized).

Nevertheless, all of this commercialization was not Munira Adhami's original project. Quite the opposite. Although Ahmed's photograph clearly captures claims of citizenship, it critiques consumerism as well, interrogating economic patriotism, wherein presidential calls to "go shopping" buried the bodies in New York in amnesia and covered the gravesites of the post-9/11 world in consumptive forgetting. For the original photo situated her next to the New York Stock Exchange, the citadel of Wall Street itself, draped with its own enormous flag. And in front of this citadel, young Ahmed stares back, her gaze framed by the flag wrapped around her hair. So her photograph challenged how money was being spent: the capitalist foundation of US wars, an *anti-imperial* stance. And citizens like Ahmed were not seen, except as problems. Thus, *Illume*'s cover photo specialized in what Ahmed calls controversial images: the main photo on the 2007 cover was not just of Ahmed but a direct challenge to the flag on the stock exchange, an icon resisting the rising war economy.

In his TED Talk, however, Adhami, the artist, makes clear that the vast digitalization of the photo and its poster image exceeded its origins in the protest by US Muslim citizens after 9/11 and in the protest over a racist administration as signified in women's marches. Beyond the mass replication of these buttons and placards of thousands upon thousands holding these images, these circulations have further shifted into other heteroglossic meanings. Indeed, his own reinscription adds a racialized citizenship to the patriotic poster: in a photo of these marches, he holds up his own sign and his own daughter's small hand. Many have reinvented these images in cosplay, kneading Fairey's resistance poster into edible products, such as bread, built it in children's toys in a re-creation of Legos. Embodied icons of resistance—filmed—posted. There have been tattoos, claiming this national aura of resistance against the Muslim bans, as well as a flag on Mt. Everest. Downloaded in over 205 countries, according to Adhami, over 350,000 times. Often ignored by archives, these embodied performances as well as their textual and digital traces provide a unique model to understand what Diana Taylor calls the "production of knowledge."[58] For if the archive does not consider these embodied and digital traces, then it will reflect only those who are the most powerful in society.[59] Expanding far beyond Fairey's poster of "We the People," online mediation and popular culture and even body art have consumed a new image of the national body. The multilayered icons resisting racist policies, while losing sight of de-imperializing meanings, have become indelibly imprinted on the nation.

But in this kaleidoscopic array of massive reproductions, Adhami's visionary projects continue protesting through these multiple identities. So when he shows the famous Fairey poster of the Women's March, for instance, it is often divided between the photo (the next-gen activist and her strong gaze) and the poster (with its whitened skin and patriotic hues). These creative visions and their resistance are not performances of "good" Muslims and their patriotism, as critics have suggested. It is, rather, a site of contestation, a splitting, and for this visionary artist, a living symbol of racialized citizenship, a digital superheroism of ingested loss and resistance agency—not a single image, but a splintering. And this dual image that combines the photo of Munira Ahmed next to the poster of Fairey Shepard is reclaiming space on Adhami's Twitter/X (with 267 likes, retweeted over 124 times, as of January 10, 2022), which spreads proportionally as the primary tweets turn into mass-reproduced media that is liked and passed onto others.[60] From initial submersions of self to survive, erupting into new forms of resistance, this is a melancholic superheroism—not a nostalgic return to some idealized American past, but continual agency that refuses to bury Muslims.

## DIGITAL SURVEILLANCE AND DEATH THREATS

For the digital activist Amani Al-Khatahtbeh, she posts images of herself with the poster of this most famous icon, Fairey's "We the People," as well as inscriptions of Rosie the Riveter, and of Muslim women as superheroes. In a video of a potential new American Muslim superhero, posting in the next gen's venue of TikTok, she introduces the mimed music piece with the caption, "If Netflix Made a Halal Superhero." The video comes with male and female voice-overs. It begins with the usual mentoring of the new female superhero: "Habibti, we believe you'll be key in saving the world. Can we count on you?" In this sketch the voice-over calls the girl dear one—*habibti* in Arabic. In response to which, the voice-over answers, God willing— *Inshallah* in Arabic. But in the video, there is an interruption, since the white actor cannot follow this simplest and most common of greetings. "What does that mean?" he asks. If you want the mission, "Just say 'yes,'" the female voice-over responds. The white male is interrupting the initiation of a female Muslim superhero. In this situation what stands in the way of the heroic image of US Muslims is his ignorance. But it also plays out a possible fantasy. For what if the majority of white men understood the most basic elements of Islam? In this reinvention, it would be this white male body who says, *Inshallah*, who believes in the possible superhero and her story. The video is made by the subsite @uncultured, which redefines a lack of culture not as a lack of sophistication, not as a missing elegance, but as a lack of understanding of cultural diversity within the US. Thus it is that these revised superheroes interrogate white power.

Extending these icons, Al-Khatahtbeh also posts artist Rabia El Mouden's racialized riveter on her site, once again flexing her powerful arm, once again set against the classic postwar yellow background, with its patriotic red-white-and-blue—but this time with a red, polka-dot scarf, positioning working women @muslimgirl. US Muslim women, specifically, "can do it!" With almost four thousand likes, the hashtag #WECanDoIt is "our forever motto." The emojis next to the caption are a muscled brown arm followed by a sparkling heart of love.

In posting these superheroic icons of power amid their own images, these next-gen activists refuse to be silenced. Like her fellow activist Linda Sarsour, who has also received death threats, as founder of MuslimGirl.com Al-Khatahtbeh has also been subjected to surveillance and attacks. But none of this activity gave her the media exposure of her run in the 2020 primary for the congressional seat of Republican Frank Pallone. The first Muslim woman in New Jersey to seek federal office, she also received death threats, which she promptly reposted on Twitter/X. One caller left an anonymous message threatening her and promising to kill her parents, listing their addresses. "This isn't my first death threat," she wrote on Twitter/X, but it's posted to see the common experience of Muslims and people of color.[61] Even as we try to construct our identities as digital selves, writes the critical theorist Bernard Harcourt, "we render ourselves exposed to the gazes of others."[62] So, digital activism comes at a high cost.

In resistance, with her followers on Twitter/X, Instagram, and even Facebook, Al-Khatahtbeh's words and images have been compiled by her fellow editors and producers, a burgeoning band of protesters, referred to as #MGArmy. These are racial solidarities that are arising. Noticing few Black Muslim authors for their website, Aamina Mohamed, one of her producers, sent out her callsign on Twitter/X, #BlackoutEid, seeking selfies of Black Muslims. The call went viral. "Black Muslims celebrate their faith—and their style—and Black Muslims from over the world joined in," Mohamed wrote.[63] "It was something that we were aching for." These calls for refashioning images of digital activism have begun to create even more racial solidarities for US Muslims and their allies. So even as protest begins with bodies, these are bodies in motion, political performances refashioning how we tell our stories, how we post ourselves. Not just measures of presence, these bodies are public claims in motion. These rites of passage are rituals of female identity, according to Della Pollock, recoding ideas of public bodies and solidarities.[64]

Similarly, there is resistance and restaging around leaders like Minnesota congresswoman Ilhan Omar. Speaking at the Civil Rights for American Muslims (CAIR) gathering, she discussed her historic campaign that drew in young people and people of color in order to bring new voices into the Democratic Party.[65] Her campaign had succeeded because of its physical and digital outreach. From the time that she announced her candidacy until election day, she reached 300,000 constituents via door knocking and texting, she said—more votes than any member of Congress in the country. She called for activism: "To agitate. To take up space. To make people uncomfortable." To build wholistic communities that are compassionate. To find the "power that we are all in search of." Even her memoir's title, *This Is What America Looks Like: My Journey from Refugee to Congresswoman*, takes a stance in defining racial inclusion.[66] And in her rally, she speaks of her ideal for this country, where members are not judged by their faith or their head dress, but by their ideals and ideas. And as a parting blow to the former president, who had called for her resignation, she celebrated love, that "ultimately trumps hate." This gathering, she said, showed that Muslims are a part of our *American fabric* and worthy of representation at the highest levels of government. The core of Islam, she continued, is this struggle to improve oneself and all of humanity.

Facing constant attacks by the former president, conservatives, and digital media alike, the congresswoman was also harassed when she posted an image of herself as a superhero. As part of the @americansuperheroproject, designed by Seattle-based artist Nate Gowdy, this print is a remake of a photograph, not unlike the revisioning of Munira Ahmed. But in this image, Omar is wearing a white business suit, ready for political action, alongside her sparkling, full-length, red gloves with white stars and a stylish Captain America tie. No more nurse with a whip, no Wonder Woman but, rather, a rescripting of postwar masculinities for a Black Muslim congresswoman. Despite almost 15,000 likes, the comments, completely unfiltered by Twitter/X, wage war against the very idea of this *counter*cultural historicization and figure of radical feminist power. Many of these attacks suggest that she is wearing an "anti-American suit"; others, mocking the chilling cries of George Floyd, issue thinly veiled threats, hoping that she soon stops "breathing."[67] Even two of her Republican colleagues called for her execution. Although many have defended her with calls to ignore these "hateful comments," the fact that these attacks are allowed to flourish in an algorithm of empire demands change from these billion-dollar platforms. In the same year, she has continually received death threats. In 2019, for instance, she was threatened with being shot at the state fair, should she attend. No stranger to these assaults, long before her election to the House of Representatives, as a policy aide to the Minneapolis City Council, she was physically attacked, hospitalized for a concussion in 2014. Even more recently a pro-Israel lobby has been running ads attacking her as a terrorist. On August 13, 2021, her spokesman responded that these Islamophobic ads place "Rep. Omar's life at risk."[68]

Fighting back and following a recent report, both Congresswomen Ilhan Omar and Rashida Tlaib have called out Twitter/X and Facebook as "complicit in anti-Muslim violence."[69] According to a study by the Social Science Research Council, almost half of the more than a 100,000 tweets about Muslim candidates in the 2018 election included hate speech.[70] In Congresswoman Omar's posting of her digital icons and in her political platforms, which calls for a commission to highlight the increasing Islamophobia in her home state and around the world, she is courageous. Not only calling for affordable housing, living wages, and immigration reform, Omar is calling us out as well—those of us who click and watch, but have yet to act—calling us in a movement that is transfiguring political identities, making room for new racial icons, even while signaling collective memories lost in empire, key components for any structural change. But the problem here is that the well-known icons, the political images, and their stories of death threats and digital assaults serve as a warning for grassroots activists, as Spring Duvall writes, a deterrent, for some, when they decide to hit the streets or even run for office themselves.[71] But what is not written are the ways that organizations have strategies—as shown in this work—their own images of icons, their own digital strategies of virtual icons, as a collective support and interracial reclaiming on the streets, rejections of these assaults.

## DIGITAL ALLIANCES AND STRUCTURAL CHANGE

As argued throughout this work, it is not enough to applaud these new super-heroes, and it is definitely not enough to watch sports commercials, calling us to #justbuyit. These activists have stepped forward into this revolt, placing not only their intelligence and their courage but, in quite concrete ways, their very lives on the line. Listen, they summon their allies. The protesters are calling to us. Back us up! Come quickly, they say. For the mothers and fathers, the sisters and brothers, the daughters and sons of these activists, the women themselves—all are in danger. Political and digital structures are crushing them. They can't breathe.

So how can interracial alliances support their work? For a start, in public and in digital alliances, the most obvious way is to support political candidates calling for change. Ilhan Omar and Rashida Tlaib have called for legislation that investigates the local and the international cases of Islamophobia. But what is often overlooked is a mode of critical thinking, calling for recognition of how spaces of power in public and in digital media are being conducted as well as contested. And these contestations are evident in recent racial iconographies. Icons are references to past sites of power, images that structure our ways of knowing, our epistemologies. On one level, while any research conducted on Google is often (mistakenly) regarded as a set of facts or a purposefully arranged and administered series of data, these sites reflect their users, and their algorithms end up as instruments of oppression, even broadcasting fake news. Even in conducting this research, websites and pop-up ads and comments all have led to hate speech—blatant attacks on Ilhan Omar, Linda Sarsour, Amani Al-Khatahtbeh, Sana Amanat, G. Willow Wilson, Mona Haydar, Blair Imani, and others. True, these search engines and social media mechanisms are no more than political fig leaves, hiding their mined data and desire to make money. True, there have been instances, as with Twitter/X, when it took a stand to block a former president when his calls led to storming the Capitol Building, threatening the lives of

Ilhan Omar and other democratic leaders. But in these decisions to block and to highlight certain data, there have been shifts in who owns and who decides, showcasing the problems in censorship, as in the recent takeover of Twitter/X. So, even in a whole army of fact-checkers who have been hired by Facebook, there is the space of uncertainty about who decides what to permit, what to publish, what to censor, what to promote. So what is needed is a new level of awareness, a new kind of training—as in a model of super-heroism with awareness of the use of icons, part of a savvy digitalization of antiracism awareness as well as in de-imperialization.

Long has there been criticism that all of this online activism is a waste of time, pointless clicks. But, as Sasha Constanza-Chock points out, it is a form of blindness, in this era of historic protests, to ignore the intimate dance of the tweets and the streets.[72] Similarly refusing the dismissive criticism of "armchair activism," #Hashtag Activism speaks of how online activism builds bonds against systemic oppression.[73] And in the online search engines, an entire generation has walked into research that remains largely based in Google searches. So there is no segregation here between politics and digital cultures.[74] Like Colin Kaepernick's taking a knee, like Beyonce's 2016 Super-bowl performance alongside her BLM sign, "Stop shooting us," followed by hashtags in the digital world—in the same way, there are influences and links in the network[75] In seeking to buy products, to find research, to locate the next film, to hear the news, we have entered into a vast network of iconog-raphies and of agendas. A new mode of understanding, as in superheroism, as it navigates in the online world, is an essential tool. And digital activism can only amplify these restructuring icons, posting iconography to dozens, if not hundreds of others, messaging these structures of oppression within virtual circles that ripple outward toward countless shores.

And along with voting for measures for restructuring the political frame-work, the sharing of these icons—not as victims, not as villains, not as sex objects—would support these politicians and activists. When we repost these images, initiative must be taken, work must be done to comment on the need for structural changes. Following #Hashtag Activism, evidence has long pointed to the need for those who continue to benefit from systems of privilege, like the postwar structures of affirmative action for whites, to join in the refusal of racist structures.[76] And this online activism works best, the authors continue, if a core group of activists is nourished by a greater circle of supporters—in terms of reach into political bastions, especially of "white allies that help advance messages of racial justice across demographic and ideological groups."[77] For this, the core work is very much happening. But what is needed in these cross-racial solidarities is an awareness of the many kinds of racism experienced on the streets,[78] in coalition work promoting new online icons and individual stories. Because of the ways in which societies with endemic racism are filtering their prejudices into oppressive algorithms, these interracial alliances may be "more important than ever."[79] This mode of digital superheroism as a study of online icons and their trans/national feminisms is a wake-up call, for clicking on superheroes and their productions and their political structures and their histories also informs algorithms. We are making meaning, we are enhancing structures, we are part of this web.

For example, when the director of the empowerment network for American Muslims, Aneelah Afzali, organized a conference, she wrote, Facebook removed her post as violating its standards . . . "so basically, someone who didn't want this event promoted reported it."[80] Her protests have been surveilled and shut down on many occasions. "It's hard when there are microaggressions against you on the streets," she said to me as we sat in a coffee shop. "But it is worse when your allies don't get it."[81] It is critical within public spaces as well as social media that there are allies who do, in fact, get it. These alliances can emerge in artistic forms, in radical icons and restructuring, spreading in public and digital formats, but what is especially needed is a broader understanding of structural inequities and continuing injustices.

Given the vast numbers of Americans who know about Muslims only from mass media, then, this decoding of the internet and its national icons is essential. And the majority culture must do more work to educate themselves, demanding new formulas for online searching, further developing a vision of who are our heroes and our superheroes. In response to the 80% of media coverage of Muslims that is negative, #TakeBacktheNarrative joins MuslimGirl.com, #MGArmy, and #BlackOutEid not only in organizing protests but also in leaning into radical feminism, in listening to a podcast of a feminist journey into the Qur'an.[82] And what are the implications for codes of gender, when the "rules of the game," as Farha Ghannam argues, are contingent on the audience as well as on the location, whether private, public, policed?[83] Further attention needs to be paid as well to the digital labor of activists in this work as part of the reclaiming of gender and sexuality. We need to understand how the early riveter, for instance, as in Rockwell's image of a buff Irish American woman, redefined femininity as a more androgynous figure, reconfiguring whiteness to include the Irish, casting a hue of romanticism over the impoverishment of the white working class.[84] Even more importantly, in a country built not by white riveters but by slaves and sharecroppers and underpaid Black labor, we need to understand Blair Imani's refashioning of LGBTQ+ icons. Messaging hope, calling on her followers to vote, reposting her racial icons—her Blairsie the Riveter, her family photos—and highlighting her grandmother's work in the Second World War, all of these *decolonizing* structures, these resistant aesthetics embody our own sexual revolution. And we need to understand as well these icons and ideas, images of gender nonconformity, which is "neither spectacular nor fetishized," following the trail of Gayatri Gopinath[85]—these new Lady Liberties, for instance, or Imani's *Smarter in Seconds* video with its over 50 million views, insisting on more space for queer Brown and Black Muslims and their sexual identities.

Using this lens of superheroism, we can call for not only a representation of identities but also a reconstruction of structures, for these online flights of superheroes and of riveters and of national icons are part of circuits of power; thus, these online icons and superstars are tied to ideas, spanning into policing and legislation.[86] These racial icons—like Blairsie the Riveter and Ms. Marvel—challenge us to join the revolution: they are doing social work, revising racial stereotypes, trying to "transform the despised into the idolized."[87] So clicking on a Black Muslim Olympic star's fencing video, for example, or buying her Barbie, is not just about Ibtihaj Muhammad but about us—not just about her actions but about our own online practices and (their political and economic) implications.[88] These digital alliances are part of a larger mobilization of citizens, part of "revolutions in the making," to quote protest theorist Zizi Papacharissi.[89] Following these icons will build a "civic intensity," writes Fleetwood in *Racial Icons*, bringing a sense of immediacy and new meaning.[90] These icons are emotive responses, compelling the public toward action.

As we analyze these digital forums, we are entering ways of making meaning, as Juana María Rodríguez envisions, refusing legacies of empire and of racism, joining these digital activists and clicking on their new national icons, we are also posting "future possibilities" in this digital media.[91] At the same time, we recognize the tensions in these online icons. Because the identity of the American Muslim as an activist, while offering a feminist sign of solidarity, also asks a high price in naming national identities over one's own racial and ethnic and personal narratives. This must be careful and nuanced work, tracing these histories as cultural archives alongside their digital impressions. Following Gopinath, their intimate photos are types of intimate data, "subnational" images that turn the "surveilling, scrutinizing gaze of the state back on itself."[92] At the same time, the details of their stories, of their artistic strategies, of their icons, of their protest posters, of their rap songs can be a form of healing in countercultural communities. But given the dearth of images of these activists, the limited individual celebrity cannot stand in for the complex multiplicities of multiracial activists. As in this work, we need to carefully consider how digital archives with their groupies and their allies and their selfies might participate in the protest products of these activists—their subscripts and reinventions challenging national structures, altering the empire of the US.

In this way, then, this book highlights the resistance of these protesters, wrapped in their red, white, and blue vestments and spilling into the streets, painting their placards, cascading into public halls; as well as a second body of artistic forms, of selfies and videos and icons and websites of women's protests, of shades of their actual bodies that are copied, cut, pasted, tinted, and then inscribed or imprinted on technological platforms—a pixilated performance of revolution in digital media. With its creative videos, its innovative texts, its digital interviews, and its protesters flourishing their megaphones, this revolution—this powerful revolt of the activist and her further revival in artistic forms and technologies—comes with its own confident stride, with its own signs, with its own contestation, alongside its own aesthetic of superheroism, its unique imprint of posted icons in a resistance aesthetic. These performed histories, these protest movements, these digital self/social inscriptions offer a radical approach, an altered iconography of the female protester, a new way of knowing in this era of protest, calling on all of us to join in an antiracist and de-imperializing movement—to critically reimagine political (be)longings.

# NOTES

## PREFACE

1. Larry Buchanan, Quoctrung Bui, and Jugal Patel, "Black Lives Matter May Be the Largest Movement in U.S. History," *New York Times*, July 3, 2020, accessed July 25, 2021, https://www.nytimes.com/interactive/2020/07/03/us/george-floyd-protests-crowd-size.html.

2. Erica Chenoweth and Jeremy Pressman, "This Is What We Learned by Counting the Women's Marches," *Washington Post*, February 7, 2017, accessed July 25, 2021, https://www.washingtonpost.com/news/monkey-cage/wp/2017/02/07/this-is-what-we-learned-by-counting-the-womens-marches.

3. From the American Muslim Poll 2020, 74 percent of US Muslim women support protests of Black Lives Matter. See website at Institute for Social Policy and Understanding, https://www.ispu.org/wp-content/uploads/2021/04/AMP-Infographic-Coalitions-8.5x11-v3-1.pdf?x46312. Fifteen million is the estimate of Kim Parker, Juliana Menasce Horowitz, and Monica Anderson, "Amid Protests, Majorities across Racial and Ethnic Groups Express Support for the Black Lives Matter Movement," Pew Research Center: Social and Demographic Trends, June 12, 2020, accessed July 25, 2021, https://www.pewsocialtrends.org/2020/06/12/amid-protests-majorities-across-racial-and-ethnic-groups-express-support-for-the-black-lives-matter-movement. Twenty-six million is the estimate of Liz Hamel, Audrey Kearney, Ashley Kirzinger, Lunna Lopes, Cailey Munana, and Mollyann Brodie, KFF Health, "KFF Health Tracking Poll—June 2020," June 26, 2020, accessed July 25, 2021, https://www.kff.org/disparities-policy/report/kff-health-tracking-poll-june-2020.

4. Kimberly Wedeven Segall, "De-imperializing Gender: Political Revivals, Shifting Beliefs, and Unexpected Trajectories," *Journal of Middle Eastern Women's Studies* 15, no. 1 (2019): 75–94; "Media Sites: Political Revivals of American Muslim Women," in *The Oxford Handbook of Politics and Performance*, ed. Shirin Rai et al. (New York: Oxford University Press, 2021), 235–50; *Performing Democracy in Iraq and South Africa: Gender, Media, and Resistance* (Syracuse, NY: Syracuse University Press, 2013); "Melancholy Ties: Intergenerational Loss and Political Exile in *Persepolis*," *Comparative Studies of South Asia, Africa, and the Middle East* 28, no. 1 (2008): 38–49; "Stories and Song in Iraq and South Africa: From Individual Trauma to Collective Mourning," *Comparative Studies of South Asia, Africa, and the Middle East* 25, no. 1 (2005): 138–51.

5. David Vine, Cala Coffman, Katalina Khoury, Madison Lovasz, Helen Bush, Rachael Leduc, and Jennifer Walkup, "Creating Refugees: Displacement Caused by the United States' Post-9/11 Wars," Brown University and Boston University, September 21, 2020, accessed October 11, 2021, https://watson.brown.edu/costsofwar/files/cow/imce/papers/2020/Dis placement_Vine%20et%20al_Costs%20of%20War%202020%2009%2008.pdf.

6. Sunaina Marr Maira, *Missing: Youth, Citizenship, and Empire after 9/11* (Durham, NC: Duke University Press, 2009), 226. Also see Lila Abu-Lughod, *Do Muslim Women Need Saving?* (Boston: Harvard University Press, 2015).

7. Maira, *Missing*, 236.

8. See Nadine Naber's excellent "Introduction: Arab Americans and U.S. Racial Formations," in *Race and Arab Americans before and after 9/11: From Invisible Citizens to Visible Subjects*, ed. Amaney Jamal and Nadine Naber, 1–45 (Syracuse, NY: Syracuse University Press, 2008). And see Michael Suleiman, "Introduction: The Arab Immigrant Experience," in *Arabs in America: Building a New Future*, ed. Michael Suleiman (Philadelphia: Temple University Press, 1999), 1–21; Neda Maghbouleh, *The Limits of Whiteness: Iranian Americans and the Everyday Politics of Race* (Stanford, CA: Stanford University Press, 2017); Sarah Gualtieri, *Arab Routes: Pathways to Syrian California* (Stanford, CA: Stanford University Press, 2020); Helen Hatab Samhan, "Not Quite White: Race Classification and the Arab-American Experience," in Suleiman, *Arabs in America*, 304–19; Louise Cainkar, "Thinking outside the Box: Arabs and Race in the United States," in Jamal and Naber, *Race and Arab Americans*, 49. Carol Fadda, *Contemporary Arab-American Literature: Transnational Reconfigurations of Citizenship and Belonging* (New York: New York University Press, 2014).

9. Maira, *Missing*, 283. See Lori Peek, *Behind the Backlash: Muslim Americans after 9/11* (Philadelphia: Temple University Press, 2011), 31. In 2005, some 191,000 incidents of hate crime were recorded by the US Department of Justice—part of what Peek describes as a post-9/11 "backlash" against US Muslims. In response, there was a "wave of solidarity" in US Muslim communities (141).

10. Nadje Al-Ali and Nicola Pratt, *What Kind of Liberation? Women and the Occupation of Iraq* (Berkeley: University of California Press, 2009).

11. For which see Sylvia Chan-Malik, *Being Muslim: A Cultural History of Women of Color in American Islam* (New York: New York University Press, 2018), 3, 5.

12. Linda Tuhiwai Smith, *Decolonizing Methodologies: Research and Indigenous Peoples*, 2nd ed. (London: Zed Books, 2012), xii. See also Nicola Pratt, *Embodying Geopolitics: Generations of Women's Activism in Egypt, Jordan, and Lebanon* (Oakland: University of California Press, 2020), 19, who emphasizes making room for "the voices of those women whose activism would not necessarily be documented," in grassroots movements, such as "small organizations that do not have resources to collect and catalog their archives."

## INTRODUCTION

1. Sana Amanat, TEDx Teen, "Myths, Misfits & Masks: Sana Amanat 2014," March 17, 2014, accessed October 16, 2022, https://www.youtube.com/watch?v=o9lev9739zQ.

And see Dave Itzkoff, "'Ms. Marvel' Introduces a New Hero (and a New Actress)," *New York Times*, June 6, 2022. Kamala's film embodiment Iman Vellani also speaks of how superheroes have been a way of surviving.

2. Marita Sturken and Lisa Cartwright, *Practices of Looking: An Introduction to Visual Culture*, 2nd ed. (New York: Oxford University Press, 2009), 357. They further ask, "For whom is this image iconic and for whom is it not?" 42.

3. Nicole Fleetwood, *Troubling Vision: Performance, Visuality, and Blackness* (Chicago: University of Chicago Press, 2011), 34. And see Sara Ahmed, *The Cultural Politics of Emotion* (New York: Routledge, 2014), 1.

4. Nicole Fleetwood, *On Racial Icons: Blackness and the Public Imagination* (New Brunswick, NJ: Rutgers University Press, 2015), 4.

5. Fleetwood, *Troubling Vision*, 10.

6. Robert Hariman and John Louis Lucaites, *No Caption Needed: Iconic Photographs, Public Culture, and Liberal Democracy* (Chicago: University of Chicago Press, 2007), 29. In Fleetwood, *Troubling Vision*, 34.

7. Leila Ahmed, *Women and Gender in Islam: Historical Roots of a Modern Debate* (New Haven: Yale University Press, 1992), 151. See also Edward Said, *Culture and Imperialism* (New York: Vintage Press, 1994); Nadje Al-Ali and Nicola Pratt, *What Kind of Liberation? Women and the Occupation of Iraq* (Berkeley: University of California Press, 2009); Evelyn Alsultany, *Arabs and Muslims in the Media: Race and Representation after 9/11* (New York: New York University Press, 2012). On sexuality, see Jasbir Puar, *Terrorist Assemblages: Homonationalism in Queer Times* (Durham, NC: Duke University Press, 2007), xiv.

8. Abu-Lughod, *Do Muslim Women Need Saving?* See also Gayatri Spivak's analysis of colonial tropes of rescuing Brown women in "Can the Subaltern Speak? Speculations on Widow Sacrifice," *Wedge* 7–8 (1985): 120–30.

9. Spring Duvall, "Becoming Celebrity Girl Activists: The Cultural Politics and Celebrification of Emma Gonzalez, Marley Dias, and Greta Thunberg," *Journal of Communication Inquiry* (August 24, 2022): 2. DOI: 10.1177/01968599221120057.

10. Jessica Taft, "Teenage Girls' Narratives of Becoming Activists," *Contemporary Social Science* 12 (1–2): 27–39. https://www.tandfonline.com/doi/abs/10.1080/21582041.2017.1324 17328.

11. Erica Austin, Rebecca Van de Vord, Bruce Pinkleton, and Evan Epstein, "Celebrity Endorsements and Their Potential to Motivate Young Voters," *Mass Communication and Society* 11, no. 4 (2008): 420–36, DOI:10.1080/15205430701866600.

12. This idea of the racial script is from Natalia Molina, *How Race Is Made in America: Immigration, Citizenship, and the Historical Power of Racial Scripts* (Berkeley: University of California Press, 2014), 7.

13. In this postwar era, popular conceptions have been of "race" as the "central problem," writes Jodi Melamed, necessitating new ways of governing, and thus this postwar structuring thrived on colonizing industries, jail complexes, and government platforms in a capitalist-driven empire, imposing its markets and military goods on other countries. In *Represent and Destroy: Rationalizing Violence in the New Racial Capitalism* (Minneapolis: University of Minnesota Press, 2011), x.

14. Elizabeth D. Samet, *Looking for the Good War: American Amnesia and the Violent Pursuit of Happiness* (New York: Picador, 2022).

15. David Vine, Cala Coffman, Katalina Khoury, Madison Lovasz, Helen Bush, Rachael Leduc, and Jennifer Walkup, "Creating Refugees: Displacement Caused by the United States' Post-9/11 Wars," Brown University and Boston University, September 21, 2020, accessed December 26, 2022. https://www.carnegie.org/publications/creating-refugees-displacement-caused-united-states-post-911-wars/.

16. Aihwa Ong, *Flexible Citizenship: The Cultural Logics of Trans-Nationality* (Durham, NC: Duke University Press, 1999), 3, 18. Nike featured an ad with Leiomy Maldona, who is known as the "Wonder Woman of Vogue." See Mariah Cooper, "Nike's New Ad Celebrates Trans Vogue Artist Leiomy Maldonado," in *Blade*, June 27, 2017, accessed January 29, 2023, https://www.washingtonblade.com/2017/06/27/nikes-pride-ad-stars-transgender-vogue-artist-leiomy-maldonado/.

17. See John Downing, *Radical Media: Rebellious Communication and Social Movements* (Thousand Oaks, CA: Sage, 2001); John Pavlik, *Journalism and New Media* (New York: Columbia University Press, 2001); Chris Atton, *An Alternative Internet: Radical Media, Politics, and Creativity* (Edinburgh: Edinburgh University Press, 2004); Marc Lynch, "Blogging the New Arab Republic," Arab Media and Society, February 2007. http://www.arabmediasociety.com/topics/index.php?t_article=32; Stuart Allan and Einar Thorsen, *Citizen Journalism: Global Perspectives* (New York: Peter Lang, 2009); Naila Hamdy, "Arab Citizen Journalism in Action: Challenging Mainstream Media, Authorities and Media Laws," *Westminster Papers in Communication and Culture* 6, no. 1 (2009): 92–112.

18. Mark Deuze, "Participation, Remediation, Bricolage: Considering Principal Components of a Digital Culture," *Information Society* 22 (2006): 66. DOI: 10.1080/01972240600567170.

19. Moya Bailey, *Misogynoir Transformed: Black Women's Digital Resistance* (New York: New York University Press, 2021), 23.

20. Dean Spade, *Mutual Aid: Building Solidarity during this Crisis (and the Next)* (New York: Verso Press, 2020), 74–75.

21. Aneelah Afzali, interview with the author, Seattle, Washington, March 2, 2019.

22. Laila Lalami, *The Moor's Account: A Lost Narrative* (New York: Pantheon Books, 2014).

23. Sylviane Diouf, "Muslims in America," February 10, 2021, accessed November 25, 2021, https://www.aljazeera.com/features/2021/2/10/muslims-in-america-always-there.

24. Sylvia Chan-Malik, *Being Muslim: A Cultural History of Women of Color in American Islam* (New York: New York University Press, 2018), 3–5. See Sylviane Diour, *Servants of Allah: African Muslims Enslaved in the Americas* (New York: New York University Press, 2013).

25. James Baldwin, "ROOTS by Alex Haley," September 26, 1976, October 21, 2021, accessed November 25, 2021, https://www.nytimes.com/2021/10/21/books/review/roots-alex-hale.html.

26. See Nadine Naber's excellent "Introduction: Arab Americans and U.S. Racial Formations," in *Race and Arab Americans Before and After 9/11: From Invisible Citizens*

to Visible Subjects, eds. Amaney Jamal and Nadine Naber (Syracuse, NY: Syracuse University Press, 2008), 1–45. And see Michael Suleiman, "Introduction: The Arab Immigrant Experience," in Arabs in America: Building a New Future, ed. Michael Suleiman (Philadelphia: Temple University Press, 1999), 1–21; Neda Maghbouleh, The Limits of Whiteness: Iranian Americans and the Everyday Politics of Race (Stanford, CA: Stanford University Press, 2017); Sarah Gualtieri, Arab Routes: Pathways to Syrian California (Stanford, CA: Stanford University Press, 2020); Helen Hatab Samhan, "Not Quite White: Race Classification and the Arab-American Experience," in Suleiman, Arabs in America, 304–19; Louise Cainkar, "Thinking Outside the Box: Arabs and Race in the United States," in Jamal and Naber, Race and Arab Americans, 49. Carol Fadda-Conrey, Contemporary Arab-American Literature: Transnational Reconfigurations of Citizenship and Belonging (New York: New York University Press, 2014).

27. Much has been written on false dichotomies of traditional/religious vs. modern/ secular, as well as Islamic feminism, for which see my article "De-imperializing Gender: Religious Revivals, Shifting Beliefs, and the Unexpected Trajectory of Laila Lalami's Hope and Other Dangerous Pursuits," Journal of Middle Eastern Women's Studies 15, no. 1 (2019): 75–94. And see Deborah Kapchan, Gender on the Market: Moroccan Women and the Revoicing of Tradition (Philadelphia: University of Pennsylvania Press, 1996); miriam cooke, Women Claim Islam: Creating Islamic Feminism through Literature (New York: Routledge, 2001); Talal Asad, Formations of the Secular: Christianity, Islam, and Modernity (Stanford, CA: Stanford University Press, 2003); Saba Mahmood, Politics of Piety: The Islamic Revival and the Feminist Subject (Princeton: Princeton University Press, 2005); Gholam Khiabany, Iranian Media: The Paradox of Modernity (New York: Routledge, 2010); Sherine Hafez, An Islam of Her Own: Reconsidering Religion and Secularism in Women's Islamic Movements (New York: New York University Press, 2011).

28. Kimberly Wedeven Segall, "Media Sites: Political Revivals of American Muslim Women," in The Oxford Handbook of Politics and Performance, ed. Shirin Rai et al. (New York: Oxford University Press, 2021), 235–50.

29. See Su'ad Abdul Khabeer, Muslim Cool: Race, Religion, and Hip Hop in the United States (New York: New York University Press, 2016). More research is needed on "interracial" solidarities—new "political vision," which must move beyond Brown Muslims as "model minorities" and "anti-Blackness" racist legacies, 231.

30. Ramzi Fawaz, The New Mutants: Superheroes and the Radical Imagination of American Comics (New York: New York University Press, 2016), 11. Fawaz originally uses this term to describe the way that the sixties comic writers had a "commitment to liberal tolerance," 20, and readers willing to "embrace the liberal project," 21. But I argue that Ms. Marvel's Kamala Khan is not part of a generic "liberal" imagination, but rather is rooted in complex inheritances and in protest traditions.

31. Stuart Hall, Jessica Evans, and Sean Nixon, Representation: Cultural Representations and Signifying Practices, 2nd ed. (Los Angeles: Sage, 2013).

32. Sasha Constanza-Chock, Out of the Shadows, into the Streets: Transmedia Organizing and the Immigration Rights Movement (Cambridge, MA: MIT Press, 2014), 7.

33. Sarah Jackson, Moya Bailey, and Brooke Foucault Welles, #Hashtag Activism: Networks of Race and Gender Justice (Cambridge, MA: MIT Press, 2020), 154. These

authors distinguish active alliances with "performative allyship" of personalized "catharsis" and "coveted identity," 155.

34. David Silver, "Introducing Cyberculture," in *Web.studies: Rewiring Media Studies for the Digital Age*, ed. David Gauntlett (Oxford: Oxford University Press, 2000), 19–30, http://www.com.washington.edu/rccs/intro.asp; Manuel Castells, *Networks of Outrage and Hope: Social Movements in the Internet Age* (Malden, MA: Polity Press, 2015); Jennifer Pybus, "Accumulating Affect: Social Networks and Their Archives of Feelings," in *Networked Affect*, ed. Ken Hillis, Susanna Paasonen, and Michael Petit (Cambridge, MA: MIT Press, 2015), 240; Ken Hillis, Susanna Paasonen, and Michael Petit, "Introduction: Networks of Transmission: Intensity, Sensation, Value," in *Networked Affect*, ed. Ken Hillis, Susanna Paasonen, and Michael Petit (Cambridge, MA: MIT Press, 2015), 1; Ganaele Langlois, "Social Media and the Care of the Self," in *Digital Existence: Ontology, Ethics, & Transcendence in Digital Culture*, ed. Amanda Lagerkvist, 156–70 (New York: Routledge, 2019).

35. Lisa Nakamura, *Cybertypes: Race, Ethnicity, and Identity on the Internet* (New York: Routledge, 2002); Siva Vaidhyanathan, *The Googlization of Everything: And Why We Should Worry* (Berkeley: University of California Press, 2011); Danah Boyd, *It's Complicated: The Social Lives of Networked Teens* (New Haven: Yale University Press, 2014); Sara Wachter-Boettcher, *Technically Wrong: Sexist Apps, Biased Algorithms, and Other Threats of Toxic Tech* (New York: W. W. Norton, 2017); Safiya Umoja Noble, *Algorithms of Oppression: How Search Engines Reinforce Racism* (New York: New York University Press, 2018).

36. Castells, *Networks of Outrage*, 8.

37. Natalie Fenton, *Digital. Political. Radical* (Cambridge, UK: Polity Press, 2016), 19.

38. L. Ayu Saraswati, *Pain Generation: Social Media, Feminist Activism, and the Neoliberal Selfie* (New York: New York University Press, 2021), 8. Her premise suggests that making money is selling out, a complete short-selling of structural changes, as pain is being "commodified" in digital activism, 42.

39. Jackson et al., *#Hashtag Activism*, xxv.

40. Austin et al., "Celebrity Endorsements."

41. As argued in my *Performing Democracy in Iraq and South Africa* (Syracuse, NY: Syracuse University Press, 2013). In fact, women's resistance is not new, "since these societies have long resisted oppression, and cultural forms have always been working out loss" (xvi). See Annabelle Sreberny and Gholam Khiabany, *Blogistan: The Internet and Politics in Iran* (New York: I. B. Tauris, 2011); Zizi Papacharissi and Sharon Meraz, "Networked Gatekeeping and Networked Framing on #Egypt," *International Journal of Press/Politics* 18, no. 2 (2013): 138–66; Ahmed Al-Rawi, *Women's Activism and New Media in the Arab World* (SUNY Press, 2020); Sara Shaban, *Iranian Feminism and Transnational Ethics in Media Discourse* (Lanham, MD: Lexington Books, 2022); Dounia Mahlouly, Dina Matar, Zahera Harb, eds. *Digital Political Cultures in the Middle East since the Arab Uprisings: Online Activism in Egypt, Tunisia and Lebanon* (I. B. Tauris, 2023). See also Robert M. Entman, *Projections of Power: Framing News, Public Opinion, and U.S. Foreign Policy* (Chicago: University of Chicago Press, 2004); W. Lance Bennett, Regina Lawrence, and Steven Livingston, *When the Press Fails: Political Power and the News Media from Iraq*

*to Katrina* (Chicago: University of Chicago Press, 2007), 8; Paul Marshall, Lela Gilbert, and Roberta Green Ahmanson, eds., *Blind Spot: When Journalists Don't Get Religion* (Oxford: Oxford University Press, 2009); Edward Said, *Covering Islam: How the Media and the Experts Determine How We See the Rest of the World* (New York: Vintage, 2015); Oluseyi Adegbola, Sherice Gearhart, and Janice Cho, "Reporting Bias in Coverage of Iran Protests by Global News Agencies," *International Journal of Press/Politics* 27, no. 1 (2022): 138–57, DOI: 10.1177/1940161220966948.

42. Wilson Wong, NBC report, "Muslim Woman Arrested in Miami Protest Forced to Remove Hijab for Booking Photo," June 19, 2020, accessed June 14, 2021, https://www.nbcnews .com/news/us-news/muslim-woman-arrested-miami-protest-forced-remove-hijab -booking-photo-n1231607.

43. Jack Elsom, "Muslim Woman Wearing a Niqab Shouts 'Shame on All of You Despicable People' in Shocking Homophobic Rant at Pride March in London," *Daily Mail*, July 29, 2019, accessed June 14, 2021, https://www.dailymail.co.uk/news/article-7294507 /Muslim-woman-shouts-shame-man-draped-LGBT-flag-Pride-march.html?ito=email _share_article-image-share.

44. Puar, *Terrorist Assemblages*, xiv.

45. Noble, *Algorithms of Oppression*, 4. See also Tarek El-Ariss, *Leaks, Hacks, and Scandals: Arab Culture in the Digital Age* (Princeton: Princeton University Press, 2019), 9, 4; Haroon Ullah, *Digital World War: Islamists, Extremists, and the Fight for Cyber Supremacy* (New Haven: Yale University Press, 2017); Guy Debord, *Society of the Spectacle*, trans. Ken Knabb (London: Aldgate, 2006).

46. Mohja Kahf, *Western Representations of the Muslim Woman: From Termagant to Odalisque* (Austin: University of Texas Press, 1999), 4.


CHAPTER 1: MS. MARVEL'S RESISTANCE ICON

1. Sana Amanat, TEDx Teen, "Myths, Misfits & Masks: Sana Amanat 2014," March 17, 2014, accessed October 16, 2022, https://www.youtube.com/watch?v=09lev9739zQ. Subsequent references in the text.

2. Framing Black/Brownness as a "monolithic identity," following *The Blacker the Ink*, while waging war on Afghanistan and Iraq and other regions, mass media almost invariably slants toward a racist lens, causing a "dislocation" and a sense of "splitting" — what Ranjana Khanna calls "colonial melancholy." See Frances Gateward and John Jennings, "Introduction: The Sweeter the Christmas," in *The Blacker the Ink: Constructions of Black Identity in Comics and Sequential Art*," ed. Frances Gateward and John Jennings (New Brunswick, NJ: Rutgers University Press, 2015), 7; Ranjana Khanna, *Dark Continents: Psychoanalysis and Colonialism* (Durham, NC: Duke University Press, 2003), 148, 145, 147. See also my work on exile and "collective melancholy" in "Melancholy Ties: Intergenerational Loss and Political Exile in *Persepolis*," *Comparative Studies of South Asia, Africa, and the Middle East* 28, no. 1 (2008): 38–49.

3. This original series, written by G. Willow Wilson, ran from 2014 to 2018, originally anticipating only ten issues, but because of its popularity there were sixty.

4. G. Willow Wilson, *Mecca*, Ms. Marvel 8 (New York: Marvel Comics, 2017). Subsequent references in text.

5. G. Willow Wilson, "The Story behind Marvel's Muslim-American Superheroine," TEDx Boulder, accessed December 1, 2020, https://www.ted.com/talks/g_willow_wilson _the_story_behind_marvel_s_muslim_american_superheroine/up-next. There were sixty thousand views.

6. My idea of the use of the superhero as a racial reinscription wherein the activist is reimagining nonwhite national identity and subverting dominant iconographies extends earlier work on citizenship. Laila Lalami uses the term "conditional citizens" to describe the ways in which nonwhite citizens are not fully accepted in the US, in *Conditional Citizens: On Belonging in America* (New York: Pantheon Books, 2020), 28. "Cultural citizenship" includes "everyday understandings of belonging and exclusion," especially as it relates to Muslim Americans, especially given the "backlash" of over seven hundred hate crimes within three weeks of 9/11, writes Sunaina Marr Maira, *Missing: Youth, Citizenship, and Empire after 9/11* (Durham, NC: Duke University Press, 2009), 10–11. Hussein Rashid stresses that the Khans are immigrants, so "power systems" try to block out their "cultural citizenship," in "Ms. Marvel Is an Immigrant," in *Ms. Marvel's America: No Normal*, ed. Jessica Baldanzi and Hussein Rashid (Jackson: University Press of Mississippi, 2020), 60. My idea of including heritage in activism is not the same as the "heritage economy" of selling certain goods, as Ahmed Afzal describes in *Lone Star Muslims: Transnational Lives in the South Asian Experience in Texas* (New York: New York University Press, 2015).

7. Mauricio Espinoza, "The Alien Is Here to Stay: Otherness, Anti-assimilation, and Empowerment in Latina Superhero Comics," in *Graphic Borders: Latino Comic Books Past, Present, and Future*, ed. Frederick Luis Aldama and Christopher Gonzalez (Austin: University of Texas Press, 2016), 192.

8. Ramzi Fawaz, *The New Mutants: Superheroes and the Radical Imagination of American Comics* (New York: New York University Press, 2016), 10, 22. Fawaz further defines the "radical imagination" as a reaction against the Cold War era and a capacity to invent despite corporate ownership in the eighties (20, 25), as part of working-class icons (11). But following Bradford Wright, *Comic Book Nation: The Transformation of Youth Culture in America* (Baltimore: Johns Hopkins University Press, 2001), although superheroes like Superman spoke out against racism in several ads, there were "not any representations of African Americans" as superheroes or even on the streets as civilians in postwar America (64). True, "Marvel attacked intolerance" but without "explicit reference" to the "struggles of African Americans." The X-Men, for instance, were oppressed by "bigots" (219).

9. Jorge Santos, *Graphic Memories of the Civil Rights Movement: Reframing History in Comics* (Austin: University of Texas Press, 2019), 4. See also Renee Romano and Leigh Raiford, "Introduction: The Struggle of Memory," in *The Civil Rights Movement in American Memory*, ed. Renee Romano and Leigh Raiford, xi–xxiv (Athens: University of Georgia Press, 2006).

10. Melinda L. de Jesus, "Liminality and Mestiza Consciousness in Lynda Barry's *One Hundred Demons*," in *Multicultural Comics: From Zap to Blue Beetle*, ed. Frederick Luis Aldama (Austin: University of Texas Press, 2010), 75.

11. G. Willow Wilson, *The Butterfly Mosque* (New York: Grove Press, 2010), 40.

12. Wilson, interview by Shabana Mir, 242. Subsequent references in text.

13. Wright, *Comic Book Nation*, 73. This era caricatured the Chinese as "sinister villains who schemed to promote racial domination from the opium dens, torture chambers, and laundries of fog-bound American Chinatowns" (49). See also Robert Petersen, *Comics, Manga, and Graphic Novels: A History of Graphic Narratives* (Santa Barbara, CA: Praeger, 2011); and Marc DiPaolo, *War, Politics, and Superheroes: Ethics and Propaganda in Comics and Film* (Jefferson, NC: McFarland Press, 2011).

14. Wright, *Comic Book Nation*, 73.

15. Jill Lepore, *The Secret History of Wonder Woman* (New York: Vintage, 2015), 233.

16. Martin Lund, "Placing Ms. Marvel and Dust: Marvel Comics, the New York Metro Area, and the 'Muslim Problem,'" in Baldanzi and Rashid, *Ms. Marvel's America*, 27. See also Jack Shaheen, *Reel Bad Arabs: How Hollywood Vilifies a People* (Northampton, MA: Olive Branch Press, 2015.)

17. Lund, "Placing Ms. Marvel and Dust," 28.

18. Lund, "Placing Ms. Marvel and Dust," 26.

19. Sophia Rose Arjana suggests Kamala Khan is on a "spiritual quest" in *Veiled Superheroes: Islam, Feminism, and Popular Culture* (Lanham, MD: Lexington Books, 2018), 48; while others, like Richard Stevens, see an "intergenerational bond" with Danvers, a dialogue of "feminist" and "postfeminist." Stevens, "Mentoring Ms. Marvel: Marvel's Kamala Khan and the Reconstitution of Carol Danvers," in Baldanzi and Rashid, *Ms. Marvel's America*, 5, 12. Other critics have not marked this as the critical juncture, calling this scene a "hallucination," in contrast to her later "attitude change"—the "rupture expected from heteroglossia." Rashid, "Ms. Marvel Is an Immigrant," 54.

20. See Rebecca Wanzo, "It's a Hero? Black Comics and Satirizing Subjection," in *The Blacker the Ink: Constructions of Black Identity in Comics and Sequential Art*, ed. Frances Gateward and John Jennings (New Brunswick, NJ: Rutgers University Press, 2015), 318.

21. A full discussion of the problems with models of assimilation arrives later in this chapter.

22. Osvaldo Oyola, "Seriality." In *Keywords for Comics Studies*, edited by Ramzi Fawaz, Shelley Streeby, and Deborah Elizabeth Whaley, 187–92. New York: New York University Press, 2021.

23. The time envisioned between panels is called "simultaneity." Scott McCloud, *Understanding Comics* (New York: Harper Perennial, 1994), 104.

24. See Henry Jenkins, *Comics and Stuff* (New York: New York University Press, 2020), 22; Matt Silady, "Panel," in *Keywords for Comics Studies*, ed. Ramzi Fawaz, Shelley Streeby, and Deborah Elizabeth Whaley (New York: New York University Press, 2021), 161.

25. Richard Rodriguez, *Brown: The Last Discovery of America* (New York: Viking Press, 2002), xii.

26. See, for instance, Mercedes Yanora, "Marked by Foreign Policy: Muslim Superheroes and the Quest for Authenticity," *Muslim Superheroes: Comics, Islam, and Representation*, ed. A. David Lewis and Martin Lund (Boston: Ilex Foundation, 2017), 129.

27. Sharing in Kamala's responses, we also negotiate complex "points of view." Oyola, "Seriality," 191.

28. Mel Gibson, "Yeah, I Think There Is Still Hope: Youth, Ethnicity, Faith, Feminism, and Fandom in Ms. Marvel," in *Gender and the Superhero Narrative*, ed. Michael Goodrum, Tara Prescott, and Philip Smith (Jackson: University Press of Mississippi, 2018), 23.

29. Bernard Lewis, *Cultures in Conflict: Christians, Muslims, and Jews in the Age of Discovery* (London: Oxford University Press, 1996).

30. Stevens, "Mentoring Ms. Marvel," 4.

31. Stevens, "Mentoring Ms. Marvel," 5.

32. Stevens, "Mentoring Ms. Marvel," 7–8. When Professor X assists her in recovering her memories, Stevens argues, she is irate that the Avengers let her leave with her rapist. In *Captain Marvel*, her 2012 revival, this amnesia is caused instead by a cancerous tumor threatening to destroy her brain (17). An explosion wipes her memory in the film *Captain Marvel*, rewritten by Anna Boden and Ryan Fleck (2019).

33. G. Willow Wilson, "Interview with G. Willow Wilson," interview by Shabana Mir (October 2017), in *Ms. Marvel's America*, ed. Jessica Baldanzi and Hussein Rashid, 230–46 (Jackson: University Press of Mississippi, 2020), 238. Subsequent references in text. The Kamala Khan series first emerged in conversations with Sana Amanat and her senior editor, Stephen Wacker. But the story's fountainhead is Amanat.

34. Wilson, interview with Mir, 241.

35. G. Willow Wilson, *No Normal*, in *Ms. Marvel* 1–4, ed. Sana Amanat (New York: Marvel Worldwide Inc, 2014). Subsequent references in text.

36. See also Victor Turner, *From Ritual to Theatre: The Human Seriousness of Play* (New York: Performing Arts Journal Publications, 1982).

37. Lauren Berlant: "Compassionate liberalism is, at best, a kind of sandpaper on the surface of the racist monument whose structural and economic solidarity endures in the intimate sphere of femininity, a kind of soft supremacy" toward exoticized others. Berlant, *The Female Complaint: The Unfinished Business of Sentimentality in American Culture* (Durham, NC: Duke University Press, 2008), 6.

38. From Willow Wilson, *The Butterfly Mosque*, quoted in Wilson, "Engagement in Cairo," *New York Times Magazine*, May 28, 2010, accessed July 7, 2021, https://www.nytimes.com/2010/05/30/magazine/30lives-t.html.

39. Fawaz, *The New Mutants*, 28; and Lauren Berlant, *The Anatomy of National Fantasy: Hawthorne, Utopia, and Everyday Life* (Chicago: University of Chicago Press, 1991), 5.

40. Sylvia Chan-Malik, *Being Muslim: A Cultural History of Women of Color in American Islam* (New York: New York University Press, 2018), 5.

41. Rachel Rinaldo, *Mobilizing Piety: Islam and Feminism in Indonesia* (Oxford: Oxford University Press, 2013), 16; and Laura Deeb, *An Enchanted Modern: Gender and Public Piety in Shi'i Lebanon* (Princeton: Princeton University Press, 2006), 9. It is not just "beliefs," argues Deeb but also "habits, skills, and styles," structuring beliefs within "strategies and action" (9).

42. L. Ayu Saraswati argues that such capitalist products present a spectacle that erases pain, which becomes a "phantasmagoria." Saraswati, *Pain Generation: Social Media, Feminist Activism, and the Neoliberal Selfie* (New York: New York University Press, 2021), 35.

43. When scrolling through advertisements, time becomes a commodity. Thomas Davenport and John Beck, *The Attention Economy: Understanding the New Currency of Business* (Boston: Harvard Business Review Press, 2002); Jonathan Beller, *The Cinematic Mode of Production: Attention Economy and the Society of the Spectacle* (Lebanon, NH: University Press of New England, 2006).

44. Fawaz, *New Mutants*, 22, 11. Also see Kishonna Gray, *Intersectional Tech: Black Users in Digital Gaming* (Baton Rouge: LSU Press, 2020).

45. Adrienne Shaw, *Gaming at the Edge: Sexuality and Gender at the Margins of Gamer Culture* (Minneapolis: University of Minnesota Press, 2014), 1.

46. Lisa Nakamura, "Afterword: Racism, Sexism, and Gaming's Cruel Optimism," in *Gaming Representation: Race, Gender, and Sexuality in Video Games*, ed. Jennifer Malkowski and TreaAndrea Russworm (Bloomington: Indiana University Press, 2017), 245.

47. TreaAndrea Russworm, "Dystopian Blackness and the Limits of Racial Empathy in *The Walking Dead* and *The Last of Us*," in Malkowski and Russworm, *Gaming Representation*, 109–28.

48. See Jennifer Malkowski, "'I Turned Out to Be Such a Damsel in Distress: Noir Games and the Unrealized Femme Fatale," in Malkowski and Russworm, *Gaming Representation*, 19–37.

49. Bonnie Ruberg, "Playing to Lose: The Queer Art of Failing at Video Games," in Malkowski and Russworm, *Gaming Representation*, 198.

50. W. E. B. Du Bois, *The Souls of Black Folk* (New York: Dover, 1903), 2–3.

51. Lisa Patty, "Entering the Picture: Digital Portraiture and the Aesthetics of Video Game Representation," in Malkowski and Russworm, *Gaming Representation*, 179.

52. Darryn Bonthuys, "Marvel's Avengers Was September's Best-Selling Game in the U.S.," October 16, 2020, accessed March 14, 2022, https://www.gamespot.com/articles /marvels-avengers-was-septembers-best-selling-game-in-the-us/1100-6483397.

53. *Call of Duty: Modern Warfare* (2019 video game), Wikipedia. See Hilary Goldstein, "Call of Duty 4: Modern Warfare Review," November 5, 2007, accessed September 11, 2021, https://web.archive.org/web/20071108223738/http://xbox360.ign.com/articles/832/832599p2 .html; John Sanbonmatsu, "Video Games: Machine Dreams of Domination," in *Gender, Race, and Class in Media*, ed. Gail Dines et al., 5th ed. (Los Angeles: Sage, 2018). The "racialization and militarization" of the video games have been located in "domestic urban landscapes" (418).

54. Sanbonmatsu, "Video Games," 419.

55. Eli Vanderbilt, interview with author, Seattle, WA, August 1, 2021. "There *are* games where you direct the character, where players can create a narrative, where you play out events. It's an adventure."

56. "Your differences are your greatest superpower." *Marvel Avengers*, Crystal Dynamics video game, September 2020.

57. YouTube, "The Avengers Really Take Care of Kamala Khan," https://youtu.be /GbKY6o_CbUU, September 7, 2020; 136,000 views.

58. Lorraine Cink, *Powers of a Girl: 65 Marvel Women Who Punched the Sky and Changed the Universe*, illus. Alice Zhang (Los Angeles: Marvel, 2019), 74–75.

59. Jeffrey Brown, *Dangerous Curves: Action Heroines, Gender Fetishism, and Popular Culture* (Jackson: University Press of Mississippi, 2011), 55.

60. Dave Itzkoff, "'Ms. Marvel' Introduces a New Hero (and a New Actress)," *New York Times*, June 6, 2022, https://www.nytimes.com/2022/06/06/arts/television/ms-marvel-iman-vellani.html?referringSource=articleShare. Subsequent quotes in text.

61. "Marvel Studios' Ms. Marvel Official Trailer," Disney+, March 15, 2022, accessed March 16, 2022, https://www.youtube.com/watch?v=m9EX0f6V11Y.

62. Patty, "Entering the Picture," in Malkowski and Russworm, *Gaming Representation*, 179, 184.

63. Catherine Ramirez, *Assimilation: An Alternative History* (Oakland: University of California Press, 2020), 9.

64. See Pierre Mayol, "The Neighborhood," in *The Practice of Everyday Life: Living and Cooking*, ed. Luce Girard, vol. 2. (Minneapolis: University of Minnesota Press, 1998), 13. These "exchanges" of various inhabitants reflect a "network of social signs that preexist."

## CHAPTER 2: ONLINE SPORT PROTEST: NIKE WONDER WOMEN

1. Spring-Serenity Duvall and Nicole Heckemeyer, "#BlackLivesMatter: Black Celebrity Hashtag Activism and the Discursive Formation of a Social Movement," *Celebrity Studies* 9, no. 3 (2018): 391–408, accessed December 2, 2022, https://doi.org/10.1080/19392397.2018.144024404.

2. Ibtihaj Muhammad, interview with Jemele Hill, "Ibtihaj Muhammad Talks about Media Treatment Heading into Rio," The Undefeated, accessed August 19, 2021, https://theundefeated.com/videos/ibtihaj-muhammad-talks-about-media-treatment-heading-into-rio.

3. Muhammad, *Proud*, 51.

4. Ibtihaj Muhammad, interview with Becky Anderson, "Authors Revealed: Ibtihaj Muhammad," *Authors Revealed*, NCTV17, August 21, 2018, accessed September 18, 2020, https://www.youtube.com/watch?v=gvVNV1X5qcg. Subsequent references in text.

5. Ibtihaj Muhammad with Lori Tharps, *Proud: My Fight for an Unlikely Dream* (New York: Hachette Books, 2018), 26.

6. Muhammad, *Proud*, 27.

7. Ibtihaj Muhammad, "Open to Possibilities," Tedx Talk, May 4, 2017, accessed January 20, 2023; 15,000 views

8. Ibtihaj Muhammad, interview with Brittany Packnet, *Politics and Prose*, YouTube, May 4, 2017, accessed January 20, 2023. Also see Muhammad, *Proud*, xii, and "Open to Possibilities," TedX Talk.

9. @Ibtihaj Muhammad, Instagram, accessed January 28, 2023. Subsequent references in text. 381,000 followers.

10. This post had 703 comments, Instagram, February 23, 2022.

11. Lina Khalifeh, posted @Ibtihaj Muhammad, Instagram, October 28, 2022.

12. Ibtihaj Muhammad, interview with Becky Anderson, "Authors Revealed: Ibtihaj Muhammad," *Authors Revealed*, NCTV17, August 21, 2018, accessed September 18, 2020, https://www.youtube.com/watch?v=gvVNV1X5qcg. Subsequent references in text.

13. Stanley Thangaraj, *Desi Hoop Dreams: Pickup Basketball and the Making of Asian American Masculinity* (New York: New York University Press, 2015), 6. Also, many thanks to this critic for his queries and suggestions throughout this chapter.

14. Many critics have traced how Muslim women have been used to justify the violence of US wars. Nadje Al-Ali and Nicola Pratt, *What Kind of Liberation? Women and the Occupation of Iraq* (Berkeley: University of California Press, 2009); Lila Abu-Lughod, *Do Muslim Women Need Saving?* (Boston: Harvard University Press, 2015).

15. Barak Obama, "Obama Praises Muslim American Olympic Fencer during Mosque Visit," *Washington Post*, March 14, 2016, accessed September 19, 2020, https://www.bing.com/videos/search?q=president+obama+ibtihaj+muhammad&&view=detail&mid=7C30F496891427FC5E2B7C30F496891427FC5E2B&&FORM=VRDGAR&ru=%2Fvideos%2Fsearch%3Fq%3Dpresident%2Bobama%2Bibtihaj%2Bmuhammad%26FORM%3DHDRSC4.

16. Stuart Hall, Jessica Evans, and Sean Nixon, eds., *Representation: Cultural Representations and Signifying Practices*, 2nd ed. (Los Angeles: Sage, 2013), 223.

17. Susan Cahn, *Coming on Strong: Gender and Sexuality in Twentieth-Century Women's Sport* (Urbana: University of Illinois Press, 1994, 2015), 112.

18. Shari Dworkin and Michael Messner, "Just Do . . . What? Sport, Bodies, Gender," in *Gender and Sport: A Reader*, ed. Sheila Scraton and Anne Flintoff (London: Routledge, 2002), 24.

19. Dworkin and Messner, "Just Do . . . What?," 24.

20. Sumaya Samie and Kim Toffoletti, "Postfeminist Paradoxes and Cultural Difference: Unpacking Media Representations of American Muslim Sportswomen Ibtihaj and Dalilah Muhammad," in *New Sporting Femininities: Embodied Politics in Postfeminist Times*, ed. Kim Toffoletti et al. (Cham, Switzerland: Palgrave Macmillan, 2018), 89.

21. Samie and Toffoletti, "Postfeminist Paradoxes and Cultural Difference," 102–3.

22. Samie and Toffoletti, "Postfeminist Paradoxes and Cultural Difference," 98–99.

23. Kathryn Lofton, *Consuming Religion* (Chicago: University of Chicago Press, 2017), xii.

24. "Ibtihaj Muhammad with Nike Women," *Nike Pro Hijab*, Nike, December 14, 2017, accessed September 12, 2021, https://www.facebook.com/watch/?v=1610860312293593

25. Ben Carrington, *Race, Sport, and Politics: The Sporting Black Diaspora* (Thousand Oaks, CA: Sage, 2010), 4.

26. Carrington, *Race, Sport, and Politics*, 3.

27. C. L. Cole and David Andrews, "America's New Son: Tiger Woods and America's Multiculturalism," in *Sports Stars: The Cultural Politics of Sporting Celebrity*, ed. David L. Andrews and Steven J. Jackson (London: Routledge, 2001), 70.

28. Jonathan Beller, *The Cinematic Mode of Production: Attention Economy and the Society of the Spectacle* (Lebanon, NH: University Press of New England, 2006), 138; Douglas Kellner, "The Sports Spectacle, Michael Jordan, and Nike: Unholy Alliance?" in David L. Andrews, ed., *Michael Jordan, Inc.: Corporate Sport, Media Culture, and Late Modern America* (Albany: State University of New York Press, 2001), 38, 39.

29. Beller, *Cinematic Mode of Production*, 138, 9.

30. Dworkin and Messner, "Just Do . . . What?," 21.

31. Toby Miller, "A Distorted Playing Field: Neoliberalism and Sport through the Lens of Economic Citizenship," in *Sport and Neoliberalism: Politics, Consumption, and Culture*, ed. David L. Andrews and Michael L. Silk (Philadelphia: Temple University Press, 2012), 25.

32. "Ibtihaj Muhammad with Nike Women," Ibtihaj Muhammad's Facebook, Nike, accessed May 20, 2020, https://www.facebook.com/watch/?v=1610860312293593.

33. Lofton, *Consuming Religion*, 4–5.

34. Lofton, *Consuming Religion*, 4.

35. See Brian Wilson and Robert Sparks, "Michael Jordan, Sneaker Commercials, and Canadian Youth Cultures," *Michael Jordan, Inc.: Corporate Sport, Media Culture, and Late Modern America*, ed. David Andrews (Albany: State University of New York Press, 2001), 220. Wilson and Sparks analyze the ways in which coding meaning by Nike is not the same as decoding meanings by varied individuals and racialized groups.

36. Emma Tarlo, *Visibly Muslim: Fashion, Politics, Faith* (Oxford: Berg, 2010), 165.

37. Tarlo, *Visibly Muslim*, 177.

38. Tarlo, *Visibly Muslim*, 165.

39. Tarlo, *Visibly Muslim*, 185.

40. Valeriya Safronova, "Nike Reveals the 'Pro Hijab' for Muslim Athletes," *New York Times*, March 8, 2017, accessed September 18, 2020, https://www.nytimes.com/2017/03/08/fashion/nike-pro-hijab-muslim-athlete.html. Subsequent references in text.

41. Samie and Toffoletti, "Postfeminist Paradoxes," 104.

42. Nike, "Nike: What Will They Say about You?" *#Believeinmore #JustDoIt*, Nike, March 6, 2017, accessed September 19, 2020, https://www.youtube.com/watch?v=F-UO9vMS7AI.

43. Ibtihaj Muhammad, "It's Only Crazy until You Do It," Sport Nike, March 8, 2019, accessed September 18, 2020, https://www.bing.com/videos/search?q=only+crazy+until+you+do+it&docid=608013274488966142&mid=102D96F27C50D6D2DEB6102D96F27C50D6D2DEB6&view=detail&FORM=VIRE.

44. Dworkin and Messner, "Just Do ... What?"

45. Colin Kaepernick narrating "Dream Crazy" for Nike commercial, "Colin Kaepernick Nike Commercial Full Video," September 7, 2018, accessed November 10, 2020, https://www.youtube.com/watch?v=lomlpJREDzw.

46. "Fashionable 50: Ibtihaj Muhammad," *Sports Illustrated*, July 17, 2017, accessed July 25, 2021, https://www.si.com/sports-illustrated/2017/07/17/fashionable-50-ibtihaj-muhammad#gid=ci02553a3bc0012580&pid=ibtihaj-muhammad.

47. Rothy's, "The Statement Makers," Rothy's Shop, paid ad in *New York Times*, May 30, 2020, accessed September 19, 2020, https://www.nytimes.com/paidpost/rothys/the-statement-makers.html. Subsequent references in text.

48. On beauty as a form of power, see Vanita Reddy, *Fashion Diaspora: Beauty, Femininity, and South Asian American Culture* (Philadelphia: Temple University Press, 2016).

49. Fleetwood, *On Racial Icons*, 11, 10.

50. Wilson and Sparks, "Michael Jordan," 224, 237, 240.

51. Minh-Ha Pham, *Asians Wear Clothes on the Internet: Race, Gender, and the Work of Personal Style Blogging* (Durham, NC: Duke University Press, 2015), 143–44.

52. "Women Shattering Stereotypes," cover of *Vogue Arabia*, April 2019, accessed December 9, 2021, https://www.google.com/search?q=april+2019+vogue+arabia+cover&rlz=1C1ZKTG_enUS907US908&source=lnms&tbm=isch&sa=X&ved=2ahUKEwi6mNjh5OTsAhUCnZ4KHRkiBwYQ_AUoAX0ECA4QAw&biw=958&bih=920#imgrc=VwXuSzIbPye1cM.

53. Ibtihaj Muhammad, "Ibtihaj Muhammad's Mirror Monologue, Brought to You by Covergirl: 'When I Look Good, I Feel Good,'" *Glamour*, August 9, 2016, accessed September 19, 2020, https://www.youtube.com/watch?v=fiwtELZbdB0.

54. Pham, *Asians Wear Clothes*, 5.

55. See Leela Fernandes, *Trans-national Feminism in the United States: Knowledge, Ethics, Power* (New York: New York University Press, 2013); Sara Shaban, *Iranian Feminism and Transnational Ethics in Media Discourse* (Lanham, MD: Lexington Books, 2022), 15.

56. Muhammad, "Authors Revealed."

57. Muhammad, *Proud*, 4.

58. Muhammad, *Proud*, 7.

59. Carolyn Rouse, *Engaged Surrender: African American Women and Islam* (Berkeley: University of California Press, 2004), xiv.

60. Muhammad, *Proud*, 7.

61. Ibtihaj Muhammad, "Secret Life of Muslims: Ibtihaj Muhammad," *Secret Life of Muslims*, May 15, 2017, accessed June 20, 2020, https://www.youtube.com/watch?v=NoFicQ_LXS0.

62. This post had 17,353 likes. Instagram, September 15, 2021.

63. This post had 9,691 likes. Instagram, July 4, 2021.

64. Ibtihaj Muhammad, "U.S. Fencer Ibtihaj Muhammad on France Hijab Row," *AFP News Agency*, March 12, 2019, accessed August 20, 2020, https://www.youtube.com/watch?v=BEBohiU77cU. Subsequent references in text.

65. Sara Ahmed, *Queer Phenomenology: Orientations, Objects, Others* (Durham, NC: Duke University Press, 2006), 20.

66. This post had 28,224 views. Instagram, July 5, 2020.

67. This post had 107 comments. Instagram, June 4, 2021.

68. This post had 16, 209 views. Instagram, May 25, 2021.

## CHAPTER 3: DIGITAL REVOLTS AND RIVETERS

1. Mona Haydar, "'Wrap My Hijab' Rapper Mona Haydar Talks Sexism, Misognyny, and Religion on the Internet," *Elle*, October 24, 2018, accessed October 15, 2021, https://www.youtube.com/watch?v=drFSP-SUl2o. Subsequent references in text.

2. Mona Haydar, "The Muslim Wrapper, Perspectives," *Huffington Post*, August 23, 2018, accessed November 30, 2021, https://www.bing.com/videos/search?q=wrap+my+hijab+elle&&view=detail&mid=B074EF3B14A561C79E51B074EF3B14A561C79E51&rvsmid=3030ACD820EF78B345EC3030ACD820EF78B345EC&FORM=VDQVAP. Subsequent references in text.

3. See posts by @blairimani Instagram and @blairimani—Campsite, "Read My FAQ," accessed April 4, 2022. Subsequent references in text.

4. See Kandice Chuh, *Imagine Otherwise: On Asian Americanist Critique* (Durham, NC: Duke University Press, 2003), 110. Jasbir Puar, *Terrorist Assemblages: Homonationalism in Queer Times* (Durham, NC: Duke University Press, 2007).

5. An arrogant racist proposal of *femonationalism* as Sara Farris suggests, *In the Name of Women's Rights: The Rise of Femonationalism* (Durham, NC: Duke University Press, 2017). See Sara Shaban, *Iranian Feminism and Transnational Ethics in Media Discourse* (Lanham, MD: Lexington Books, 2022).

6. See Kimberly Wedeven Segall, "De-imperializing Gender: Political Revivals, Shifting Beliefs, and Unexpected Trajectories," *Journal of Middle Eastern Women's Studies* 15, no. 1 (2019): 75–94.

7. Allison Stubblebine, "25 Top Feminist Anthems," *Pride*, Billboard, November 8, 2017, accessed September 17, 2020, https://www.billboard.com/articles/news/pride/8022687/top -feminist-anthems-songs.

8. Mona Haydar, "Islamophobe Is Just a New Way of Saying White Supremacist," *Mona Haydar—Love, Always*, October 12, 2010, accessed June 7, 2020, http://www.monahaydar .com/2010/10.

9. Mona Haydar, interview with Celine Seman, "Mona Haydar Is a Syrian, American, Muslim, Woman, Mother, Chaplain, Activist . . . and Rapper," in *Elle*, October 25, 2018, accessed September 17, 2020, https://www.elle.com/culture/music/a24112253/mona-haydar -new-album-barbarican-interview. Subsequent references in text.

10. Fatema Mernissi, *Scheherazade Goes West: Different Cultures, Different Harems* (New York: Washington Square Press, 2001), 46.

11. Mohja Kahf, *Western Representations of the Muslim Woman: From Termagant to Odalisque* (Austin: University of Texas Press, 1999), 4.

12. Various scholars have analyzed religious icons of Eve. See, for instance, Mary Condren's *The Serpent and the Goddess: Women, Religion, and Power in Celtic Ireland* (San Francisco: Harper and Row, 1989).

13. Judith Butler, *Notes towards a Performative Theory of Assembly* (Cambridge: Harvard University Press, 2015), 2.

14. See Laura Mulvey, "Visual Pleasure and Narrative Cinema," *Film Theory and Criticism*, ed. Leo Braudy and Marshall Cohen, 6th ed. (New York: Oxford University Press, 2004), 841.

15. See the alternate histories of women's protest in dancing of Assia Djebar, *Fantasia: An Algerian Cavalcade* (London: Heinemann, 2003).

16. Junaid Rana, *Terrifying Muslims: Race and Labor in the South Asian Diaspora* (Durham, NC: Duke University Press, 2011), 25–26.

17. Lori Peek, *Behind the Backlash: Muslim Americans after 9/11* (Philadelphia: Temple University Press, 2011), 141.

18. Mona Haydar, interview with Jennifer Chowdhury, "Conservative Muslims and Islamophobes Have One Thing in Common: Hating Mona Haydar," *Marie Claire*, November 20, 2017, accessed September 17, 2020, https://www.marieclaire.com/culture /a13122846/mona-haydar-interview. Subsequent references in text.

19. Leslie Camhi, "Model Halima Aden Is Redefining the Idea of Modest Style on the Runway," *Vogue*, June 16, 2017, accessed November 2, 2020, https://www.vogue.com/article /halima-aden-runway-model-yeezy.

20. Mona Haydar, interview with Tsafi Saar, "The U.S.-Syrian Rapper Who Hits Back at Those Who Would Tell Her to Take Off Her Hijab," *Haaretz Magazine*, April 21, 2017, accessed December 9, 2021, https://www.haaretz.com/life/.premium.MAGAZINE-the -fiery-hijabi-music-video-that-takes-aim-at-all-the-racists-1.5463161. See also posts: "Flowers 4U," August 13, 2011, accessed December 9, 2021, http://www.monahaydar.com /2011/08; "Mahalia Jackson: He Knows Just How Much We Can Bear," May 13, 2009, accessed December 9, 2021, http://www.monahaydar.com/2009/05.

21. Hisham Aidi, *Rebel Music: Race, Empire, and the New Muslim Youth Culture* (New York: Vintage, 2014), xxiii.

22. Haydar, interview with Saar.

23. Su'ad Abdul Khabeer, *Muslim Cool: Race, Religion, and Hip Hop in the United States* (New York: New York University Press, 2016), 71.

24. Elizabeth Bucar, *Pious Fashion: How Muslim Women Dress* (Cambridge: Harvard University Press, 2017), 172.

25. Khabeer, *Muslim Cool*, 115.

26. Khabeer, *Muslim Cool*, 115.

27. Stanley Thangaraj, "Racing the Muslim: Strategies for Teaching Race and Ethnic Studies in the Education Curriculum," *Urban Education* 56, no. 7 (2021): 1042–66.

28. See J. L. Austin, *How to Do Things with Words* (Cambridge: Harvard University Press, 1975), 5.

29. Haydar, "Conservative Muslims."

30. Clara Rodriguez, *Changing Race: Latinos, the Census, and the History of Ethnicity in the United States* (New York: New York University Press, 2000), 92.

31. Lisa Suhair Majaj, "Arab Americans and the Meaning of Race," in *Postcolonial Theory and the United States: Race, Ethnicity, and Literature*, ed. Amaritjit Singh and Peter Schmidt (Jackson: University Press of Mississippi, 2000), 321.

32. Sarah Gualtieri, *Between Arab and White: Race and Ethnicity in the Early Syrian American Diaspora* (Berkeley: University of California Press, 2009), 54.

33. Rodriguez, *Changing Race*, 92. See also Helen Hatab Samhan, "Not Quite White: Race Classification and the Arab-American Experience," in *Arabs in America: Building a New Future*, ed. Michael Suleiman (Philadelphia: Temple University Press, 1999), 217; Ian Haney-Lopez, *White by Law: The Legal Construction of Race* (New York: New York University Press, 1996); Lisa Suhair Majaj, "Arab-American Ethnicity: Locations, Coalitions and Cultural Negotiations," in *Arabs in America: Building a New Future*, ed. Michael Suleiman (Philadelphia: Temple University Press, 1999).

34. On lynching, see Sarah Gualtieri, "Strange Fruit? Syrian Immigrants, Extralegal Violence and Racial Formation in the Jim Crow South," *Arab Studies Quarterly* 26, no. 3 (2004): 63. Please note, following Gualtieri, that this exceptional case resides within horrific numbers of Black lynchings—around 3,220 between 1880–1930 in the United States. On racial "ambiguities," see Nadine Naber, "Introduction: Arab Americans and U.S. Racial Formations," in *Race and Arab Americans before and after 9/11: From Invisible Citizens to Visible Subjects*, ed. Amaney Jamal and Nadine Naber (Syracuse, NY: Syracuse University Press, 2008), 23.

35. Mona Haydar, "Muslim Woman Raps about Choosing to Cover Up: My Hijab, My Choice," Fusion Media Group TV, Fusion, April 6, 2017, accessed December 19, 2021,

https://www.bing.com/videos/search?q=mona+haydar+youtube&&view=detail&mid=02
F756BA1D6785F0E10602F756BA1D6785F0E106&&FORM=VDRVRV. And see also Mona
Haydar's Malcolm X in "Ajeebness," Mona Haydar—Love, Always, February 26, 2011,
accessed October 7, 2020, http://www.monahaydar.com/2011/02.

36. Stefano Allievi, "Islam in the Public Space: Social Networks, Media and Neo-
Communities," in *Muslim Networks and Transnational Communities in and across Europe*,
ed. Stefano Allievi and Jorgen Nielsen (Leiden, NL: Brill, 2003), 8.

37. Anne McClintock, "'No Longer in a Future Heaven': Gender, Race and
Nationalism," in *Dangerous Liaisons: Gender, Nation, and Postcolonial Perspectives*,
ed. Anne McClintock, Aamir Mufti, and Ella Shohat (Minneapolis: University of
Minnesota Press, 1997), 89.

38. Mona Haydar, "Your Heart Is the Only True Authority," TedxTalk, accessed January 25,
2023, https://www.ted.com/talks/mona_haydar_your_heart_is_the_only_true_authority.

39. Haydar, "Wrap My Hijab." Subsequent references in text.

40. Mona Haydar, "#Syria," Mona Haydar—Love, Always, May 30, 2012, accessed June 30,
2020, http://www.monahaydar.com/2012/05/30/syria.

41. Michelle Hartman, *Breaking Broken English: Black-Arab Literary Solidarities and
the Politics of Language* (Syracuse, NY: Syracuse University Press, 2019), 6–7. See also Theri
Pickens, *New Body Politics: Narrating Arab and Black Identity in the Contemporary United
States* (New York: Routledge, 2014).

42. Tricia Rose, *The Hip Hop Wars: What We Talk about When We Talk about Hip
Hop—and Why It Matters* (New York: Basic Books, 2008), 202, 203.

43. *Amaliah*, July 20, 2017, accessed June 14, 2022, https://www.amaliah.com/post
/28424/controversy-mona-haydar.

44. Khabeer, *Muslim Cool*, 25.

45. Khabeer, *Muslim Cool*, 228.

46. Khabeer, *Muslim Cool*, 228.

47. Su'ad Abdul Khabeer, interview with Mark Anthony Neal, *Left of Black*, season 9,
episode 9, November 19, 2018, accessed June 14, 2022.

48. Mona Haydar, *Dog*, July 17, 2017, accessed November 30, 2021, https://www.bing
.com/videos/search?q=wrap+my+hijab+elle&&view=detail&mid=0B4D28354CC736E126
CA0B4D28354CC736E126CA&rvsmid=3030ACD820EF78B345EC3030ACD820EF78B345
EC&FORM=VDQVAP. Subsequent references in the text.

49. Wendy Chun, *Updating to Remain the Same: Habitual New Media* (Cambridge:
MIT Press, 2017), xi, 3.

50. See posts by @blairimani Instagram and @blairimani—Campsite, "Read My FAQ,"
accessed April 4, 2022. Subsequent references in text.

51. Blair Imani, *Modern HERStory: Stories of Women and Nonbinary People Rewriting
History* (Berkeley, CA: Ten Speed Press, 2018).

52. Penny Coleman, *Rosie the Riveter: Women Working on the Home Front in World
War II* (New York: Yearling, 1995), 27.

53. Maureen Honey, *Creating Rosie the Riveter: Class, Gender and Propaganda during
World War II* (Boston: University of Massachusetts Press, 1984), 215.

54. Honey, *Creating Rosie the Riveter*, 23.

55. Kimberlé Crenshaw, "Demarginalizing the Intersection of Race and Sex: A Black Feminist Critique of Antidiscrimination Doctrine, Feminist Theory and Antiracist Politics," *Feminist and Queer Theory: An Intersectional and Transnational Reader*, ed. L. Ayu Saraswati and Barbara Shaw (New York: Oxford University Press, 2021), 141–49.

56. Honey, *Creating Rosie the Riveter*, 214.

57. Elspeth Brown, *Work! A Queer History of Modeling* (Durham, NC: Duke University Press, 2019), 176.

58. Brown, *Work!*, 177.

59. Leigh-Ann Jackson, "Like a Boss: The Work Diary of Blair Imani, 'Herstory,' Historian," *New York Times*, November 13, 2020, accessed October 6, 2021, https://www.nytimes.com/2020/11/13/business/blair-imani.html?smid=em-share.

60. Nicole Fleetwood, *On Racial Icons: Blackness and the Public Imagination* (New Brunswick, NJ: Rutgers University Press, 2015).

61. This post had 28,223 likes on Instagram, June 17, 2021.

62. Safiya Umoja Noble, *Algorithms of Oppression: How Search Engines Reinforce Racism* (New York: New York University Press, 2018). See also Ruha Benjamin, *Race after Technology* (Cambridge: Polity, 2019).

63. Michael Goodman, "Celebrity Politics, Neoliberal Sustainabilities, and the Terrains of Care," in *Age of Icons: Exploring Philanthrocapitalism in the Contemporary World*, ed. Gavin Fridell and Martijn Konings (Toronto: University of Toronto Press, 2013), 84. "Celebrity politics," according to Goodman, involves the star becoming a type of "commodity," a model of "care," distracting from the work needed by the state (73).

64. Minh-Ha Pham, *Asians Wear Clothes on the Internet: Race, Gender, and the Work of Personal Style Blogging* (Durham, NC: Duke University Press, 2015), 22, 151.

65. Pham, *Asians Wear Clothes*, 32, 25.

66. Pham, *Asians Wear Clothes*, 133.

67. Pham, *Asians Wear Clothes*, 135.

68. Pham, *Asians Wear Clothes*, 145, 147.

69. José Esteban Muñoz, *Disidentifications: Queers of Color and the Performance of Politics* (Minneapolis: University of Minnesota Press, 1999), 89.

70. This post had 22,308 likes on Instagram, September 23, 2021.

71. This post had 16,053 likes on Instagram, July 19, 2020.

72. Muñoz, *Disidentifications*, 39.

73. Juana María Rodríguez, *Sexual Futures, Queer Gestures, and Other Latina Longings* (New York: New York University Press, 2014), 5.

74. Rodríguez, *Sexual Futures, Queer Gestures*, 2.

75. Marlon Bailey, *Butch Queens up in Pumps* (Ann Arbor: University of Michigan Press, 2013), 16, 17.

76. Blair Imani, "One Month Ago in Baton Rouge," *Huffington Post*, August 10, 2016, accessed October 25, 2021, https://www.huffpost.com/entry/one-month-ago-in-baton-rouge_b_57a7d416e4b0c94bd3c9ce0c. Subsequent references in text.

77. Blair Imani, "One Month Ago in Baton Rouge," *Huffington Post*, August 10, 2016, accessed October 25, 2021, https://www.huffpost.com/entry/one-month-ago-in-baton-rouge_b_57a7d416e4b0c94bd3c9ce0c.

78. @TuckerCarlson, "Activist Advocates for Muslim 'Safe Spaces' Here in the U.S.," June 9, 2017, accessed October 6, 2021, https://twitter.com/tuckercarlson/status/873346438 788517889?s=10.

79. Blair Imani with Brandon Wolf, "Accelerating Acceptance for LGBTQ People," Tweet@glaad, accessed December 5, 2021, https://twitter.com/glaad/status/9929372 07437508609?ref_src=twsrc%5Etfw%7Ctwcamp%5Etweetembed%7Ctwterm%5E99293720 7437508609%7Ctwgr%5E%7Ctwcon%5Es1_c10&ref_url=https%3A%2F%2Fwww.glaad .org%2Fblog%2Fpulse-survivor-brandon-wolf-and-queer-muslim-activist-blair-imani -call-out-tucker-carlson-glaad. Subsequent references in text.

80. Puar, *Terrorist Assemblages*, 93.

81. This post had 24,657 likes on Instagram, April 17, 2021.

82. FAQ--@blairimani.com, accessed October 6, 2021.

83. See Kareem Khubchandani, *Ishtyle: Accenting Gay Indian Nightlife* (Ann Arbor: University of Michigan Press, 2020) on the pleasures of performing in "queer" spaces.

84. Clare Croft, "Introduction," in *Queer Dance: Meanings and Makings* (New York: Oxford University Press, 2017), 1.

85. "Queer and Muslim: Nothing to Reconcile," TedXTalk, Boulder, CO, accessed December 9, 2022, https://www.youtube.com/watch?v=8IhaGUlmO_k

86. See Ellen J. Amster, *Medicine and the Saints: Science, Islam, and the Colonial Encounter in Morocco, 1877–1956* (Austin: University of Texas Press, 2013), 3. Amster documents how diseases were coded as resulting from Muslims and their sexual practices, as Moroccans were treated as a "disease environment rather than a public to protect" (13).

87. Roderick Ferguson, *Aberrations in Black: Toward a Queer of Color Critique* (Minneapolis: University of Minnesota Press, 2004), 138.

88. This post had 15,534 likes on Instagram, October 5, 2021.

89. Gayatri Gopinath, *Unruly Visions: The Aesthetic Practices of Queer Diaspora* (Durham, NC: Duke University Press, 2018), 21.

90. Blair Imani, *Read This to Get Smarter: About Race, Class, Gender, Disability & More* (Berkeley, CA: Ten Speed Press, 2021).

91. Celine Parenas Shimizu, *The Hypersexuality of Race: Performing Asian/American Women on Screen and Scene* (Durham, NC: Duke University Press, 2007), 267.

92. Sara Ahmed, *Queer Phenomenology: Orientations, Objects, Others* (Durham, NC: Duke University Press, 2006), 117.

## CHAPTER 4: GRASSROOTS ICONS: FACEBOOK RESISTANCE

1. Aneelah Afzali, interview with author, Seattle, WA, June 30, 2021. Several interviews with author have been cited throughout this chapter. See also Malcolm X interview, YouTube, "Malcolm X—If You Stick a Knife in My Back," November 5, 2011, accessed November 21, 2021, https://www.youtube.com/watch?v=XiSiHRNQlQo; 76,895 views.

2. Voted one of the "Most Influential Seattleites" in 2017, Afzali received the Humanitarian Leadership Award in 2018, and the Achievement Award for Community Service in 2019. Also see Aneelah Afzali, "Biography," Muslim Association of Puget Sound,

accessed November 25, 2021, https://mapsredmond.org/aneelah-afzali-bio. See also
Alison Krupneck, "Most Influential Seattleites of 2017: Aneelah Afzali," *Seattle Magazine*,
November 2017, accessed November 22, 2021, https://www.seattlemag.com/news-and
-features/most-influential-seattleites-2017-aneelah-afzali.

3. Aneelah Afzali, Facebook heading, June 10, 2019.

4. Aneelah Afzali, interview with Charissa Soriano, "Conversations on Tech and Social
Justice: Aneelah Afzali," *Seattle Globalist*, May 31, 2019, accessed September 1, 2021, https://
seattleglobalist.com/2019/05/31/conversations-on-tech-and-social-justice-aneelah-afzali
/85304. Subsequent references in text.

5. From the American Muslim Poll 2020, 74 percent of US Muslim women support
protests of Black Lives Matter. See website at Institute for Social Policy and Understanding,
https://www.ispu.org/wp-content/uploads/2021/04/AMP-Infographic-Coalitions-8.5x11
-v3-1.pdf?x46312. Fifteen million is the estimate of Kim Parker, Juliana Menasce Horowitz,
and Monica Anderson, "Amid Protests, Majorities across Racial and Ethnic Groups
Express Support for the Black Lives Matter Movement," Pew Research Center: Social and
Demographic Trends, June 12, 2020, accessed July 25, 2021, https://www.pewsocialtrends
.org/2020/06/12/amid-protests-majorities-across-racial-and-ethnic-groups-express
-support-for-the-black-lives-matter-movement. Twenty-six million is the estimate of Liz
Hamel, Audrey Kearney, Ashley Kirzinger, Lunna Lopes, Cailey Munana, and Mollyann
Brodie, "KFF Health Tracking Poll—June 2020," KFF Health, June 26, 2020, accessed July 25,
2021, https://www.kff.org/disparities-policy/report/kff-health-tracking-poll-june-2020

6. Mona Baker and Bolette Blaagaard, "Reconceptualizing Citizen Media: A
Preliminary Charting of a Complex Domain," in *Citizen Media and Public Spaces: Diverse
Expressions of Citizenship and Dissent*, ed. Mona Baker and Bolette Blaagaard (London:
Routledge, 2016), 1.

7. Zizi Papacharissi and Sharon Meraz, "Networked Gatekeeping and Networked
Framing on #Egypt," *International Journal of Press/Politics* 18, no. 2 (2013): 138.

8. Zizi Papacharissi, *Affective Publics: Sentiment, Technology, and Politics* (Oxford:
Oxford University Press, 2015), 101.

9. Aneelah Afzali, Facebook entries, accessed January 25, 2023.

10. Aneelah Afzali, "The Superpower I Call Home Cannot Abandon the Afghan
'Supergirls' of My Homeland," *Seattle Times*, September 24, 2021, accessed November 21,
2021, https://www.seattletimes.com/opinion/the-superpower-i-call-home-cannot-abandon
-the-afghan-supergirls-of-my-homeland.

11. Aneelah Afzali, interview with author, Seattle, WA, June 30, 2021.

12. Malcolm X interview, "If You Stick a Knife."

13. Aneelah Afzali, "The Superpower I Call Home," https://www.seattletimes.com
/opinion/the-superpower-i-call-home-cannot-abandon-the-afghan-supergirls-of-my
-homeland. Subsequent references in text.

14. See introduction that situates the research of Lila Abu-Lughod, *Do Muslim Women Need
Saving?* (Boston: Harvard University Press, 2015); Nadje Al-Ali and Nicola Pratt, *What Kind of
Liberation? Women and the Occupation of Iraq* (Berkeley: University of California Press, 2009).

15. Craig Whitlock, interview with Amy Goodman, "Democracy Now," August 20,
2021, on his new book, *The Afghanistan Papers: A Secret History of the War* (New York:

Simon & Schuster, 2021), https://www.democracynow.org/2021/8/19/the_afghanistan
_papers_craig_whitlock.

16. Moya Bailey, *Misogynoir Transformed: Black Women's Digital Resistance* (New York: New York University Press, 2021), 24.

17. Kevin Nadal et al., "Subtle and Overt Forms of Islamophobia: Microaggressions toward Muslim Americans," *Journal of Muslim Mental Health* 6, no. 2 (2012): 17, http://dx.doi.org/10.3998/jmmh.10381607.0006.203

18. Aneelah Afzali, "Telling Our Stories" workshop, February 2, 2019.

19. Jane Smith, *Islam in America* (New York: Columbia University Press, 2009), xv.

CHAPTER 5: SOLIDARITY ICONS: A VIRTUAL REVOLUTION

1. See Erica Austin, Rebecca Van de Vord, Bruce Pinkleton, and Evan Epstein, "Celebrity Endorsements and Their Potential to Motivate Young Voters," *Mass Communication and Society* 11, no. 4 (2008): 420–36, DOI:10.1080/15205430701866600. And see Spring Duvall, "Becoming Celebrity Girl Activists: The Cultural Politics and Celebrification of Emma Gonzalez, Marly Dias, and Greta Thunberg," *Journal of Communication Inquiry* 2, DOI: 10.1177/0196859922; Jessica Taft, "Teenage Girls' Narratives of Becoming Activists," *Contemporary Social Science* 12 (1–2): 27–39, https://www.tandfonline.com, DOI:P 10.1080/2 1582041.2017.132417328.

2. Richard Schechner, *Performance Theory* (New York: Routledge, 2003), 69.

3. Shirin Rai and Janelle Reinelt, "Introduction," in *The Grammar of Politics and Performance*, ed. Shirin Rai and Janelle Reinelt (London: Routledge, 2015), 4.

4. All of these interviews and forums in this chapter are with the author. "Telling Our Stories: Workshop," unpublished video recordings, February 2, March 2, and March 30, 2019. And from the interviews and panel at Seattle Pacific University, "Panel of American Muslim Women," unpublished video recordings, April 5, 2019, and MAPS-AMEN Mosque Visit, April 6, 2019. These videos and transcripts include the written permissions of participants, the director, and the videographer.

5. Kevin Nadal, Marie-Anne Issa, Katie E. Griffin, Sahran Hamit, and Oliver B. Lyons, "Religious Microaggressions in the United States: Mental Health Implications for Religious Minority Groups," in *Microaggressions and Marginality: Manifestations, Dynamics, and Impact*, ed. Derald Wing Sue (Hoboken, NJ: John Wiley & Sons, 2010), 304.

6. Nadal et al., "Religious Microaggressions in the United States," 288.

7. Derald Wing Sue, "Microaggressions, Marginality, and Oppression: An Introduction," in *Microaggresions and Marginality: Manifestations, Dynamics, and Impact*, ed. Derald Wing Sue (Hoboken, NJ: John Wiley & Sons, 2010), 3, 6.

8. Kevin Nadal, *Microaggressions and Traumatic Stress: Theory, Research, and Clinical Treatment* (Washington, DC: American Psychological Association, 2018), 43.

9. Brian Massumi, *Parables for the Virtual: Movement, Affect, Sensation* (Durham, NC: Duke University Press, 2002), 48–49.

10. Ibrahim Hooper, "CAIR Report: Anti-Muslim Bias Incidents, Hate Crimes Spike in Second Quarter of 2018," *Cision*, PR Newswire, July 12, 2018, accessed September 4, 2020,

https://www.prnewswire.com/news-releases/cair-report-anti-muslim-bias-incidents-hate
-crimes-spike-in-second-quarter-of-2018-300680320.html.

11. For earlier work that suggested that this revival among women was in solidarity against the 9/11 backlash, see especially Louise Cainkar, "Islamic Revival among Second-Generation Arab-Americans: The American Experience and Globalization Intersect," *Bulletin of the Royal Institute for Inter-Faith Studies* 6, no. 2 (2004): 99–120. See also Leila Ahmed, *A Quiet Revolution: The Veil's Resurgence from the Middle East to America* (New Haven: Yale University Press, 2011), 8–9. "Why had the veil made such a comeback," Ahmed asks, "and how had it spread with such remarkable swiftness?" Ahmed interviews women, following Jane Smith's argument on Islam in the US. Smith, *Islam in America* (New York: Columbia University Press, 1999), 46. These public solidarities are the subject of Lori Peek's *Behind the Backlash: Muslim Americans after 9/11* (Philadelphia: Temple University Press, 2011).

12. See Leela Fernandes, *Trans-National Feminism in the United States: Knowledge, Ethics, Power* (New York: New York University Press, 2013); Sara Shaban, *Iranian Feminism and Transnational Ethics in Media Discourse* (Lanham, MD: Lexington Books, 2022), 15.

See also Rachel Rinaldo, *Mobilizing Piety: Islam and Feminism in Indonesia* (Oxford: Oxford University Press, 2013); Saba Mahmood, *The Politics of Piety: The Islamic Revival and the Feminist Subject* (Princeton, NJ: Princeton University Press, 2005); Lara Deeb, *An Enchanted Modern: Gender and Public Piety in Shi'i Lebanon* (Princeton: Princeton University Press, 2006).

13. Sherry Turkle claims that identities are shifting because of the internet, with a changing relationship between a person and their presence on a computer, a "second self." Sherry Turkle, *Life on the Screen: Identity in the Age of the Internet* (New York: Touchstone, 1995), 9.

14. Alyssa Rippy and Elana Newman, "Perceived Religious Discrimination and Its Relationship to Anxiety and Paranoia among Muslim Americans," *Journal of Muslim Mental Health* 1, no. 1 (2006): 7; Lorraine Sheridan, "Islamophobia Pre-and Post-September 11th, 2001," *Journal of Interpersonal Violence* 21, no. 3 (2006): 334.

15. John Protevi, *Political Affect: Connecting the Social and the Somatic* (Minneapolis: University of Minnesota Press, 2009), xi, 49.

16. Protevi, *Political Affect*, vii.

17. On visibility in the wake of 9/11, see Therese Saliba, "Resisting Invisibility: Arab Americans in Academia and Activism," in *Arabs in America: Building a New Future*, ed. Michael Suleiman (Philadelphia: Temple University Press, 1999), 304–19. And see Louise Cainkar, *Homeland Insecurity: The Arab American and Muslim American Experience after 9/11* (New York: Russell Sage Foundation, 2009); Nadine Naber, "Introduction: Arab Americans and U.S. Racial Formations," in *Race and Arab Americans before and after 9/11: From Invisible Citizens to Visible Subjects*, ed. Amaney Jamal and Nadine Naber (Syracuse, NY: Syracuse University Press, 2008), 1–45.

18. W. E. B. Du Bois, "Strivings of the Negro People," *Atlantic Monthly*, August 1897, accessed September 11, 2020, https://www.theatlantic.com/magazine/archive/1897/08/strivings-of-the-negro-people/305446. See also Paul Gilroy, *The Black Atlantic: Modernity and Double Consciousness* (Cambridge: Harvard University Press, 1993).

19. Kevin Nadal, Katie Griffin, Sahran Hamit, Jayleen Leon, Michael Tobio, and David Rivera, "Subtle and Overt Forms of Islamophobia: Microaggressions toward Muslim Americans," *Journal of Muslim Mental Health* 6, no. 2 (2012): 29, accessed April 1, 2022, https://academicworks.cuny.edu/cgi/viewcontent.cgi?article=1314&context=gc_pubs.

20. Nadal et al., "Subtle and Overt Forms of Islamophobia," 29.

21. Nadal, "Religious Microaggressions," 303.

22. Nadal et al., "Subtle and Overt Forms of Islamophobia," 288.

23. Derald Wing Sue, "Microaggressions, Marginality, and Oppression: An Introduction," in *Microaggresions and Marginality: Manifestations, Dynamics, and Impact*, edited by Derald Wing Sue, 3–24. Hoboken, NJ: John Wiley & Sons, 2010, 15–16.

24. Massumi, *Parables*, 59.

25. Massumi, *Parables*, 59.

26. Massumi, *Parables*, 50.

## CONCLUSION: DIGITALIZING WONDER WOMEN

1. Safiya Umoja Noble, *Algorithms of Oppression: How Search Engines Reinforce Racism* (New York: New York University Press, 2018), 1.

2. Sarah Jackson, Moya Bailey, and Brooke Foucault Welles, *#HashtagActivism: Networks of Race and Gender Justice* (Cambridge, MA: MIT Press, 2020), 191.

3. Nicole Fleetwood, *On Racial Icons: Blackness and the Public Imagination* (New Brunswick: Rutgers University Press, 2015), 2.

4. Fleetwood, *On Racial Icons*, 13.

5. Audre Lorde, *Sister Outsider: Essays and Speeches* (Trumansburg, NY: Crossing Press, 1984), 116. "This norm is usually defined as white, thin, male, young, heterosexual, Christian, and financially secure. It is with this mythical norm that the trappings of power reside within this society. Those of us who stand outside that power often identify one way in which we are different, and we assume that to be the primary cause of all oppression, forgetting other distortions around difference, some of which we ourselves may be practicing" (ibid.).

6. See Ann Cvetkovich, *An Archive of Feelings: Trauma, Sexuality, and Lesbian Public Cultures* (Durham, NC: Duke University Press, 2003), 7; Jennifer Pybus, "Accumulating Affect: Social Networks and Their Archives of Feelings," in *Networked Affect*, ed. Ken Hillis, Susanna Paasonen, and Michael Petit (Cambridge, MA: MIT Press, 2015), 240.

7. See Sunaina Marr Maira, *Missing: Youth, Citizenship, and Empire after 9/11* (Durham, NC: Duke University Press, 2009), 283.

8. John Protevi, *Political Affect: Connecting the Social and the Somatic* (Minneapolis: University of Minnesota Press, 2009), iv.

9. Protevi, *Political Affect*, v–vi.

10. Maurice Halbwachs, *On Collective Memory*, ed. and trans. Lewis Coser (Chicago: University of Chicago Press, 1992), 47.

11. W. E. B. Du Bois, "A Negro Nation within the Nation," *Current History* 4 (1935), in Eric J. Sundquist, ed., *The Oxford W. E. B. Du Bois Reader* (New York: Oxford University Press, 1996), 431.

12. Ira Katznelson, *When Affirmative Action Was White: The Untold History of Racial Inequality in Twentieth-Century America* (New York: W. W. Norton, 2005), x.

13. Katznelson, *When Affirmative Action Was White.*

14. Richard Rothstein, *The Color of Law: A Forgotten History of How Our Government Segregated America* (New York: W. W. Norton, 2017), xi.

15. Rothstein, *Color of Law*, xii.

16. Rothstein, *Color of Law*, xi.

17. Rothstein, *Color of Law*, viii.

18. Charles Lawrence, "The Id, the Ego, and Equal Protection Reckoning with Unconscious Racism," in *Critical Race Theory: The Key Writings That Formed the Movement*, ed. Kimberlé Crenshaw, Neil Gotanda, Gary Peller, and Kendall Thomas (New York: The New Press, 1995), 239.

19. Elspeth Brown, *Work! A Queer History of Modeling* (Durham, NC: Duke University Press, 2019), 176. But the postwar era was a turning point in icons, according to Elspeth Brown, since Black marketing experts were aware of the potential $16 billion market in Black communities. "Brand loyalty," they suggested, would require movement away from these overt stereotypes, in order to cash in on the "big money of postwar consumption." *Work!*, 185, 184.

20. Brown, *Work!*, 170.

21. G. Willow Wilson, "The Story behind Marvel's Muslim-American Superhero," TEDx Rainier, November 2015, accessed November 5, 2021, https://www.ted.com/talks/g_willow _wilson_the_story_behind_marvel_s_muslim_american_superheroine/up-next.

22. Wilson, "The Story behind Marvel's Muslim-American Superhero." See the attacks of Anonymous, *The Fourth Age*, "Who Is Sana Amanat: A Portrait of the Power Behind the 'Progressive' Power Industry," accessed September 16, 2020, https://www.youtube.com /watch?v=5zPrDJo5apk.

23. G. Willow Wilson, "Interview with G. Willow Wilson," interview by Shabana Mir (October 2017), in *Ms. Marvel's America: No Normal*, ed. Jessica Baldanzi and Hussein Rashid, 230–46 (Jackson: University Press of Mississippi, 2020).

24. Sara Wachter-Boettcher, *Technically Wrong: Sexist Apps, Biased Algorithms, and Other Threats of Toxic Tech* (New York: W. W. Norton, 2017), 141.

25. See Bisha K. Ali on Twitter/X, announcing that she is "so tired of the 5 million podcasts by all white men" attacking her and other women of color. And see conservative backlash against this writer, calling her a "raging feminist," as in the video by Douglas Ernest, "Bisha K. Ali, Ms. Marvel showrunner, deletes 5K tweets in a blink." Some 8,400 watch his video. https://youtu.be/XiFoqMWsGcY.

26. Roman Gerodimos, "Reclaiming the Urban Landscape, Rebuilding the Civic Culture: Online Mobilization, Community Building, and Public Space in Athens, Greece," in *Mediated Communities: Civic Voices, Empowerment, and Media Literacy in the Digital Era*, ed. Moses Shumov (New York: Peter Lang, 2015), 108.

27. Mahmood Mamdani, *Neither Settler nor Native: The Making and Unmaking of Permanent Minorities* (Cambridge: Belknap Press, 2020), 95. In Mamdani's analysis of white policies, his distinction is that "Blacks have been sources of labor, and Indians sources of land" (95).

28. Shepard Fairey, interview with Edward Helmore, "Munira Ahmed: The Woman Who Became the Face of the Trump Resistance," *The Guardian*, January 23, 2017, accessed January 7, 2021, https://www.theguardian.com/us-news/2017/jan/23/womens-march -poster-munira-ahmed-shepard-fairey-interview. Subsequent references in text.

29. Michelle Garcia, "Meet the Muslim Woman Who's Become the Face of Anti-Trump Resistance," VOX, February 10, 2017, accessed January 3, 2022, https://www.vox.com/identities /2017/2/10/14508820/muslim-poster-protest-munira-ahmed-ridwan-adhami-shepard-fairey

30. See also documentation of this backlash in Lori Peek's *Behind the Backlash: Muslim Americans after 9/11* (Philadelphia: Temple University Press, 2011).

31. Rob Frehse and Amir Vera, "A Man Was Charged with Hate Crimes for Attacks on Muslims in New York City," CNN, July 29, 2021, accessed September 22, 2021, https://www .msn.com/en-us/news/crime/a-man-was-charged-with-hate-crimes-for-attacks-on -muslims-in-new-york-city/ar-AAMGKji.

32. Munira Ahmed, interview in The Young Turks, "Meet the Face of the Resistance," *Facebook*, February 23, 2020, https://www.bing.com/videos/search?q=munira+ahmed&do cid=608046972738493995&mid=21742B4E4F24513098A821742B4E4F24513098A8&view =detail&FORM=VIRE." Subsequent quotes in text.

33. Ridwan Adhami, TEDxTysons—Creating Art with Purpose and Patience, August 11, 2017, accessed September 22, 2021, https://www.ridwanadhami.com/#5. Subsequent references in text.

34. Ridwan Adhami, interview with Edward Helmore, "Munira Ahmed: The Woman Who Became the Face of the Trump Resistance," *The Guardian*, January 23, 2017, accessed January 7, 2021, https://www.theguardian.com/us-news/2017/jan/23/womens-march -poster-munira-ahmed-shepard-fairey-interview. Subsequent references in text.

35. Anne Anlin Cheng, *The Melancholy of Race: Psychoanalysis, Assimilation, and Hidden Grief* (New York: Oxford University Press, 2001), 10.

36. Ranjana Khanna, *Dark Continents: Psychoanalysis and Colonialism* (Durham, NC: Duke University Press, 2003), 11, 166.

37. Khanna, *Dark Continents*, 23–24.

38. Molly McCluskey, "Inaugural Protest Poster Stirs Debate among Muslim American Women," Middle East Eye, January 20, 2017, accessed September 21, 2021. Subsequent quotes in text. https://www.middleeasteye.net/news/inaugural-protest-poster-stirs-debate -among-muslim-american-women.

39. Elora Shehabuddin, *Sisters in the Mirror: A History of Muslim Women and the Global Politics of Feminism* (Oakland: University of California Press, 2021), 283.

40. Shehabuddin, *Sisters in the Mirror*, 283. See also Mahmood Mamdani, *Good Muslim, Bad Muslim: America, the Cold War, and the Roots of Terror* (New York: Pantheon, 2004); Nadine Naber, "Introduction: Arab Americans and U.S. Racial Formations," in *Race and Arab Americans before and after 9/11: From Invisible Citizens to Visible Subjects*, ed. Amaney Jamal and Nadine Naber (Syracuse, NY: Syracuse University Press, 2008).

41. Carol Fadda-Conrey, *Contemporary Arab-American Literature: Transnational Reconfigurations of Citizenship and Belonging* (New York: New York University Press, 2014), 154–55.

42. Heidi Safia Mirza, "A Second Skin: Embodied Intersectionality, Transnationalism, and Narratives of Identity and Belonging among Muslim Women in Britain," in *Feminist and Queer Theory: An Intersectional and Transnational Reader*, ed. L. Ayu Saraswati and Barbara Shaw (New York: Oxford University Press, 2021), 314.

43. McCluskey, "Inaugural Protest Poster."

44. McCluskey, "Inaugural Protest Poster."

45. Sasha Lekach, "The Woman in the Iconic Shepard Fairey Poster Was at the Women's March," Mashable, January 23, 2017, accessed September 22, 2017, https://mashable.com /article/inauguration-womens-march-poster-woman.

46. Shehabuddin, *Sisters in the Mirror*, 283. Subsequent quotes from this page.

47. Shehabuddin, *Sisters in the Mirror*, 283.

48. "Munira Ahmed Marches for Women's Rights." *Facebook*, accessed September 22, 2021, https://www.bing.com/videos/search?q=munira+ahmed+facebook&&view=detail& mid=2375833D927D1C9BE0092375833D927D1C9BE009&&FORM=VRDGAR&ru=%2Fvi deos%2Fsearch%3Fq%3Dmunira%2Bahmed%2Bfacebook%26FORM%3DHDRSC3.

49. Catherine Ramirez, *Assimilation: An Alternative History* (Berkeley: University of California Press, 2020), 9.

50. Ramirez, *Assimilation*, 14.

51. Ramirez, *Assimilation*, 11, 3.

52. Munira Ahmed, Facebook, January 20, 2017, accessed January 7, 2022. https://www .facebook.com/photo/?fbid=10154824619910586&set=ecnf.694620585.

53. Munira Ahmed, "Face of Resistance," directed and produced by Amina Chaudary, Tim Media Production, ArcDocs, accessed August 1, 2023. https://www.youtube.com /watch?v=jrSdsb5E0C8.

54. Sasha Lekach, "The Woman in the Iconic Shepard Fairey Poster was at the Women's March," Mashable, January 23, 2017, accessed September 22, 2017, https://mashable.com /article/inauguration-womens-march-poster-woman.

55. Amani Al-Khatahtbeh, *Muslim Girl: A Coming of Age* (New York: Simon & Schuster, 2016).

56. Shehabuddin, *Sisters in the Mirror*, 285.

57. Jude Gardner, "Women's March Official Poster 2017," *REDBUBBLE*, accessed August 15, 2020, https://www.redbubble.com/i/poster/Women-s-March-Official-Poster-2017-HD -by-judegardner/25919169.LVTDI.

58. Diana Taylor, *The Archive and the Repertoire: Performing Cultural Memory in the Americas* (Durham, NC: Duke University Press, 2003), xviii–xix.

59. Taylor, *Archive and the Repertoire*, xvii.

60. Ridwan Adhami, Twitter/X, January 19, 2017, accessed November 17, 2021.

61. Hannan Adely, "'This Is What It Feels Like': NJ Muslim Candidate, Media Figure Recounts Death Threat," NorthJersey.com, April 22, 2020, accessed January 7, 2021, https:// www.northjersey.com/story/news/new-jersey/2020/04/22/muslimgirl-founder-con gressional-candidate-shares-racist-death-threat/3005319001.

62. Bernard Harcourt, *Exposed: Desire and Disobedience in the Digital Age* (Cambridge: Harvard University Press, 2015), 109–10.

63. Aamina Mohamed, editor, producer, screenwriter, post on Instagram in #MGArmy, July 31, 2020. See also Nena Beecham, "#BlackoutEid: Celebrating Being Black and Muslim," *Al Jazeera*, June 4, 2019, accessed October 2, 2020, https://www.aljazeera.com /opinions/2019/6/4/blackouteid-celebrating-being-black-and-muslim.

64. Della Pollock, *Telling Bodies, Performing Birth* (New York: Columbia University Press, 1999), 8.

65. Author's transcript, "Unapologetically US—Building Muslim Power for 2020 and Beyond," CAIR fundraising event, Seattle, Washington, May 25, 2019.

66. Ilhan Omar, *This Is What America Looks Like: My Journey from Refugee to Congresswoman* (New York: Dey Street, 2020).

67. Yet another insulting comment on this "Captain Anti-American" site urges her to return to Somalia. A wide range of these attacks center on the supposed "cult of Islam" and the "inhumane chains" that shackle Muslim women, repeated propaganda that has flourished in this empire of sexual fetishism.

68. "AIPAC Doubles Down on Ad about US Rep. Omar," *AL-Monitor*, August 13, 2021, accessed January 6, 2021, https://www.al-monitor.com/originals/2021/08/aipac-doubles -down-ad-about-us-rep-omar.

69. ABC Religion and Ethics Report, cited in Alejandra Molina, "Ilhan Omar, Rashida Tlaib Denounce Facebook as Complicit in Anti-Muslim Violence," RNS: Religion News Service, October 22, 2020, accessed November 17, 2020, https://christiannewsnow.com /ilhan-omar-rashida-tlaib-denounce-facebook-as-complicit-in-anti-muslim-violence.

70. Craig Timberg, "Twitter Fueled Attacks on Muslim Candidates in 2018, Study Finds," *Washington Post*, November 4, 2019, accessed November 6, 2021, https://www .washingtonpost.com/business/economy/twitter-fueled-attacks-on-muslim-candidates -in-2018-study-finds/2019/11/04/be0bf432-ff51-11e9-9518-1e76abc088b6_story.html

71. Duvall, "Becoming Celebrity Girl Activists," 2.

72. Sasha Constanza-Chock, *Out of the Shadows, into the Streets! Transmedia Organizing and the Immigration Rights Movement* (Cambridge, MA: MIT Press, 2014), 7.

73. Jackson, *#HashtagActivism*, 154. Authors distinguish active alliances with "performative allyship" of personalized "catharsis" and "coveted identity" (155).

74. Jackson, *#HashtagActivism*, 151.

75. Jackson, *#HashtagActivism*, 151.

76. Jackson, *#HashtagActivism*, 156.

77. Jackson, *#HashtagActivism*.

78. Segregation is virtual and physical. Danah Boyd, *It's Complicated: The Social Lives of Networked Teens* (New Haven: Yale University Press, 2014), 155.

79. Jackson, *#HashtagActivism*, 156.

80. Aneelah Afzali, "Intersectional Dialogue on Weaponizing Charges of Antisemitism," May 2, 2019, accessed August 31, 2021, https://www.facebook.com/events/5720.

81. Aneelah Afzali, interview with author, Seattle, Washington, February 15, 2020.

82. Sara Marsso, "*PODCAST*: Reading the Qur'an for Ourselves: *A Feminist Journey*," June 3, 2019, accessed January 7, 2022, https://www.musawah.org/blog/webinar-feminist -quest-for-quranic-justice-beauty-spiritual-care.

83. Farha Ghannam, *Live and Die like a Man: Gender Dynamics in Urban Egypt* (Stanford, CA: Stanford University Press, 2013), 10.

84. See Penny Coleman, *Rosie the Riveter: Women Working on the Home Front in World War II* (New York: Yearling, 1998).

85. Gayatri Gopinath, *Unruly Visions: The Aesthetic Practices of Queer Diaspora* (Durham, NC: Duke University Press, 2018), 160.

86. Stuart Hall, Jessica Evans, and Sean Nixon, eds. *Representation: Cultural Representations and Signifying Practices*, 2nd ed. (Los Angeles: Sage, 2013), xviii.

87. Fleetwood, *Racial Icons*, 3, 4.

88. See Kathryn Lofton, *Consuming Religion* (Chicago: University of Chicago Press, 2017), xii.

89. Zizi Papacharissi, *Affective Publics: Sentiment, Technology, and Politics* (Oxford: Oxford University Press, 2015), 4.

90. Papacharissi, *Affective Publics*, 25.

91. Juana María Rodríguez, *Sexual Futures, Queer Gestures, and Other Latina Longings* (New York: New York University Press, 2014), 1.

92. Gopinath, *Unruly Visions*, 21.

# BIBLIOGRAPHY

Abu-Lughod, Lila. *Do Muslim Women Need Saving?* Boston: Harvard University Press, 2015.

Adegbola, Oluseyi, Sherice Gearhart, and Janice Cho. "Reporting Bias in Coverage of Iran Protests by Global News Agencies." *International Journal of Press/Politics* 27, no. 1 (2022): 138–57. DOI: 10.1177/1940161220966948.

Afzal, Ahmed. *Lone Star Muslims: Transnational Lives in the South Asian Experience in Texas*. New York: New York University Press, 2015.

Ahmed, Leila. *A Quiet Revolution: The Veil's Resurgence from the Middle East to America*. New Haven: Yale University Press, 2011.

Ahmed, Leila. *Women and Gender in Islam: Historical Roots of a Modern Debate*. New Haven: Yale University Press, 1992.

Ahmed, Sara. *The Cultural Politics of Emotion*. New York: Routledge, 2014.

Ahmed, Sara. *Queer Phenomenology: Orientations, Objects, Others*. Durham, NC: Duke University Press, 2006.

Aidi, Hisham. *Rebel Music: Race, Empire, and the New Muslim Youth Culture*. New York: Vintage, 2014.

Al-Ali, Nadje, and Nicola Pratt. *What Kind of Liberation? Women and the Occupation of Iraq*. Berkeley: University of California Press, 2009.

Aldama, Frederick Luis, ed. "Multi-Cultural Comics Today: A Brief Introduction." In *Multicultural Comics: From Zap to Blue Beetle*, 1–26. Austin: University of Texas Press, 2010.

Al-Khatahtbeh, Amani. *Muslim Girl: A Coming of Age*. New York: Simon and Schuster, 2016.

Allan, Stuart, and Einar Thorsen. *Citizen Journalism: Global Perspectives*. New York: Peter Lang, 2009.

Allievi, Stefano. "Islam in the Public Space: Social Networks, Media and Neo-Communities." In *Muslim Networks and Transnational Communities in and across Europe*, edited by Stefano Allievi and Jorgen Nielsen, 1–27. Leiden, The Netherlands: Brill, 2003.

Al-Rawi, Ahmed. *Women's Activism and New Media in the Arab World*. Suny Press, 2020.

Alsultany, Evelyn. *Arabs and Muslims in the Media: Race and Representation after 9/11*. New York: New York University Press, 2012.

Amster, Ellen J. *Medicine and the Saints: Science, Islam, and the Colonial Encounter in Morocco, 1877–1956*. Austin: University of Texas Press, 2013.

Andrews, David L., ed. *Michael Jordan, Inc.: Corporate Sport, Media Culture, and Late Modern America*. Albany: State University of New York Press, 2001.

Arjana, Sophia Rose. *Veiled Superheroes: Islam, Feminism, and Popular Culture*. Lanham, MD: Lexington Books, 2018.

Asad, Talal. *Formations of the Secular: Christianity, Islam, and Modernity*. Stanford, CA: Stanford University Press, 2003.

Atton, Chris. *An Alternative Internet: Radical Media, Politics, and Creativity*. Edinburgh: Edinburgh University Press, 2004.

Austin, Erica, Rebecca Van de Vord, Bruce Pinkleton, and Evan Epstein. "Celebrity Endorsements and their Potential to Motivate Young Voters." *Mass Communication and Society* 11, no. 4 (2008): 420–36. DOI:10.1080/15205430701866600.

Austin, J. L. *How to Do Things with Words*. Cambridge: Harvard University Press, 1975.

Bailey, Marlon. *Butch Queens up in Pumps*. Ann Arbor: University of Michigan Press, 2013.

Bailey, Moya. *Misogynoir Transformed: Black Women's Digital Resistance*. New York: New York University Press, 2021.

Baker, Mona, and Bolette Blaagaard. "Reconceptualizing Citizen Media: A Preliminary Charting of a Complex Domain." In *Citizen Media and Public Spaces: Diverse Expressions of Citizenship and Dissent*, edited by Mona Baker and Bolette Blaagaard, 1–28. London: Routledge, 2016.

Baldanzi, Jessica, and Hussein Rashid, eds. *Ms. Marvel's America: No Normal*. Jackson: University Press of Mississippi, 2020.

Beller, Jonathan. *The Cinematic Mode of Production: Attention Economy and the Society of the Spectacle*. Lebanon, NH: University Press of New England, 2006.

Benjamin, Ruha. *Race after Technology*. Cambridge: Polity, 2019.

Benjamin, Walter. "The Work of Art in the Age of Mechanical Reproduction." In *Illuminations*, edited by Hannah Arendt, translated by Harry Zohn. New York: Schocken Books, 1969.

Bennett, W. Lance, Regina Lawrence, and Steven Livingston. *When the Press Fails: Political Power and the News Media from Iraq to Katrina*. Chicago: University of Chicago Press, 2007.

Berlant, Lauren. *The Anatomy of National Fantasy: Hawthorne, Utopia, and Everyday Life*. Chicago: University of Chicago Press, 1991.

Berlant, Lauren. *The Female Complaint: The Unfinished Business of Sentimentality in American Culture*. Durham, NC: Duke University Press, 2008.

Birchall, Clare. *Radical Secrecy: The Ends of Transparency in Datafied America*. Minneapolis: University of Minnesota Press, 2021.

Bolter, Jay David, and Richard Grusin. *Remediation: Understanding New Media*. Cambridge, MA: MIT Press, 1999.

Boyd, Danah. *It's Complicated: The Social Lives of Networked Teens*. New Haven: Yale University Press, 2014.

Brown, Elspeth. *Work! A Queer History of Modeling*. Durham, NC: Duke University Press, 2019.

Brown, Jeffrey. *Dangerous Curves: Action Heroines, Gender Fetishism, and Popular Culture*. Jackson: University Press of Mississippi, 2011.

Bucar, Elizabeth. *Pious Fashion: How Muslim Women Dress*. Cambridge: Harvard University Press, 2017.

Butler, Judith. *Notes toward a Performative Theory of Assembly*. Cambridge: Harvard University Press, 2015.

Cahn, Susan. *Coming on Strong: Gender and Sexuality in Twentieth-Century Women's Sport*. 2nd ed. Urbana: University of Illinois Press, 1994.

Cainkar, Louise. "American Muslims at the Dawn of the 21st Century: Hope and Pessimism in the Drive for Civic and Public Inclusion." In *Muslims in the West after 9/11: Religion, Politics, and Law*, edited by Jocelyne Cesair, 176–97. New York: Routledge, 2010.

Cainkar, Louise. *Homeland Insecurity: The Arab American and Muslim American Experience after 9/11*. New York: Russell Sage Foundation, 2009.

Cainkar, Louise. "Islamic Revival among Second-Generation Arab-Americans: The American Experience and Globalization Intersect." *Bulletin of the Royal Institute for Inter-faith Studies* 6, no. 2 (2004): 99–120.

Cainkar, Louise. "Thinking outside the Box: Arabs and Race in the United States." In *Race and Arab Americans before and after 9/11: From Invisible Citizens to Visible Subjects*, edited by Amaney Jamal and Nadine Naber, 46-80. Syracuse, NY: Syracuse University Press, 2008.

Carrington, Ben. *Race, Sport, and Politics: The Sporting Black Diaspora*. Thousand Oaks, CA: Sage, 2010.

Castells, Manuel. *Networks of Outrage and Hope: Social Movements in the Internet Age*. Malden, MA: Polity Press, 2015.

Chan-Malik, Sylvia. *Being Muslim: A Cultural History of Women of Color in American Islam*. New York: New York University Press, 2018.

Cheng, Anne Anlin. *The Melancholy of Race: Psychoanalysis, Assimilation, and Hidden Grief*. New York: Oxford University Press, 2001.

Chuh, Kandice. *Imagine Otherwise: On Asian Americanist Critique*. Durham, NC: Duke University Press, 2003.

Chun, Wendy Hui Kyong. *Updating to Remain the Same: Habitual New Media*. Cambridge, MA: MIT Press, 2017.

Cink, Lorraine. *Powers of a Girl: 65 Marvel Women Who Punched the Sky and Changed the Universe*. Illustrated by Alice Zhang. Los Angeles: Marvel, 2019.

Cole, C. L., and David Andrews. "America's New Son: Tiger Woods and America's Multiculturalism." In *Sports Stars: The Cultural Politics of Sporting Celebrity*, edited by David L. Andrews and Steven J. Jackson, 70–87. London: Routledge, 2001.

Coleman, Penny. *Rosie the Riveter: Women Working on the Home Front in World War II*. New York: Yearling, 1998.

Condren, Mary. *The Serpent and the Goddess: Women, Religion, and Power in Celtic Ireland*. San Francisco: Harper and Row, 1989.

Constanza-Chock, Sasha. *Out of the Shadows, into the Streets! Transmedia Organizing and the Immigration Rights Movement*. Cambridge, MA: MIT Press, 2014.

cooke, miriam. *Women Claim Islam: Creating Islamic Feminism through Literature*. New York: Routledge, 2001.

Crenshaw, Kimberlé. "Demarginalizing the Intersection of Race and Sex: A Black Feminist Critique of Antidiscrimination Doctrine, Feminist Theory and Antiracist Politics." In *Feminist and Queer Theory: An Intersectional and Transnational Reader*, edited by L. Ayu Saraswati and Barbara Shaw, 141–49. New York: Oxford University Press, 2021.

Croft, Clare, ed. "Introduction." *Queer Dance: Meanings and Makings*, 1–36. New York: Oxford University Press, 2017.

Cvetkovich, Ann. *An Archive of Feelings: Trauma, Sexuality, and Lesbian Public Cultures.* Durham, NC: Duke University Press, 2003.

Davenport, Thomas, and John Beck. *The Attention Economy: Understanding the New Currency of Business.* Boston: Harvard Business Review Press, 2002.

Debord, Guy. *Society of the Spectacle.* Translated by Ken Knabb. London: Aldgate, 2006.

Deeb, Lara. *An Enchanted Modern: Gender and Public Piety in Shi'i Lebanon.* Princeton: Princeton University Press, 2006.

De Jesus, Melinda L. "Liminality and Mestiza Consciousness in Lynda Barry's One Hundred Demons." In *Multicultural Comics: From* Zap *to* Blue Beetle, edited by Frederick Luis Aldama, 73-92. Austin: University of Texas Press, 2010.

Deuze, Mark. "Participation, Remediation, Bricolage: Considering Principal Components of a Digital Culture." *Information Society* 22 (2006): 63–75. DOI: 10.1080/01972240600567170.

Dines, Gail, Jean Humez, Bill Yousman, and Lori Bindig Yousman, eds. *Gender, Race, and Class in Media.* 5th ed. Los Angeles: Sage, 2018.

Diour, Sylviane. *Servants of Allah: African Muslims Enslaved in the Americas.* New York: New York University Press, 2013.

DiPaolo, Marc. *War, Politics, and Superheroes: Ethics and Propaganda in Comics and Film.* Jefferson, NC: McFarland Press, 2011.

Djebar, Assia. *Fantasia: An Algerian Cavalcade.* London: Heinemann, 2003.

Downing, John. *Radical Media: Rebellious Communication and Social Movements.* Thousand Oaks, CA: Sage, 2001.

Du Bois, W. E. B. "A Negro Nation within the Nation (1934)." Black Past. March 13, 2012. Accessed April 6, 2022. https://www.blackpast.org/african-american-history /speeches-african-american-history/1934-w-e-b-du-bois-negro-nation-within-nation/.

Du Bois, W. E. B. *The Souls of Black Folk.* Mineola, NY: Dover, 1994.

Duvall, Spring. "Becoming Celebrity Girl Activists: The Cultural Politics and Celebrification of Emma Gonzalez, Marley Dias, and Greta Thunberg." *Journal of Communication Inquiry* (August 24, 2022): 1–21. DOI: 10.1177/01968599221120057.

Duvall, Spring-Serenity, and Nicole Heckemeyer. "#BlackLivesMatter: Black Celebrity Hashtag Activism and the Discursive Formation of a Social Movement." *Celebrity Studies* 9, no. 3 (2018): 391–408. https://doi.org/10.1080/19392397.2018.144024404.

Dworkin, Shari, and Michael Messner. "Just Do . . . What? Sport, Bodies, Gender." In *Gender and Sport: A Reader*, edited by Sheila Scraton and Anne Flintoff, 17–29. London: Routledge, 2002.

El-Ariss, Tarek. *Leaks, Hacks, and Scandals: Arab Culture in the Digital Age.* Princeton: Princeton University Press, 2019.

El Guindi, Fadwa. *Veil: Modesty, Privacy, and Resistance.* Oxford: Berg, 1999.

Entman, Robert M. *Projections of Power: Framing News, Public Opinion, and U.S. Foreign Policy*. Chicago: University of Chicago Press, 2004.

Espinoza, Mauricio. "The Alien Is Here to Stay: Otherness, Anti-assimilation, and Empowerment in Latino/a Superhero Comics." In *Graphic Borders: Latino Comic Books Past, Present, and Future*, edited by Frederick Luis Aldama and Christopher Gonzalez, 181–202. Austin: University of Texas Press, 2016.

Fadda-Conrey, Carol. *Contemporary Arab-American Literature: Transnational Reconfigurations of Citizenship and Belonging*. New York: New York University Press, 2014.

Farris, Sara. *In the Name of Women's Rights: The Rise of Femonationalism*. Durham, NC: Duke University Press Books, 2017.

Fawaz, Ramzi. *The New Mutants: Superheroes and the Radical Imagination of American Comics*. New York: New York University Press, 2016.

Fawaz, Ramzi, Shelley Streeby, and Deborah Elizabeth Whaley, eds. *Keywords for Comics Studies*. New York: New York University Press, 2021.

Fenton, Natalie. *Digital. Political. Radical.* John Wiley & Sons, 2016.

Fenton, Natalie. "Left Out? Digital Media, Radical Politics and Social Change." *Information Communication and Society* 19, no. 3 (2015): 346–61. DOI:10.1080/13691 18X.2015.1109698.

Ferguson, Roderick. *Aberrations in Black: Toward a Queer of Color Critique*. Minneapolis: University of Minnesota Press, 2004.

Fernandes, Leela. *Trans-national Feminism in the United States: Knowledge, Ethics, Power*. New York: New York University Press, 2013.

Fleetwood, Nicole. *On Racial Icons: Blackness and the Public Imagination*. New Brunswick, NJ: Rutgers University Press, 2015.

Fleetwood, Nicole. *Troubling Vision: Performance, Visuality, and Blackness*. Chicago: University of Chicago Press, 2011.

Gateward, Frances, and John Jennings. "Introduction: The Sweeter the Christmas." In *The Blacker the Ink: Constructions of Black Identity in Comics and Sequential Art*, edited by Frances Gateward and John Jennings, 1–18. New Brunswick, NJ: Rutgers University Press, 2015.

Gerodimos, Roman. "Reclaiming the Urban Landscape, Rebuilding the Civic Culture: Online Mobilization, Community Building, and Public Space in Athens, Greece." In *Mediated Communities: Civic Voices, Empowerment, and Media Literacy in the Digital Era*, edited by Moses Shumov, 93–113. New York: Peter Lang, 2015.

Ghannam, Farha. *Live and Die like a Man: Gender Dynamics in Urban Egypt*. Stanford, CA: Stanford University Press, 2013.

Gibson, Mel. "Yeah, I Think There Is Still Hope: Youth, Ethnicity, Faith, Feminism, and Fandom in Ms. Marvel." In *Gender and the Superhero Narrative*, edited by Michael Goodrum, Tara Prescott, and Philip Smith, 23–44. Jackson: University Press of Mississippi, 2018.

Gilroy, Paul. *The Black Atlantic: Modernity and Double Consciousness*. Cambridge: Harvard University Press, 1993.

Gluck, Sherna Berger. *Rosie the Riveter Revisited: Women, the War, and Social Change*. Boston: Twayne, 1987.

Göle, Nilüfer. *The Forbidden Modern: Civilization and Veiling*. Ann Arbor: University of Michigan Press, 1996.

Goodman, Michael. "Celebrity Politics, Neoliberal Sustainabilities, and the Terrains of Care." In *Age of Icons: Exploring Philanthrocapitalism in the Contemporary World*, edited by Gavin Fridell and Martijn Konings, 72–92. Toronto: University of Toronto Press, 2013.

Gopinath, Gayatri. *Unruly Visions: The Aesthetic Practices of Queer Diaspora*. Durham, NC: Duke University Press, 2018.

Gray, Kishonna. *Intersectional Tech: Black Users in Digital Gaming*. Baton Rouge: LSU Press, 2020.

Gualtieri, Sarah. *Arab Routes: Pathways to Syrian California*. Stanford, CA: Stanford University Press, 2020.

Gualtieri, Sarah. *Between Arab and White: Race and Ethnicity in the Early Syrian American Diaspora*. Berkeley: University of California Press, 2009.

Gualtieri, Sarah. "Strange Fruit? Syrian Immigrants, Extralegal Violence and Racial Formation in the Jim Crow South." *Arab Studies Quarterly* 26, no. 3 (2004): 63–85.

Haddad, Yvonne Yazbeck, Jane Smith, and Kathleen Moore. *Muslim Women in America: The Challenge of Islamic Identity Today*. Oxford: Oxford University Press, 2006.

Hafez, Sherine. *An Islam of Her Own: Reconsidering Religion and Secularism in Women's Islamic Movements*. New York: New York University Press, 2011.

Halberstam, Jack. *In a Queer Time and Place: Transgender Bodies, Subcultural Lives*. New York: New York University Press, 2005.

Halberstam, Jack. *The Queer Art of Failure*. Durham, NC: Duke University Press, 2011.

Halbwachs, Maurice. *On Collective Memory*. Edited and translated by Lewis Coser. Chicago: University of Chicago Press, 1992.

Hall, Stuart, Jessica Evans, and Sean Nixon, eds. *Representation: Cultural Representations and Signifying Practices*. 2nd ed. Los Angeles: Sage, 2013.

Hamdy, Naila. "Arab Citizen Journalism in Action: Challenging Mainstream Media, Authorities and Media Laws." *Westminster Papers in Communication and Culture* 6, no. 1 (2009): 92–112.

Haney-Lopez, Ian. *White by Law: The Legal Construction of Race*. New York: New York University Press, 1996.

Harcourt, Bernard. *Exposed: Desire and Disobedience in the Digital Age*. Cambridge: Harvard University Press, 2015.

Hariman, Robert, and John Louis Lucaites. *No Caption Needed: Iconic Photographs, Public Culture, and Liberal Democracy*. Chicago: University of Chicago Press, 2007.

Hartman, Michelle. *Breaking Broken English: Black-Arab Literary Solidarities and the Politics of Language*. Syracuse, NY: Syracuse University Press, 2019.

Hillis, Ken, Susanna Paasonen, and Michael Petit. "Introduction: Networks of Transmission, Intensity, Sensation, Value." In *Networked Affect*, edited by Ken Hillis, Susanna Paasonen, and Michael Petit, 1–26. Cambridge, MA: MIT Press, 2015.

Holliday, Ruth. "(Dis)Comforting Identities." In *Pleasure Zones: Bodies, Cities, Spaces*, edited by David Bell, Jon Binnie, Ruth Holliday, Robyn Longhurst, and Robin Peace, 55–83. Syracuse, NY: Syracuse University Press, 2001.

Honey, Maureen. *Creating Rosie the Riveter: Class, Gender and Propaganda during World War II*. Boston: University of Massachusetts Press, 1984.

Hui, Yuk. *On the Existence of Digital Objects*. Minneapolis: University of Minnesota Press, 2016.

Imani, Blair. *Modern HERStory: Stories of Women and Nonbinary People Rewriting History*. Berkeley, CA: Ten Speed Press, 2018.

Imani, Blair. *Read This to Get Smarter: About Race, Class, Gender, Disability & More*. Berkeley, CA: Ten Speed Press, 2021.

Jackson, Sarah, Moya Bailey, and Brooke Foucault Welles. *#Hashtag Activism: Networks of Race and Gender Justice*. Cambridge, MA: MIT Press, 2020.

Jamal, Amaney, and Nadine Naber, eds. *Race and Arab Americans before and after 9/11: From Invisible Citizens to Visible Subjects*. Syracuse, NY: Syracuse University Press, 2008.

Jenkins, Henry. *Comics and Stuff*. New York: New York University Press, 2020.

Kahf, Mohja. *Western Representations of the Muslim Woman: From Termagant to Odalisque*. Austin: University of Texas Press, 1999.

Kapchan, Deborah. *Gender on the Market: Moroccan Women and the Revoicing of Tradition*. Philadelphia: University of Pennsylvania Press, 1996.

Katznelson, Ira. *When Affirmative Action Was White: The Untold History of Racial Inequality in Twentieth-Century America*. New York. W. W. Norton, 2005.

Kellner, Douglas. "The Sports Spectacle, Michael Jordan, and Nike: Unholy Alliance?" In *Michael Jordan, Inc.: Corporate Sport, Media Culture, and Late Modern America*, edited by David L. Andrews, 37–64. Albany: State University of New York Press, 2001.

Khabeer, Su'ad Abdul. *Muslim Cool: Race, Religion, and Hip Hop in the United States*. New York: New York University Press, 2016.

Khanna, Ranjana. *Dark Continents: Psychoanalysis and Colonialism*. Durham, NC: Duke University Press, 2003.

Khiabany, Gholam. *Iranian Media: The Paradox of Modernity*. New York: Routledge, 2010.

Khubchandani, Kareem. *Ishtyle: Accenting Gay Indian Nightlife*. Ann Arbor: University of Michigan Press, 2020.

Lagerkvist, Amanda, ed. *Digital Existence: Ontology, Ethics, & Transcendence in Digital Culture*. New York: Routledge, 2019.

Lalami, Laila. *Conditional Citizens: On Belonging in America*. New York: Pantheon Books, 2020.

Lalami, Laila. *The Moor's Account: A Lost Narrative*. New York: Pantheon Books, 2014.

Langlois, Ganaele. *Meaning in the Age of Social Media*. New York: Palgrave, 2014.

Langlois, Ganaele. "Social Media and the Care of the Self." In *Digital Existence: Ontology, Ethics, & Transcendence in Digital Culture*, edited by Amanda Lagerkvist, 56–170. New York: Routledge, 2019.

Lawrence, Charles. "The Id, the Ego, and Equal Protection Reckoning with Unconscious Racism." In *Critical Race Theory: The Key Writings that Formed the Movement*, edited by Kimberlé Crenshaw, Neil Gotanda, Gary Peller, and Kendall Thomas, 235–56. New York: New Press, 1995.

Lepore, Jill. *The Secret History of Wonder Woman*. New York: Vintage, 2015.

Lewis, Bernard. *Cultures in Conflict: Christians, Muslims, and Jews in the Age of Discovery.* Oxford: Oxford University Press, 1996.

Lofton, Kathryn. *Consuming Religion.* Chicago: University of Chicago Press, 2017.

Lorde, Audre. *Sister Outsider: Essays and Speeches.* Trumansburg, NY: Crossing Press, 1984.

Lund, Martin. "Placing Ms. Marvel and Dust: Marvel Comics, the New York Metro Area, and the 'Muslim Problem.'" In *Ms. Marvel's America: No Normal,* edited by Jessica Baldanzi and Hussein Rashid, 21–46. Jackson: University Press of Mississippi, 2020.

Lynch, Marc. "Blogging the New Arab Republic." *Arab Media & Society,* February 2007. http://www.arabmediasociety.com/topics/index.php?t_article=32.

Maghbouleh, Neda. *The Limits of Whiteness: Iranian Americans and the Everyday Politics of Race.* Stanford, CA: Stanford University Press, 2017.

Magubane, Zine. *Bringing the Empire Home: Race, Class, and Gender in Britain and Colonial South Africa.* Chicago: University of Chicago Press, 2004.

Mahlouly, Dounia, Dina Matar, Zahera Harb, eds. *Digital Political Cultures in the Middle East since the Arab Uprisings: Online Activism in Egypt, Tunisia and Lebanon.* New York: I. B. Tauris, 2023.

Mahmood, Saba. *The Politics of Piety: The Islamic Revival and the Feminist Subject.* Princeton: Princeton University Press, 2005.

Maira, Sunaina Marr. *Missing: Youth, Citizenship, and Empire after 9/11.* Durham, NC: Duke University Press, 2009.

Majaj, Lisa Suhair. "Arab-American Ethnicity: Locations, Coalitions and Cultural Negotiations." In *Arabs in America: Building a New Future,* edited by Michael Suleiman, 321–36. Philadelphia: Temple University Press, 1999.

Majaj, Lisa Suhair. "Arab Americans and the Meaning of Race." In *Postcolonial Theory and the United States: Race, Ethnicity, and Literature,* edited by Amaritjit Singh and Peter Schmidt, 320–37. Jackson: University Press of Mississippi, 2000.

Malkowski, Jennifer. "'I Turned Out to Be Such a Damsel in Distress': Noir Games and the Unrealized *Femme Fatale.*" In *Gaming Representation: Race, Gender, and Sexuality in Video Games,* edited by Jennifer Malkowski and TreaAndrea Russworm, 19–37. Bloomington: Indiana University Press, 2017.

Mamdani, Mahmood. *Good Muslim, Bad Muslim: America, the Cold War, and the Roots of Terror.* New York: Pantheon, 2004.

Mamdani, Mahmood. *Neither Settler nor Native: The Making and Unmaking of Permanent Minorities.* Cambridge: Belknap Press, 2020.

Marshall, Paul, Lela Gilbert, and Roberta Green Ahmanson, eds. *Blind Spot: When Journalists Don't Get Religion.* Oxford: Oxford University Press, 2009.

Massumi, Brian. *Parables for the Virtual: Movement, Affect, Sensation.* Durham, NC: Duke University Press, 2002.

Mayol, Pierre. "The Neighborhood." In *The Practice of Everyday Life: Living and Cooking,* edited by Luce Girard, 2:7–15. Minneapolis: University of Minnesota Press, 1998.

McClintock, Anne. "'No Longer in a Future Heaven': Gender, Race and Nationalism." In *Dangerous Liaisons: Gender, Nation, and Postcolonial Perspectives,* edited by Anne McClintock, Aamir Mufti, and Ella Shohat, 89–112. Minneapolis: University of Minnesota Press, 1997.

McCloud, Scott. *Understanding Comics*. New York: Harper Perennial, 1994.

Melamed, Jodi. *Represent and Destroy: Rationalizing Violence in the New Racial Capitalism*. Minneapolis: University of Minnesota Press, 2011.

Mernissi, Fatema. *Scheherazade Goes West: Different Cultures, Different Harems*. New York: Washington Square Press, 2001.

Miller, Toby. "A Distorted Playing Field: Neoliberalism and Sport through the Lens of Economic Citizenship." In *Sport and Neoliberalism: Politics, Consumption, and Culture*, edited by David L. Andrews and Michael L. Silk, 23–37. Philadelphia: Temple University Press, 2012.

Mirza, Heidi Safia. "A Second Skin: Embodied Intersectionality, Transnationalism, and Narratives of Identity and Belonging among Muslim Women in Britain." In *Feminist and Queer Theory: An Intersectional and Transnational Reader*, edited by L. Ayu Saraswati and Barbara Shaw, 314–29. New York: Oxford University Press, 2021.

Molina, Natalia. *How Race Is Made in America: Immigration, Citizenship, and the Historical Power of Racial Scripts*. Berkeley: University of California Press, 2014.

Monshipouri, Mahmood, ed. "Introduction: Protests and Human Rights in Context." In *Information Politics, Protests, and Human Rights in the Digital Age*, 1–20. Cambridge: Cambridge University Press, 2016.

Muhammad, Ibtihaj. *Proud: My Fight for an Unlikely Dream*. With Lori Tharps. New York: Hachette Books, 2018.

Mulvey, Laura. "Visual Pleasure and Narrative Cinema." In *Film Theory and Criticism*, 6th ed., edited by Leo Braudy and Marshall Cohen, 837–48. New York: Oxford University Press, 2004.

Muñoz, José Esteban. *Cruising Utopia: The Then and There of Queer Futurity*. New York: New York University Press, 2009.

Muñoz, José Esteban. *Disidentifications: Queers of Color and the Performance of Politics*. Minneapolis: University of Minnesota Press, 1999.

Naber, Nadine. *Arab America: Gender, Cultural Politics, and Activism*. New York: New York University Press, 2012.

Naber, Nadine. "Introduction: Arab Americans and U.S. Racial Formations." In *Race and Arab Americans before and after 9/11: From Invisible Citizens to Visible Subjects*, edited by Amaney Jamal and Nadine Naber, 1-45. Syracuse, NY: Syracuse University Press, 2008.

Nadal, Kevin. *Microaggressions and Traumatic Stress: Theory, Research, and Clinical Treatment*. Washington, DC: American Psychological Association, 2018.

Nadal, Kevin, Katie Griffin, Sahran Hamit, Jayleen Leon, Michael Tobio, and David Rivera. "Subtle and Overt Forms of Islamophobia: Microaggressions toward Muslim Americans." *Journal of Muslim Mental Health* 6, no. 2 (2012): 16–37. https://academic works.cuny.edu/cgi/viewcontent.cgi?article=1314&context=gc_pubs.

Nadal, Kevin, Marie-Anne Issa, Katie E. Griffin, Sahran Hamit, and Oliver B. Lyons. "Religious Microaggressions in the United States: Mental Health Implications for Religious Minority Groups." In *Microaggressions and Marginality*, edited by Derald Wing Sue, 287–312. Hoboken, NJ: John Wiley & Sons, 2010.

Nakamura, Lisa. "Afterward: Racism, Sexism, and Gaming's Cruel Optimism." In *Gaming Representation: Race, Gender, and Sexuality in Video Games*, edited by Jennifer

Malkowski and TreaAndrea Russworm, 245–50. Bloomington: Indiana University Press, 2017.

Nakamura, Lisa. *Cybertypes: Race, Ethnicity, and Identity on the Internet*. New York: Routledge, 2002.

Negroponte, Nicholas. *Being Digital*. New York: Vintage Books, 1995.

Noble, Safiya Umoja. *Algorithms of Oppression: How Search Engines Reinforce Racism*. New York: New York University Press, 2018.

Omar, Ilhan. *This Is What America Looks Like: My Journey from Refugee to Congresswoman*. New York: Dey Street, 2020.

Ong, Aihwa. *Flexible Citizenship: The Cultural Logics of Trans-Nationality*. Durham, NC: Duke University Press, 1999.

Oyola, Osvaldo. "Seriality." In *Keywords for Comics Studies*, edited by Ramzi Fawaz, Shelley Streeby, and Deborah Elizabeth Whaley, 187–92. New York: New York University Press, 2021.

Papacharissi, Zizi. *Affective Publics: Sentiment, Technology, and Politics*. Oxford: Oxford University Press, 2015.

Papacharissi, Zizi, and Sharon Meraz. "Networked Gatekeeping and Networked Framing on #Egypt." *International Journal of Press/Politics* 18, no. 2 (2013): 138–66.

Patty, Lisa. "Entering the Picture: Digital Portraiture and the Aesthetics of Video Game Representation." In *Gaming Representation: Race, Gender, and Sexuality in Video Games*, edited by Jennifer Malkowski and TreaAndrea Russworm, 179–96. Bloomington: Indiana University Press, 2017.

Pavlik, John. *Journalism and New Media*. New York: Columbia University Press, 2001.

Peek, Lori. *Behind the Backlash: Muslim Americans after 9/11*. Philadelphia: Temple University Press, 2011.

Petersen, Robert. *Comics, Manga, and Graphic Novels: A History of Graphic Narratives*. Santa Barbara, CA: Praeger, 2011.

Pham, Minh-Ha. *Asians Wear Clothes on the Internet: Race, Gender, and the Work of Personal Style Blogging*. Durham, NC: Duke University Press, 2015.

Pickens, Theri. *New Body Politics: Narrating Arab and Black Identity in the Contemporary United States*. New York: Routledge, 2014.

Pollock, Della. *Telling Bodies, Performing Birth*. New York: Columbia University Press, 1999.

Pratt, Nicola. *Embodying Geopolitics: Generations of Women's Activism in Egypt, Jordan, and Lebanon*. Oakland: University of California Press, 2020.

Protevi, John. *Political Affect: Connecting the Social and the Somatic*. Minneapolis: University of Minnesota Press, 2009.

Puar, Jasbir. *Terrorist Assemblages: Homonationalism in Queer Times*. Durham, NC: Duke University Press, 2007.

Pybus, Jennifer. "Accumulating Affect: Social Networks and Their Archives of Feelings." In *Networked Affect*, edited by Ken Hillis, Susanna Paasonen, and Michael Petit, 235–50. Cambridge, MA: MIT Press, 2015.

Rai, Shirin, and Janelle Reinelt, eds. "Introduction." In *The Grammar of Politics and Performance*. London: Routledge, 2015.

Ramadan, Tariq. *Islam and the Arab Awakening*. Oxford: Oxford University Press, 2012.

Ramirez, Catherine. *Assimilation: An Alternative History*. Oakland: University of California Press, 2020.

Rana, Junaid. *Terrifying Muslims: Race and Labor in the South Asian Diaspora*. Durham, NC: Duke University Press, 2011.

Rancière, Jacques. *The Politics of Aesthetics: The Distribution of the Sensible*. Translated by Gabriel Rockhill. London: Bloomsbury, 2004.

Rashid, Hussein. "Ms. Marvel Is an Immigrant." In *Ms. Marvel's America: No Normal*, edited by Jessica Baldanzi and Hussein Rashid, 47–64. Jackson: University Press of Mississippi, 2020.

Reddy, Vanita. *Fashion Diaspora: Beauty, Femininity, and South Asian American Culture*. Philadelphia: Temple University Press, 2016.

Rinaldo, Rachel. *Mobilizing Piety: Islam and Feminism in Indonesia*. Oxford: Oxford University Press, 2013.

Rippy, Alyssa, and Elana Newman. "Perceived Religious Discrimination and Its Relationship to Anxiety and Paranoia among Muslim Americans." *Journal of Muslim Mental Health* 1, no. 1 (2006): 5–20.

Rodriguez, Clara. *Changing Race: Latinos, the Census, and the History of Ethnicity in the United States*. New York: New York University Press, 2000.

Rodríguez, Juana María. *Sexual Futures, Queer Gestures, and Other Latina Longings*. New York: New York University Press, 2014.

Rodriguez, Richard. *Brown: The Last Discovery of America*. New York: Viking Press, 2002.

Romano, Renee, and Leigh Raiford. "Introduction: The Struggle of Memory." In *The Civil Rights Movement in American Memory*, edited by Renee Romano and Leigh Raiford, xi–xxiv. Athens: University of Georgia Press, 2006.

Rose, Tricia. *The Hip Hop Wars: What We Talk about When We Talk about Hip Hop—and Why It Matters*. New York: Basic Books, 2008.

Rothstein, Richard. *The Color of Law: A Forgotten History of How Our Government Segregated America*. New York: W. W. Norton, 2017.

Rouse, Carolyn. *Engaged Surrender: African American Women and Islam*. Berkeley: University of California Press, 2004.

Ruberg, Bonnie. "Playing to Lose: The Queer Art of Failing at Video Games." In *Gaming Representation: Race, Gender, and Sexuality in Video Games*, edited by Jennifer Malkowski and TreaAndrea Russworm, 197–211. Bloomington: Indiana University Press, 2017.

Russworm, TreaAndrea. "Dystopian Blackness and the Limits of Racial Empathy in 'The Walking Dead' and 'The Last of Us.'" In *Gaming Representation: Race, Gender, and Sexuality in Video Games*, edited by Jennifer Malkowski and TreaAndrea Russworm, 109–28. Bloomington: Indiana University Press, 2017.

Said, Edward. *Covering Islam: How the Media and the Experts Determine How We See the Rest of the World*. New York: Vintage, 2015.

Said, Edward. *Culture and Imperialism*. New York: Vintage Press, 1994.

Saliba, Therese. "Resisting Invisibility: Arab Americans in Academia and Activism." In *Arabs in America: Building a New Future*, edited by Michael Suleiman, 304–19. Philadelphia: Temple University Press, 1999.

Samet, Elizabeth D. *Looking for the Good War: American Amnesia and the Violent Pursuit of Happiness*. New York: Picador, 2022.

Samhan, Helen Hatab. "Not Quite White: Race Classification and the Arab-American Experience." In *Arabs in America: Building a New Future*, edited by Michael Suleiman, 209–26. Philadelphia: Temple University Press, 1999.

Samie, Sumaya, and Kim Toffoletti. "Postfeminist Paradoxes and Cultural Difference: Unpacking Media Representations of American Muslim Sportswomen Ibtihaj and Dalilah Muhammad." In *New Sporting Femininities: Embodied Politics in Postfeminist Times*, edited by K. Toffoletti, Jessica Francombe-Webb, and Holly Thorpe, 87–110. Cham, Switzerland: Palgrave Macmillan, 2018.

Sanbonmatsu, John. "Video Games: Machine Dreams of Domination." In *Gender, Race, and Class in Media*, 5th ed., edited by Gail Dines, Jean Humez, Bill Yousman, and Lori Bindig Yousman, 413–27. Los Angeles: Sage, 2018.

Santos, Jorge. *Graphic Memories of the Civil Rights Movement: Reframing History in Comics*. Austin: University of Texas Press, 2019.

Saraswati, L. Ayu. *Pain Generation: Social Media, Feminist Activism, and the Neoliberal Selfie*. New York: New York University Press, 2021.

Schechner, Richard. *Performance Theory*. New York: Routledge, 2003.

Segall, Kimberly Wedeven. "Contestational Spaces and the Nervous Conditions of Postcolonial Theories." In *Teaching the African Novel*, edited by Gaurav Desai, 371–85. MLA Series. New York: Modern Language Association, 2009.

Segall, Kimberly Wedeven. "De-imperializing Gender: Political Revivals, Shifting Beliefs, and Unexpected Trajectories." *Journal of Middle Eastern Women's Studies* 15, no. 1 (2019): 75–94.

Segall, Kimberly Wedeven. "Media Sites: Political Revivals of American Muslim Women." In *The Oxford Handbook of Politics and Performance*, edited by Shirin Rai, Milija Gluhovic, Sivija Jestrovic, and Michael Saward, 235–50. New York: Oxford University Press, 2021.

Segall, Kimberly Wedeven. "Melancholy Ties: Intergenerational Loss and Political Exile in *Persepolis*." *Comparative Studies of South Asia, Africa, and the Middle East* 28, no. 1 (2008): 38–49.

Segall, Kimberly Wedeven. *Performing Democracy in Iraq and South Africa: Gender, Media, and Resistance*. Syracuse, NY: Syracuse University Press, 2013.

Shaban, Sara. *Iranian Feminism and Transnational Ethics in Media Discourse*. Lanham, MD: Lexington Books, 2022.

Shaheen, Jack. *Reel Bad Arabs: How Hollywood Vilifies a People*. Northampton, MA: Olive Branch Press, 2015.

Shaw, Adrienne. *Gaming at the Edge: Sexuality and Gender at the Margins of Gamer Culture*. Minneapolis: University of Minnesota Press, 2014.

Shehabuddin, Elora. *Sisters in the Mirror: A History of Muslim Women and the Global Politics of Feminism*. Oakland: University of California Press, 2021.

Sheridan, Lorraine. "Islamophobia Pre- and Post-September 11th, 2001." *Journal of Interpersonal Violence* 21, no. 3 (2006): 317–36.

Shimizu, Celine Parenas. *The Hypersexuality of Race: Performing Asian/American Women on Screen and Scene.* Durham, NC: Duke University Press, 2007.

Shumov, Moses. "Foreword: Developing Global Perspectives through Media Literacy and Civic Engagement." In *Mediated Communities: Civic Voices, Empowerment, and Media Literacy in the Digital Era,* edited by Moses Shumov, 1–13. New York: Peter Lang, 2015.

Silady, Matt. "Panel." In *Keywords for Comics Studies,* edited by Ramzi Fawaz, Shelley Streeby, and Deborah Elizabeth Whaley, 160–64. New York: New York University Press, 2021.

Smith, Jane. *Islam in America.* New York: Columbia University Press, 1999.

Smith, Linda Tuhiwai. *Decolonizing Methodologies: Research and Indigenous Peoples.* 2nd ed. London: Zed Books, 2012.

Spade, Dean. *Mutual Aid: Building Solidarity during This Crisis (and the Next).* New York: Verso Press, 2020.

Spivak, Gayatri. "Can the Subaltern Speak? Speculations on Widow Sacrifice." *Wedge* 7–8 (1985): 120–30.

Sreberny, Annabelle, and Gholam Khiabany. *Blogistan: The Internet and Politics in Iran.* New York: I. B. Taurus, 2010.

Stevens, Richard. "Mentoring Ms. Marvel: Marvel's Kamala Khan and the Reconstitution of Carol Danvers." In *Ms. Marvel's America: No Normal,* edited by Jessica Baldanzi and Hussein Rashid, 3–20. Jackson: University Press of Mississippi, 2020.

Sturken, Marita, and Lisa Cartwright. *Practices of Looking: An Introduction to Visual Culture.* 2nd ed. New York: Oxford University Press, 2009.

Sue, Derald Wing. "Microaggressions, Marginality, and Oppression: An Introduction." In *Microaggressions and Marginality: Manifestations, Dynamics, and Impact,* edited by Derald Wing Sue, 3–24. Hoboken, NJ: John Wiley & Sons, 2010.

Suleiman, Michael. "Introduction: The Arab Immigrant Experience." In *Arabs in America: Building a New Future,* edited by Michael Suleiman, 1–21. Philadelphia: Temple University Press, 1999.

Taft, Jessica. "Teenage Girls' Narratives of Becoming Activists." *Contemporary Social Science* 12, no. 1–2 (1999): 27–39.

Tarlo, Emma. *Visibly Muslim: Fashion, Politics, Faith.* Oxford: Berg, 2010.

Taylor, Diana. *The Archive and the Repertoire: Performing Cultural Memory in the Americas.* Durham, NC: Duke University Press, 2003.

Thangaraj, Stanley. *Desi Hoop Dreams: Pickup Basketball and the Making of Asian American Masculinity.* New York: New York University Press, 2015.

Thangaraj, Stanley. "Racing the Muslim: Strategies for Teaching Race and Ethnic Studies in the Education Curriculum." *Urban Education* 56, no. 7 (2021): 1042–66.

Tobin, Sarah. *Everyday Piety: Islam and Economy in Jordan.* Ithaca: Cornell University Press, 2016.

Tufekci, Zeynep. *Twitter and Tear Gas: The Power and Fragility of Networked Protest.* New Haven: Yale University Press, 2017.

Turkle, Sherry. *Life on the Screen: Identity in the Age of the Internet.* New York: Touchstone, 1995.

Turner, Victor. *From Ritual to Theatre: The Human Seriousness of Play*. New York: Performing Arts Journal Publications, 1982.

Tzanelli, Rodanthi. *Heritage in the Digital Era: Cinematic Tourism and the Activist Cause*. London: Routledge, 2013.

Ullah, Haroon. *Digital World War: Islamists, Extremists, and the Fight for Cyber Supremacy*. New Haven: Yale University Press, 2017.

Vaidhyanathan, Siva. *The Googlization of Everything: And Why We Should Worry*. Berkeley: University of California Press, 2011.

Wachter-Boettcher, Sara. *Technically Wrong: Sexist Apps, Biased Algorithms, and Other Threats of Toxic Tech*. New York: W. W. Norton, 2017.

Wanzo, Rebecca. "It's a Hero? Black Comics and Satirizing Subjection." In *The Blacker the Ink: Constructions of Black Identity in Comics and Sequential Art*, edited by Frances Gateward and John Jennings, 314–32. New Brunswick, NJ: Rutgers University Press, 2015.

Warner, Michael. *Publics and Counterpublics*. New York: Zone Books, 2002.

Wickham, Carrie Rosefsky. *Mobilizing Islam: Religion, Activism, and Political Change in Egypt*. New York: Columbia University Press, 2002.

Williams, Raymond. *Culture & Society: 1780–1950*. New York: Columbia University Press, 1983.

Wilson, Brian, and Robert Sparks. "Michael Jordan, Sneaker Commercials, and Canadian Youth Cultures." In *Michael Jordan, Inc*. Albany: State University of New York Press, 2001.

Wilson, G. Willow. *The Butterfly Mosque*. New York: Grove Press, 2010.

Wilson, G. Willow. "Interview with G. Willow Wilson." Interview by Shabana Mir. In *Ms. Marvel's America: No Normal*, edited by Jessica Baldanzi and Hussein Rashid, 230–46. Jackson: University Press of Mississippi, 2020.

Wilson, G. Willow. *Mecca*, Ms. Marvel 8. New York: Marvel Comics, 2017.

Wilson, G. Willow. *No Normal*, in *Ms. Marvel 1–4*. Edited by Sana Amanat. New York: Marvel Worldwide, 2014.

Wright, Bradford. *Comic Book Nation: The Transformation of Youth Culture in America*. Baltimore: Johns Hopkins University Press, 2001.

Yanora, Mercedes. "Marked by Foreign Policy: Muslim Superheroes and the Quest for Authenticity." In *Muslim Superheroes: Comics, Islam, and Representation*, edited by A. David Lewis and Martin Lund, 110–32. Boston: Ilex Foundation, 2017.

Zakaria, Rafia. *Against White Feminism: Notes on Disruption*. New York: W. W. Norton, 2021.

# INDEX

Page numbers in **bold** refer to illustrations.

# ABOUT THE AUTHOR

**Kimberly Wedeven Segall** is professor of literature and cultural studies at Seattle Pacific University and affiliate faculty of gender, women, and sexuality studies at the University of Washington. As director of the social justice and cultural studies major and Morocco study abroad and South Africa study abroad program, Segall specializes in trans/national protest, digital media, and gender studies. Her book *Performing Democracy in Iraq and South Africa: Gender, Media, and Resistance* (Syracuse University Press, 2013) is based on long-term fieldwork and analysis of creative and digital media of resistance, including protests of Iraqi women in blogs and poetic laments, of Iranian women in their graphic novels and videos, in their political performances of Islamic feminism, and in their rejections of (neo)colonization.

Her approach is an interdisciplinary intervention in gender studies, cultural studies, and digital activism. *Superheroes in the Streets: Muslim Women Activists and Protest in the Digital Age* is about online icons of superheroes and their foundations in protest and radical feminism—what she calls "radical superheroism"—and reflects her experiences in South Africa, Syria, Iraq, and elsewhere, as well as her work with grassroots organizations, demonstrating for their rights, especially in the wake of the murder of George Floyd and ongoing police violence against minorities. As a scholar activist for the past three decades, her experience includes workshops for racial reparations in South Africa and cofacilitating workshops at the American Muslim Empowerment Network in the Pacific Northwest with Aneelah Afzali. Her recent articles on "de-imperializing gender" and on "media sites" have been published in Oxford University Press's *Handbook of Politics and Performance*; *Comparative Studies of South Asia, Africa, and the Middle East*; *Journal of Middle Eastern Women's Studies*; *Public Culture*; and other academic compilations.

www.ingramcontent.com/pod-product-compliance
Lightning Source LLC
Chambersburg PA
CBHW030325270326
41926CB00010B/1505